Learning to Collaborate
for the Global Common Good

Fernando M. Reimers

With

Noah A. Barr, Jessica Bergmann, Katy Bullard, Isabelle Byusa,
Allison Casey, June Chung, Pilar Cuesta,
Gillian Foster Wilkinson, Beatriz Giraldo, Ben Gulla,
Rachel Hunkler, Idia F. Irele, Aakriti Kalra, Ameya Kamath,
Ashira Khera, Jennifer Kuang, Josué Lavandeira,
Hui Helen Liu, Ana Marcela Lozano, Dahlia Maarouf,
Florencia Mingo, Victoria Gale Modesto, Tina Owen-Moore,
Mitsuko "Mimi" Peters, Shannon O'Brien, Nell O'Donnell,
Aarati Rao, Lauralee Y. Roddy, Tatiana Shevchenko,
Aarushi Singhania, Sonya Temko, Sarah Thang,
Michelle A. Ward, Veena K. Wulfekuhle, Jesella Zambrano,
Shengnan "Cicy" Zhang

Book Format and Design: Kristin Foster-

Book Cover: Paulo Costa

ISBN-13: 978-1718677883

ISBN-10: 171867788X

Library of Congress Control Number: 2018905617

CreateSpace Independent Publishing Platform
North Charleston, South Carolina

This book presents a compelling case for why teachers and school leaders must urgently prioritize the development of competencies for active democratic citizenship in our schools. The curriculum resources developed by Fernando and his students provide an actionable way to translate those aspirations into powerful instruction.

Arne Duncan. Former US Secretary of Education

This book makes plain, what we've all suspected to be true; here in the US and across the world, the link between free education and a free democracy is inextricable and co-dependent. This book reminds us that we cannot take democracy or civility for granted and gives us historical guideposts and practical resources to help ensure we don't.

Lily Eskelsen Garcia, President National Education Association
1989 Utah Teacher of the Year

If education is the docking station that powers all of our common global goals, then collaborative efforts among teachers *such as this book* are our best hope to ensure that the power, civic engagement and critical thinking are distributed equitably, democratically and for the common good. *Learning to Collaborate for the Global Common Good* is an important contribution to the development of a teacher-led way out of the current morass of xenophobia, isolationism and growing inequality.

David Edwards, Ph.D., General Secretary, Education International

Learning to Collaborate for the Global Common Good' successfully and ambitiously brings humanity's best goals into the classroom, with utility for teachers and heart for global citizenstudents, the stewards of our future.

Naomi Volain, Science teacher and educator,
Global Teacher Prize Top 10 Finalist 2015, www.plantsgoglobal.com

Education is the backbone of a healthy democracy. Now, in this time of political unrest, unprecedented technological innovation and societal disruption, our schools must lead the way in protecting our democratic norms. 'Learning to Colaborate for the Global Common Good' gives teachers the tools they need to empower students as the civically-engaged, positive change agents that we need.

Michael Soskil, 2017-2018 Pennsylvania Teacher of the Year
2016 Global Teacher Prize Top-10 Finalist

The future of the world lies in our teachers' ability to unlock the doors of creativity in the minds of our children and teach them how to collaborate with one another to solve complex problems. Dr. Reimers' new book, Learning to Collaborate for the Global Common Good, will serve as their guide.

Joseph Fatheree, Top 10 Finalist 2016 Global Teacher Prize

Education for democracy, civic education, or human rights education, are vital for creating and sustaining of a culture of peace, as is fully recognised in Transforming our World: the 2030 Agenda for Sustainable Development. At the same time it recognizes that education provides the bedrock for delivering not only on the SDGs core promise of equality and eradication of poverty but for effective democratic participation and governance. This book by Professor Reimers and his students is most timely and a true expression of global collaboration in education in a globally interdependent, volatile and uncertain world. Given the shrinking space for transparent public democratic debate with the rising wave of populism, it is ever more important that education institutions enable students to take on local and global challenges with the appropriate skills and as the book states "become democratic cosmopolitans". It is a welcome contribution to the field as it is practical providing curriculum guidance and tools for teachers to engage students in deep learning to empower them to be democratic citizens and ambassadors for peace and tolerance.

Jordan Naidoo, UNESCO Director, Division for Education 2030

Table of Contents

14

Education for a democratic and cosmopolitan future

Fernando M. Reimers

This book is a collection of curriculum resources aligned with some of the United Nations (UN) Sustainable Development Goals, designed to help develop the agency of elementary and secondary school students to meet these aspirations.

These resources were developed by graduate students at the Harvard Graduate School of Education who took my course in Education Policy Analysis and Research in Comparative Perspective. My hope is that these resources will be useful to teachers around the world interested in using active pedagogies that help students develop skills to understand how their world is deeply local as well as global, and to develop understanding and care for the challenges we share.

In a world that is increasingly globally interdependent, volatile and uncertain, cultivating the capabilities of students to not just understand the world in which they live, but to improve it, is especially critical. It is also necessary that we offer these opportunities to all students, not just to the privileged few. The accomplishment of this task will require designing student-centered curriculum and pedagogies aligned with an ambitious set of learning outcomes, guided in turn by ambitious goals of societal improvement. This is hard and complex work which calls for collaboration among many teachers and others who can support them to design, experiment, and revise curriculum and pedagogical approaches that successfully empower students with a breath of skills necessary for civic and economic participation in our complex, volatile and uncertain times. This volume is a modest contribution to that much needed larger effort of generating collective intelligence to transform education in ways aligned to the pressing needs of our times, and of the future.

This volume follows two previous volumes in which, my graduate students and I developed a rigorous global citizenship curriculum aligned with the UN Sustainable Development Goals and the Universal Declaration of Human Rights (Reimers et al, 2016, 2017a). As a result of feedback received from many of the teachers who have used those resources I have become aware of how valuable instructional resources such as this can be to those who are trying to help their students understand and find their place in the rapidly changing world in which they live. I believe universities have a special responsibility to collaborate with elementary and secondary schools in empowering students to improve the world. I hope that this effort will inspire others in academia as an example of one of the ways in which we can collaborate with school teachers and leaders in supporting the important and challenging work they do.

In this introductory chapter I discuss why intentional education to help students become effective democratic citizens is necessary in the United States and in other democracies around the world. I then discuss why 21st century engaged democratic citizenship is also, inevitably, global citizenship. Finally, I describe the approach and process we followed in the design of this curriculum.

Education, democracy and cosmopolitanism

Public education, especially in its aspiration to serve all children, is part and parcel of the project to build a social order with a foundation on the powerful ideas that ordinary people can rule themselves and that they can collaborate with others in improving their own circumstances and those of the communities of which they are a part. These ideas are the foundation of democracy, an institution joined at the hip with public schools and with modern research universities (Reimers, 2017b).

The global expansion of public education, as well as the expansion of democracy and of modern research universities, is a cosmopolitan project, one that connects people across the boundaries of the nation-state in learning from each other and collaborating in various ways to build these institutions to improve the world. Such global collaborations take variegated forms, from the simple exchange of ideas, to the development of institutional partnerships to accelerate the diffusion of the practices that sustain schools, universities, or more importantly, democracy.

In the 18th and 19th centuries, travelers and books transferred many of these ideas across the world. The establishment of the democratic republics in the 18th centuries benefited from the dissemination of the works of the philosophers of the Enlightenment. Their establishment also benefited from exchanges among those who led the creation of the first democratic republics, such as those Benjamin Franklin sustained during the years he lived in England and France, or such as Thomas Jefferson's correspondence with Alexander Humboldt and other European scientists and philosophers or his time, or such as the correspondence between Francisco de Miranda and Thomas Jefferson and Alexander Hamilton, or the exchanges Miranda sustained during his visit to North America, in particular to visit education and government institutions.

Similarly, the creation of public schools and of universities aligned with the liberating and cosmopolitan goals of the Enlightenment benefited from similar exchanges. In 1759, British writer Oliver Goldsmith published 'An Enquiry into the Present State of Polite Learning in Europe' (Goldsmith, 1759) in which he analyzes and criticizes educational institutions, publishing and theater, in Italy, Germany, Holland, France and England. Illustrative of the cosmopolitan spirit guiding such comparative studies, Goldsmith also penned an essay titled 'The citizen of the World' (Goldsmith, 1820).

In 1804, John Quincy Adams, serving as ambassador to the court of Berlin, wrote a treaty examining educational institutions in Silesia and discussing how similar institutions would help consolidate the democratic experiment in the United States (Adams, 1804). In a letter to John Jebb, dated September 10th, 1785, his father, John Adams, had already made a case for public education as central to a project that empowered ordinary people:

> "The social science will never be much improved untill the People unanimously know and Consider themselves as the fountain of Power and untill they Shall know how to manage it Wisely and honestly. reformation must begin with the Body of the People which can be done only, to affect, in their Educations. the Whole People must take upon themselvs the Education of the Whole People and must be willing to bear the expences of it. there should not be a district of one Mile Square without a

school in it, not founded by a Charitable individual but maintained at the expence of the People themselvs they must be taught to reverence themselvs instead of adoreing their servants their Generals Admirals Bishops and Statesmen." (Adams 1785)

In 1817, Marc Antoine Jullien, a French journalist and educator politically active in the pre-revolutionary period in France, published a treaty on comparative education, making the case for and suggesting methods for the comparative analysis of education systems as a way to support the expansion of public education. Knowledgeable of the educational innovations developed by Pestalozzi –with whom he corresponded and to whom he sent his first three sons to be educated at the school Pestalozzi founded at Yverdon– he promoted the monitorial system of education, a low-cost method to educate all people (Jullien, 1817).

These developments in Europe influenced educational developments in the Americas. In 1810, Simon Bolivar and his former tutor Andres Bello visited London to seek support for their efforts in the independence movement in South America. There, Francisco de Miranda, who lived in London, introduced them to Joseph Lancaster, who had founded a school based on the monitorial system of education. Those exchanges influenced the views of the two Venezuelans. Bolivar would a few years later bring Lancaster to Venezuela to start a normal school. Andres Bello would some years later move to Chile to establish the first University in that country, where he supported the development of ideas to advance public education, supporting the work of Domingo Faustino Sarmiento, whom he hired as faculty member at the university he established, and who published a thesis advocating for popular education. Similarly, American professor John Griscom published two volumes with observations of institutions in several countries he visited in Europe, including schools (Griscom, 1823).

In 1843, based on a study trip to those countries, Horace Mann published an analysis of educational institutions and practices in England, Scotland, Ireland, France, Holland and Germany, which he used to support his case for public education to the Massachusetts legislature. In 1849, Domingo Faustino Sarmiento published *De la Educación Popular*, a treaty making the case for public education based on his travels to Europe and to the United States, and on his exchanges with Horace Mann and Mary Peabody Mann.

The advancement of public education was cosmopolitan not only in that it benefited from these types of transnational exchanges and collaborations, but in that it sought to cultivate a cosmopolitan spirit, informed by ideas of the Enlightenment that placed in the cultivation of human reason and of a scientific understanding of the world, a central role in the democratic project of self-improvement and societal improvement.

This cosmopolitan project accelerated with the inclusion of the right to education as one of the rights in the Universal Declaration adopted by the United Nations on December 10 of 1948. The creation of the United Nations, and of specialized agencies such as UNESCO, systematized and supported cross-national exchanges for the explicit purpose of advancing public education. In turn, the right to education was guided by the purpose of cultivating in students a commitment to universal human rights, as a cornerstone of global stability and peace.

Modern universities developed also, as did schools, to advance the goals of empowering individuals for self-rule. In the United States, the founding fathers who led the American experiment in self-rule created the first academic societies. In 1743, Benjamin Franklin established the American Philosophical Society, and six years later an institution of higher learning which would become the University of Pennsylvania. In 1780, John Adams chartered the American Academy of Arts and Sciences, tasked to promote scientific inquiry to advance the public good. The charter of the American Academy recognizes that scientists have an obligation to educate the public so that people can govern themselves. The same year that the American Academy was chartered, John Adams wrote the Massachusetts constitution, whose first article expands on the civic purposes of our universities:

> "Wisdom, and knowledge, as well as virtue, diffused generally among the body of the people, being necessary for the preservation of their rights and liberties; and as these depend on spreading the opportunities and advantages of education in the various parts of the country, and among the different orders of

the people, it shall be the duty of legislators and magistrates, in all future periods of this Commonwealth, to cherish the interests of literature and the sciences, and all seminaries of them; especially the university at Cambridge, public schools, and grammar schools in the towns; to encourage private societies and public institutions, rewards and immunities, for the promotion of agriculture, arts, sciences, commerce, trades, manufactures, and a natural history of the country; to countenance and inculcate the principles of humanity and general benevolence, public and private charity, industry and frugality, honesty and punctuality in their dealings; sincerity, good humour, and all social affections, and generous sentiments among the people." (Massachusetts Constitution).

These civic purposes of the 'modern' university crystalized with the founding of the first modern research university in Berlin by Wilhelm von Humboldt in 1820, a university that would advance three interrelated goals: the advancement of truth through research, the promotion of independent and critical thinking, and the education of the public. A year earlier, in 1819, Thomas Jefferson founded the University of Virginia, an idea he had been developing for at least two decades, to create an institution on the most extensive liberal scale possible.

Public schools and universities, insofar as they seek to cultivate the capacity to reason, an understanding of science, a desire to find truth, and intellectual autonomy and agency, are thus essentially instruments of the democratic project of the Enlightenment, as described by John Adams in his letter to John Jebb in 1785.

This is not to say that schools and universities have intentionally and consistently sought to align their purposes with the purpose of sustaining and deepening democracy. This is first because democracy as a form of political organization is contested by various forms of political organization around the world, such as communism, fascism or other forms of autocratic rule, and secondly because of the fluid nature of the understanding of the forms of participation that democracy requires and of the capacities necessary for such participation. Democracy is, in many ways, an evolving project, and therefore understanding of how public schools can prepare students to participate in democracy are evolving as well. In the words of John Dewey (1916):

> "It is no accident that all democracies have put a high estimate upon education; that schooling has been their first care and enduring charge. Only through education can equality of opportunity be anything more than a phrase. Accidental inequalities of birth, wealth, and learning are always tending to restrict the opportunities of some as compared with those of others. Only free and continued education can counteract those forces which are always at work to restore, in however changed a form, feudal oligarchy. Democracy has to be born anew every generation, and education is its midwife." (Dewey 1916).

In established democracies, there are at least four ways in which schools and universities can prepare students for democratic participation:

1. Educating all students, and in this way provide all people opportunities to develop their reason and the capacities which will enable them to gain autonomy and to participate in society. This was an idea recognized from the inception of the notion that the emergent republics required providing all people the opportunity to develop their reasoning skills. It is the idea expressed in John Adams's letter of 1785 and it is the power Marc Antoine Jullien, Andres Bello, Simon Bolivar and others saw in the method devised by Joseph Lancaster for educating the poor.

2. Providing students an opportunity to learn about others who are different from themselves, and to recognize similarities as well as appreciate differences, so they can develop the dispositions and the capacity to collaborate with others in a diverse democracy. This is an idea that is at the heart of the cosmopolitan nature of the project of the Enlightenment, the notion that our humanity allows us to transcend tribal identities and find common purpose with others across the divides created by our identities. Jan Amos Comenius first articulated this idea in his Didactica Magna, published in 1657, when he argued that educating all would be a way to help reduce the violence that people exercised against others. This idea was central to

21

Horace Mann's argument for public education as the United States experienced one of its most significant waves of immigration. Mann saw public schools as the place where those with different cultural and religious identities would learn to recognize one another as having shared interests and develop an identity that transcended the divides created by nationality of origin, language and religion. As democracies have evolved to recognize equal rights for various groups, schools have become crucial avenues to make such inclusion real by providing opportunities for students from different backgrounds to come together. This was a central tenet of the civil rights movement in the United States in promoting racial integration in schools.

3. Providing students with knowledge and appreciation about the institutions and norms that govern democratic life such as the constitution, the division of powers, and the rights and duties of government and citizens. This has been a core idea of democratic civic education and is central in the contributions of John Dewey.

4. Helping students gain the competencies to participate in the democratic process, not only participating in elections, but also engaging in the many forms of civic duty and service which make democracy a way of life. This idea stems from the recognition that democracy requires more than formal participation in elections and acceptance of the institutions of democracy: it requires active engagement from citizens through an active civil society that regularly and effectively participates in the project of societal improvement.

Democracy at risk

Democracies, as other forms of government, are fluid. They can become stronger, deepening the opportunities for participation and receiving increasing support from citizens, and they can also become weaker and even break down. Examples of the deepening of American democracy include George Washington's famous letter (1790) to Moses Seixas, assuring him that in this new democracy, political rights extend to people of different religious faiths, and that the government would give bigotry no sanction:

The Citizens of the United States of America have a right to applaud themselves for having given to mankind examples of an enlarged and liberal policy: a policy worthy of imitation. All possess alike liberty of conscience and immunities of citizenship. It is now no more that toleration is spoken of, as if it was by the indulgence of one class of people, that another enjoyed the exercise of their inherent natural rights. For happily the Government of the United States, which gives to bigotry no sanction, to persecution no assistance, requires only that they who live under its protection should demean themselves as good citizens, in giving it on all occasions their effectual support.

It would be inconsistent with the frankness of my character not to avow that I am pleased with your favorable opinion of my Administration, and fervent wishes for my felicity. May the children of the Stock of Abraham, who dwell in this land, continue to merit and enjoy the good will of the other Inhabitants; while everyone shall sit in safety under his own vine and fig-tree, and there shall be none to make him afraid. May the father of all mercies scatter light and not darkness in our paths and make us all in our several vocations useful here, and in his own due time and way everlastingly happy (Washington 1790).

Other examples of the deepening of American democracy include the movement for the political rights of women and the civil rights movement, for the political rights of African Americans and of other ethnic minorities and socioeconomically disadvantaged groups.

Efforts to limit rights to people of particular identities by denying them to "others" run counter to efforts to make democracy live true to its founding ideals of the recognition of equality among all people. This was the tactic used by the Nazis as they rose to power to strip German Jews of their legal rights.

A recent study of the breakdown of democratic regimes, and an analysis of the risks of a breakdown of American democracy, argues that contemporary democracies break down constitutionally, not as a result of a military coup as some did in the past, but as elected leaders use the instruments of the democratic process to progressively curtail freedoms and democratic checks and balances (Levitsky and Ziblatt, 2018). In their analysis of how democracies die, Levitsky and Ziblatt argue that two specific norms are central to sustaining democratic rule: mutual toleration (the acceptance of those with different views) and self-restraint on the part of those who have political power in any of the branches of government. These norms are, I argue, squarely the product of what educational institutions do, or fail to do. It is no accident, for example, that one of Hitler's first targets to begin the process of 'othering' as he rose to power were schools and universities. As mentioned earlier, the modern research university had been born in Germany in 1820 to advance the goals of the Enlightenment; a century later, German universities had a well-deserved reputation for educating independent thinkers. Academic freedom and research in German universities were a model that many universities followed, in the United States as well as in other nations. But as politicians began to stimulate tribalism and 'othering', a form of ultra-nationalism developed in German universities. Large numbers of German professors applauded Germany's war ambitions in 1915, and few supported the Weimar government that emerged after Germany surrendered in 1918. They may have underestimated the evil force into which the nascent populist-nationalism would eventually transform.

Hitler saw academics as an enemy who would resist his attempts to impose an ideology of racial supremacy. Once appointed Chancellor, he achieved control of the university curriculum to eliminate education in the humanities and to control appointments of university faculty and leaders, firing faculty who were Jewish, social democrats or liberals. Academics who spoke against the regime were brought to concentration camps. Many professors and administrators became collaborators of the Nazi regime, aligning teaching and research with the efforts to create a society based in white supremacy. Many German academics went into exile.

A recent issue of the journal *Foreign Affairs* reflects in the title of a special dossier "Is Democracy Dying?" a question and concern increasingly asked in academic and political circles in response to the recent wave of elections around the world in which populist leaders who have advocated clear antidemocratic views, have been elected.

The most recent Freedom House survey on the state of democracy around the world concludes that democracy faces its most serious crisis in decades as its core tenets –free and fair elections, rights of minorities, freedom of the press and the rule of law– are under attack around the world. In the past year, seventy-one countries suffered declines in political rights and civil liberties, while only 35 experienced gains. This makes 2017 the 12th consecutive year in decline in global freedom. The report indicates that the United States retreated from its traditional role as a champion and exemplar of democracy as political rights and civil liberties decline in the United States (Freedom House, 2018.)

In an op-ed discussing the report, the President of Freedom House (Abramowitz and Willkie, 2017) concludes:

> In practice, President Trump has largely discarded the principles that formed the basis for American leadership over the previous seven decades. His animating slogan, America First, harks back to the United States' dangerous flirtation with isolationism in the period leading up to World War II. While he has correctly invoked human rights to criticize a handful of countries such as Iran, Cuba and Venezuela, in general the president has showered his most lavish praise on noxious strongmen and autocrats. Trump continues to offer accolades to Russian President Vladimir Putin, a brutal dictator who represses dissent and seeks to disrupt democracy in the United States and Europe, and he commended President Rodrigo Duterte of the Philippines on his anti-drug efforts, which have featured a campaign of extrajudicial killings.

Also concerning is the administration's silence in the face of renewed repression in China. Any independent speech on sensitive issues is now subject to severe punishment. The Internet, which had begun to facilitate the development of an independent civil society, has been transformed into an instrument of state control. Beijing has indicated that it will continue to develop its system of repression by incorporating the latest innovations in

25

surveillance technology and artificial intelligence. China has already shared its existing techniques with other regimes; we should assume that any new methods will also be available for export. " (Abramowitz and Willkie 2017).

The same conclusion is reached by University of Michigan Professor Ronald Inglehart (2018), drawing on the analysis of multiple waves of data from the World Values Survey, a series of polls surveying adults on political views and cultural values:

> After 1980…support for authoritarian parties surged. By 2015, they were drawing an average of more than 12 percent of the vote across [the 32 western democracies that contained at least one such party]. In Denmark, the Netherlands, and Switzerland, authoritarian parties became the largest or second largest political bloc. In Hungary and Poland, they won control of government. Since then, they have grown even stronger in some countries. In the 2016 U.S. presidential election, the Republican candidate Donald Trump campaigned on a platform of xenophobia and sympathy toward authoritarianism. (pp. 22-24)

This global democratic setback is the most severe since the rise of fascism in the 1930s (Inglehart, 2018). It includes the rise of populism, authoritarian and xenophobic movements in France, Germany, the Netherlands, Sweden and the United Kingdom (Ibid). Inglehart's analysis of the global democratic decline attributes it to a reaction against immigration and increasing racial equality, and declining job security. "If the developed world continues on its current course, democracy could wither away. If there is nothing inevitable about democratic decline, there is also nothing inevitable about democratic resurgence" (Inglehart, 2018, 20).

Alongside democratic decline and increase in support for authoritarianism, there is rising 'othering' of people from diverse ethnic and religious identities. Several recent reports document an increase in religious and ethnic hatred in the United States since the presidential election, as white nationalist groups grow (Beirich and Buchanan, 2018). The Anti-Defamation's yearly publication, for example, notes the following (2018):

In its annual *Audit of Anti-Semitic Incidents*, [the Anti-Defamation League] found that the number of anti-Semitic incidents in the U.S. rose 57 percent in 2017 – the largest single-year increase on record and the second highest number reported since ADL started tracking such data in 1979. The sharp rise was in part due to a significant increase in incidents in schools and on college campuses, which nearly doubled for the second year in a row. (ADL 2018).

Along with decline in support for democratic institutions and increase in 'othering' and attacks on the rights of some groups, rising populist movements are undermining the value of reason and of the institutions that enhance it, such as science and education. Political debates now include references to 'alternative facts', and some politicians question the value of education. In the last Presidential campaign, candidate Donald Trump made virtue out of the lack of education of some of his supporters: "I love the uneducated," he said in several campaign rallies.

Michael Hayden, a former director of the Central Intelligence Agency, has warned of the dangers that this assault on facts and intelligence poses to US national security (2018):

It was no accident that the Oxford Dictionaries' word of the year in 2016 was 'post-truth' a condition were facts are less influential in shaping opinion than emotion and personal beliefs. To adopt post-truth thinking is to depart from Enlightenment ideas, dominant in the West since the 17th century, that value experience and expertise, the centrality of fact, humility in the face of complexity, the need for study and a respect for ideas. President Trump both reflects and exploits this kind of thinking (Hayden 2018).

In a recent book (2018), former US Secretary of State Madeleine Albright explains that the rise of fascism is a more serious threat today than at any time since the end of World War II:

Warning signs include the relentless grab for more authority by governing parties in Hungary, the Philippines, Poland and Turkey — all United States allies. The raw anger that feeds fascism is evident across the Atlantic in the growth of nativist movements opposed to the idea of a united Europe, including in Germany, where the right-wing Alternative für Deutschland has emerged as the principal opposition party. The danger of despotism is on display in the Russia of Vladimir Putin — invader of Ukraine, meddler in foreign democracies, accused political assassin, brazen liar and proud son of the K.G.B. Putin has just been re-elected to a new six-year term, while in Venezuela, Nicolás Maduro, a ruthless ideologue, is poised to triumph in sham balloting next month. In China, Xi Jinping has persuaded a docile National People's Congress to lift the constitutional limit on his tenure in power." (Albright 2018).

Global risks

These challenges experienced by democracy around the world will obstruct our ability to address other challenges such as growing inequality, poverty, climate change, health challenges, and national and global conflicts, including the threat of nuclear war. Effectively addressing those challenges requires that we leverage all the power of human reason, enhanced by science and technology and by collaboration across institutions and borders. It requires also that we engage in the kind of deliberation that can bring people with diverse ideas to collaborate in solving these problems. In short, today as yesterday, improving the world requires that we depend on the institutions created on the foundation of Enlightenment values. As those values and institutions are challenged, as expertise, knowledge and science are devalued, as globalism is under attack, and as we lose the toleration which makes collaboration across divides possible it will become more difficult to sustain progress. Our collective descent into tribalism, xenophobia and populism will undermine the very foundations of human progress, exacerbating the sources of malaise that are at the root of the rise in populism. In a recent essay on the risks of descending into Tyranny, Yale History Professor Timothy Snyder warns of the risks of a post-truth world: "You submit to tyranny when you renounce the difference between what you want to hear and what is actually the case. Post-truth is pre-fascism, and to abandon facts is to abandon freedom" (Snyder, 2017).

In a recent book, former US secretary of labor and Berkeley Professor argues that we have lost our commitment to the common good, a shared value of our obligations to each other which rest on our core democratic values:

respect for the rule of law and democratic institutions, toleration of our differences, and belief in equal rights and opportunity (Reich, 2018). Such erosion of the common good will challenge our ability to address rising economic and social inequality, which in turn undermines the democratic process.

One of the most authoritative analysis of global risks is a report produced each year by the World Economic Forum, the "Global Risks Report". The 2017 report identifies as the top five trends that will determine global developments:

1) Rising income and wealth disparity,
2) Changing climate,
3) Increasing polarization of societies,
4) Rising cyberdependency, and
5) An ageing population.

These trends in turn interact with each other, leading to the following most important risks: 1) unemployment and underemployment, leading to profound social instability; 2) large-scale voluntary migration leading to state collapse or crisis; 3) failure of climate change mitigation and adaptation leading to water crisis; 4) failure of national governance, leading to profound social instability; and 5) interstate conflict with regional consequences leading to large-scale involuntary migration (World Economic Forum, 2017).

All of these trends and their interactions are in part shaped by education. For instance, rising income and wealth disparities are already a result of differences in education and skills. The continued development of artificial intelligence will likely continue to erode jobs, further dislocating and marginalizing workers, and thus increasing social inequality and poverty. One way to address this is by investing in higher-quality education so that people can continuously adapt to new labor market demands and gain the skills to create new work for themselves and others as we transition to a post-industrial economy and new occupations emerge after a transitional period that is likely to bring considerable occupational instability as the jobs of the 20th century are replaced by computational algorithms until new jobs emerge. The development of the skills and dispositions to navigate this transition require schools and opportunities for lifelong learning that guarantee all students a breath of competencies which far exceed anything public schools have done at scale since they were invented. Not insignificantly, schools will need to develop a commitment to the common good so that those who most benefit from the transition to a post-industrial economy lead efforts of solidarity to include and support those most adversely affected by the disruptions caused by the development of artificial intelligence.

Similarly, education can contribute to slowing down global warming, one of the most significant challenges humanity faces. There is indisputable scientific evidence that temperatures are rising at rates that will challenge the capacity of living species in our planet to adapt. While complete undoing of the damage already caused to climate is highly improbable, significantly reducing the rate at which climate is changing is within reach, provided humans change their patterns of consumption and life, and provided we pay the necessary costs to bring about such changes.

Fundamentally, reversing global warming requires a planetary shift in consciousness, culture and lifestyle which can help achieve certain goals in mitigating climate change, goals which many scientists consider insufficient: to bring the increase in global temperatures to less than two degrees centigrade of the temperature of the planet before the industrial era.

There are abundant resources to help teachers educate their students about climate change and about sustainability, resources that provide access to high quality content on scientific evidence, such as the National Oceanic Atmospheric Administration, or NASA, or the Climate Literacy and Energy Awareness Network. MIT has also developed the 'World Climate Simulation Game' a tool developed by the Systems Dynamics Group at the Sloan School https://www.climateinteractive.org/programs/world-climate/

Developing high quality curriculum to teach about global topics such as climate change is within the reach of all teachers.

Reducing the polarization of societies also fits squarely within the mandate of schools. This was Comenius vision when he advocated that all should be educated, and it was Horace Mann's motivation in advancing public

30

education in Massachusetts. This was also the primary reason to include education as one of the rights in the Universal Declaration adopted in 1948.

But our schools have, for some time now, abrogated their civic mission. Questions of means have taken precedence over clarity of purpose. Most of our public discourse and education politics have been and are focused on resources and immediate goals, such as enrollments, attendance, graduation or student performance on the basic domains of language or mathematics. These are important, for sure, especially if they are well-aligned with a profile of high school graduates who have developed the essential competencies to actively participate in a democratic society.

However, more schools, districts and states need to be debating what exactly this means as polarization and intolerance grow in American society. Schools are certainly not doing their job in cultivating a democratic citizenry if students learn the basics and perform well on tests, but bully each other over differences in their identities, while the adults in the building turn a blind eye. Schools are not preparing students to understand that in a democracy all persons have the same rights, if African American and Latino students are disciplined at disproportionately higher rates than their white counterparts, as documented in a recent report by the General Accounting Office. School district leaders are not delivering on their obligations to a democratic society if they are focused on getting schools to improve student performance in language and math, while extremist groups challenge the inclusion of books in the curriculum which promote critical thinking and an appreciation of racial and cultural diversity.

Similarly, powerfully effective education can prepare our citizenry to manage a world characterized by rising cyberdependency, and to prepare an ageing population to live healthy lives of purpose and with inclusion.

Education Challenges

While our education institutions can help address, at least in part, some of the most serious risks we face, and in particular the challenge of the breakdown of democracy which will compound all other risks, schools and universities are in turned challenged by the emerging breakdown of democracy and rising

31

populism. As populism devalues ideas, knowledge and expertise, it also devalues the role of schools and universities. Public funding for these institutions is likely to diminish. In the United States the teaching profession has been under attack for some time now, and as a result the nation is facing a looming teaching shortage. Limits in school funding constrain the ability of districts and schools to invest in the preparation of teachers to enhance their skills in supporting the deeper learning necessary for students to develop the competencies to engage in a contested democracy and to address the risks mentioned earlier.

Furthermore, the very same polarization which characterizes political debate today is extending into schools, with the result that there are increasing risks for teachers to address any themes which might be perceived as partisan. Extremists groups are hijacking the curriculum by declaring as partisan topics which in times of greater toleration would have been perceived as part of the preparation to live in a pluralistic democracy.

The Responsibility of Educators

Today, as democracy is challenged around the world, education must be its midwife, as Dewey declared a century ago. To do this, teachers and school leaders must create opportunities for students to study the important challenges facing their communities and the world, and to develop the skills to address them. Teachers must educate their students to understand and to improve the world. They must help them become democratic cosmopolitans because the world is ever more integrated. Students should be helped to overcome the forces of tribalism which push them to reject 'the other' and to hunker down into narrowly defined identities and bigotry, instead replacing them with a capacity to work across all lines of difference for societal improvement.

Teachers should help the students understand the world and find a place for themselves and their voice in the world, in improving the world. Learning to improve the world will inevitably mean learning by doing, accepting complexity and ambiguity, collaborating with others, and taking responsibility. This will make education relevant, activate their intrinsic motivation to learn, help them develop healthy identities in a world that is diverse and pluralistic and prepare them to be engage and effective citizens in democratic pluralistic societies. Developmental studies show that when parents can help students understand how their education relates to future success, this fosters engagement with school and academic achievement, diminishes problematic behavior and reduces depressive symptoms:

"linking education to future success, a core component of academic socialization, also increased across middle and high school. As a parental involvement strategy, it also capitalizes on teen's emerging cognitive capabilities. As brain structures develop over the course of adolescence, teens are better able to manipulate multiple viewpoints simultaneously, learn from their own and others' mistakes, and envision the future outcomes of current decisions (Keating, 2004). This means that parental involvement that communicates the value and utility of schoolwork and links it to youth's future success and goals serves to bolster emerging self-identities (Bandura et al., 2001) and gives purpose to their work." (Wang, Hill and Hofkens 2014, 2163).

Powerful curriculum is essential for teachers to engage their students in such deep learning. Over the last few years I have developed, together with my graduate students, ambitious and coherent curriculum aligned with the United Nations Sustainable Development Goals and with the United Nations Universal Declaration of Human Rights. In 2016 I published *Empowering Global Citizens*, a K-12 resource with over 300 units. The feedback I received from the teachers who read and used it was that the vision of the curriculum, which proposed devoting about eight hours a week from kindergarten to high school to a *World Course*, made its adoption challenging. Also, the effective adoption of such curriculum required a school-wide commitment to the enterprise and extensive teacher professional development.

That book was followed by another curriculum, *Empowering Students to Improve the World in Sixty Lessons*, published in 2017, which was much better received because it could be adopted more easily. This second book included a protocol to design a process of school adoption of a school-wide effort for global citizenship education, a prototype of a curriculum similar in aspirations to the *World Course*, but streamlined to five lessons per grade. The feedback I have received from teachers and school leaders about this new curriculum is that this streamlined prototype is much more usable because it conveys to teachers that effective global citizenship education is within their reach and it inspires them to communicate with colleagues, across various grades and school subjects, on an ambitious vision to empower their students as change-makers.

I am persuaded that as we deepen efforts to educate cosmopolitan democratic citizens we will need to continue to develop ambitious curriculum and that teachers will have to play a significant role in such task. But the task is too complex and fluid to be effectively addressed by individual teachers working in isolation, and so we will have to build effective forms to enable teacher collaboration that leverage the power of collective intelligence and improvement networks. I am currently studying such efforts.

The various resources offered in this book support these ongoing efforts of educators in the United States, and around the world, who understand that schools exist to empower students for democratic citizenship. Unlike the previous two books I published on this subject, this one presents not a single integrated curriculum, but an array of approaches to educating students with activities and content aligned to the United Nations Sustainable Development Goals. We seek to illustrate that there are multiple pathways to prepare students for the responsible exercise of citizenship in a world that is increasingly interdependent, and we recognize that teachers work in a multiplicity of contexts which require that they make deliberate professional judgements about what is feasible in their schools and with their students. We hope to facilitate such professional judgements by expanding the range of resources from which they can draw.

These resources were developed by graduate students in a course on education policy analysis in comparative development I teach at the Harvard Graduate School of Education and at the Harvard Extension School. I teach this course with the skilled support of a group of outstanding teaching fellows. Last year, they were: Isabelle Byusa, Nell O'Donnell, Tatiana Shevchenko and Sonya Temko. The course attracts students who have had experience working in school systems in many different education systems around the world. A core goal of the course is to help students develop the capacity to learn from comparative analysis of educational experiences, including curriculum. A central tenet of the course is that education policy must begin with clear purposes for students, and with well thought out theories of the kind of activities that students and teachers will participate in, guided by curriculum to help students develop specific competencies. We emphasize how the increasing demands of civic and economic participation call for deeper learning and for the development of a breath of skills in the cognitive, intrapersonal and interpersonal domains. This is also the focus of the Global Education Innovation Initiative, the research and practice collaborative I lead with the mission of understanding how to support the transformation of education systems to increase their relevance and effectiveness (Reimers & Chung, 2016, 2018).

My students learn to map backwards the kinds of supports, programs and policies that will help teachers and students follow a deeper learning curriculum, guided by the clarity with which the instructional core should align with intended learning goals, which in turn should align with longer-term goals for individuals and societies. In that context, I engage them in the design of curriculum, a task that is familiar to those of them who have taught and been prepared as teachers, usually about two thirds of the students in the course. In guiding them to develop curriculum, I draw on the principles of design thinking, which emphasize communicating and receiving feedback from teachers, so that students can revise and improve their prototypes. Once students develop a prototype of a curriculum, they then discuss it with at least one teacher, receive feedback and revise it. At that point, their prototypes are shared with the entire class and revised yet again, before they receive feedback from me and from the teaching fellows who assist me in teaching the course. At this point students are invited, but not required, to take their curriculum a step further in revision and development, an invitation only some of them accept. They bring their revised prototypes to a Hackathon at the Harvard Innovation Lab, an intensive five-hour session where they receive feedback from a larger group of educators and practitioners. Based on this feedback, they then revise their lessons and share with a cooperating teacher, provide feedback to them that is used to make final revisions. The resources presented in this book are the product of this process of development.

As with the previous two books, the most important contribution our resources will make will come not from following these lessons as scripts. Rather, the most important contribution will come from seeing these resources as examples or prototypes, on which teachers will build and which they will adapt, engaging in a process of continuous experimentation and improvement with their colleagues, in professional networks, until they produce materials that may bear little resemblance to these initial prototypes, except in their alignment with an ambitious vision for education that sees students as capable of taking responsibility for the improvement of themselves and the many communities of which they are a part, in a world increasingly interconnected.

It is my hope that these resources my students and I have developed illustrate also the promise of a pedagogical approach in which graduate students are engaged in experiences that invite them to collaborate with other students and with practitioners to address challenging and complex problems, such as how to design powerful curriculum for students in the K-12 level aligned with the United Nations Sustainable Development Goals. Complex problems are solved not by contemplation or mere study, but by taking action and learning from the results of such action, even better if done as part of diverse teams. If graduate students who are preparing to lead educational change experience such pedagogies and can evaluate their results, they may be more likely to subsequently advance reforms that provide school teachers and students similar opportunities to learn from action. I can think of no better way to empower students to improve the world, which is to say to become engaged democratic citizens in times when the very foundations of democracy are challenged.

References

John Adams, "From John Adams to John Jebb, 10 September 1785," https://founders.archives.gov/documents/Adams/06-17-02-0232

John Q. Adams, 1804. *Letters on Silesia* (London: Printed for J. Budd at the Crown and Mitre, Pall Mall, 1804).

Michael J. Abramowitz and Wendell L. Willkie, "We looked at the state of democracy around the world, and the results are grim," *Washington Post* January 17, 2017. https://www.washingtonpost.com/news/democracy-

post/wp/2018/01/17/we-looked-at-the-state-of-democracy-around-the-world-and-the-results-are-grim/?noredirect=on&utm_term=.5b4846d10829

Madeleine Albright, "Will We Stop Trump Before it is too late?" *The New York Times* April 6, 2018. https://www.nytimes.com/2018/04/06/opinion/sunday/trump-fascism-madeleine-albright.html

Anti Defamation League, *Audit of Anti-Semitic Incidents.* https://www.adl.org/resources/reports/2017-audit-of-anti-semitic-incidents

Heidi Beirich and Susy Buchanan, *The Year in Extremism.* https://www.splcenter.org/fighting-hate/intelligence-report/2018/2017-year-hate-and-extremism

John Dewey, "The Need of an Industrial Education in an Industrial Democracy," *Manual Training and Vocational Education* 17 (1916): 409-14.

Freedom House. *Freedom in the World 2018. Democracy in Crisis.* https://freedomhouse.org/report/freedom-world/freedom-world-2018

Oliver Goldsmith, *An enquiry into the present state of polite learning.* (London: Printed for R. and J. Dodsley in Pall Mall, 1759).

Oliver Goldsmith, *The citizen of the world.* (Bungay: Printed by J. and R. Childs, 1820).

John Griscom, *A year in Europe comprising a journal of observations in England, Scotland, Ireland, France, Switzerland, the North of Italy and Holland.* (New York: Published by Collins and Co. 1823).

Michael Hayden, "The End of Intelligence," *The New York Times* April 29, 2018.

Ronald Inglehart, "The Age of Insecurity. Can democracy save itself?" *Foreign Affairs.* May/June 2018. Pages 20-28.

Marc Antoine Jullien, *Esquisse et vues preliminaires d'un ouvrage sur l'education comparée.* (Paris: Imprimerie de Fain. Rue de Racine. Place de L'Odeon, 1817).

Steven Levitsky and Daniel Ziblatt, *How Democracies Die*. (New York: Crown Publishing, 2018).

Massachusetts Constitution. https://malegislature.gov/Laws/Constitution

Ming-Te Wang, Nancy Hill and Tara Hofkens, "Parental Involvement and African American and European American Adolescents' Academic, Behavioral, and Emotional Development in Secondary School." Child Development, November/December 2014, Vol 85. Number 6. Pages 2151-2168.

Robert Reich, The Common Good. (New York: Alfred Knopf, 2018).

Fernando Reimers et al., Empowering Global Citizens. (Charleston, SC: CreateSpace, 2016).

Fernando Reimers et al., Empowering Students to Improve the World in Sixty Lessons. (Charleston, SC: CreateSpace, 2017a).

Fernando Reimers, One Student at a Time. Leading the Global Education Movement. (Charleston, SC: Create Space, 2017b).

Fernando Reimers and Connie K. Chung (Eds.), Teaching and Learning in the Twenty First Century. (Cambridge, MA: Harvard Education Press, 2016).

Fernando Reimers and Connie K. Chung (Eds). Preparing Teachers to Educate Whole Children. (Cambridge, MA: Harvard Education Press, 2018).

Domingo F. Sarmiento, De la Educación Popular. (Santiago: Imprenta de Julio Belin y Compania, 1849).

Timonty Sneider, On Tyranny (New York: Tim Duggan Books, 2017).

George Washington, Letter to Moses Sexas August 17, 1790. . http://www.mountvernon.org/digital-encyclopedia/article/moses-seixas/

World Economic Forum. *The Global Risks Report*. https://www.weforum.org/reports/the-global-risks-report-2017

Empowering Students to Improve the World Lesson Plan: SDG 14 Life Below Water

Noah A. Barr & Ashira Khera

With more than 70 percent of the earth covered in water, the oceans are crucial to our planet. While people know that forests produce most of our oxygen, the fact that oceans and seas serve a very similar function is often overlooked. The oceans provide storage and absorb 30 percent of the world's carbon dioxide. Marine phytoplankton generates 50 percent of the oxygen needed for survival. Another startling statistic is that 3.1 billion of the world's population lives within 100 kilometres of the ocean or sea, and about 3 billion depend heavily on marine resources. In fact, marine resources not only provide food and oxygen, but have many ramifications in the global economy.

UN Sustainable Development Goal 14 deals with the conservation and sustainable management of the oceans, seas, and marine resources. Whilst it is a standalone goal, it is strongly connected with the other SDGs and, in particular, SDG 2 (ending hunger and achieving food security, improved nutrition, and sustainable agriculture) and SDG 12 (sustainable production and consumption). Oceans therefore have a clear contribution to poverty eradication by providing opportunities for sustainable livelihoods. SDG 14 is a linchpin, and the lesson plans below will not only introduce the topic but will also attempt to leave a lasting impression that we must be the actors of change.

Lessons Overview

Students embark on a five-lesson course which will culminate in the presentation of a group project. The first lesson will lay out the foundations of what is life below water and why it is important. It will complement or expand on any knowledge possibly gained through introductory classes given at a lower grade. This lesson will allow students with greater maturity to gain a better understanding of key concepts and reflect on critical issues affecting oceans, seas and marine life, e.g. what is climate change, the flora and fauna of the ocean, fishing, pollution and its impact on the oceans and the seas.

The second lesson is the educational discovery, uncovering threats to the oceans, seas and marine resources. There will be an understanding of the impact of these threats as well as the issues on a global context. During the third lesson, students will formulate thoughts on the responsibilities of conservation and sustainability. They will reflect on the two previous lessons and gain a deeper understanding of how they can be agents of change.

The fourth lesson sets out the proposals for a group project, subject to the teacher's approval. Alternatively, students will be allocated a given team/topic, absent any proposal. The final lesson is where the students present their group project. There will be a sense of achievement as students will be ultimately awarded a certificate of completion on "Student Awareness on Sustainable Development for Life Below Water."

These lessons will raise students' awareness on the beauty and diversity of oceans, seas and marine life, the dependency of human life upon marine resources, and the key values regarding conservation and need to preserve the status quo in an environmental setting. Learning will be based around the fundamentals of sustainable resources and the need to preserve the ecosystem. Students will learn and debate the different approaches followed by countries to protect the marine environment. Some discussion should prompt students to think about how economic needs, industry and culture frame human views on life below water. They will discuss which values are more important to them, why these values should take priority over others, and why the sustainable management of marine resources should be viewed as a global concern.

Learning Goals

Students will explore life below water and why it matters. They will learn about the important global role of the oceans, seas and marine resources: the provision of natural resources, the environmental effects of coastal ecosystems, and the impact on health, poverty and tourism. Students will also learn about some of the threats to marine life and the impact that this may have on the world. Students will show their understanding by designing and presenting a project based on what they have learned.

Lessons

Lesson 1	What can the sea see: Life below water
Lesson 2	What can the sea see: A view of the horizon
Lesson 3	What the sea saw: A balancing act
Lesson 4	A prescription for sea-sickness: Project design
Lesson 5	A prescription for sea-sickness: Project implementation

Learning Objectives

- Students will understand the important global role of the oceans, seas, and marine resources.
- Students will become cognizant with the issues that threaten our waters and marine life and the impact of this on everyday life.
- Students will design and present a project to promote the conservation and sustainability of the oceans, seas and marine resources.

Standards

SDG 14 (Life below water), SDG 1 (no poverty), SDG 2 (zero hunger), SDG 3 (good health and well-being), SDG 6 (clean water and sanitation), SDG 7 (affordable and clean energy), SDG 8 (decent work and economic growth), SDG 9 (industry, innovation and infrastructure), SDG 10 (reduced inequalities), SDG 11 (sustainable cities and communities), SDG 12 (responsible consumption and production)

Lesson 1: What can the sea see: Life below water

Grade: 6   Time Frame: 60 - 70 minutes

Summary and Rationale:

To provide students with an overview of the ocean's resources, ecosystems and role in the environment. This will serve as a foundation for the following lessons in which students will begin to uncover threats to the oceans, seas and marine resources and understand what the impact of these threats may be.

Empowering Students to Improve the World Lesson Plan: SDG 14
Life Below Water

During this session, students will be organised into cooperative learning groups of mixed ability. These groups will work together for the duration of the project.

Instructional Goal:

Students will gain a greater understanding of the important global role of the oceans, seas and marine life.

Understanding Goals:

- Oceans provide key natural resources including food, medicines, biofuels and other products.
- Coastal ecosystems play a role in protecting the environment, supporting the removal of waste, reduction of pollution and climate change mitigation.
- Marine protected areas contribute to poverty reduction by increasing fish catches and income and improving health.

Essential Questions:

- What key natural resources do the oceans provide?
- How do oceans help with the breakdown and removal of waste and pollution?
- How do coastal ecosystems protect the coast?
- How do healthy oceans support the mitigation of climate change?
- How do marine protected areas contribute to poverty reduction?
- What kinds of creatures and organisms live in the marine environment?

Student Learning Objectives:

Students will be able to:

- Collaboratively research oceans, seas and marine resources using printed and online resources
- Name the key natural resources that the oceans provide
- Explain some of the important roles the oceans, seas and marine resources play in supporting and protecting the environment

- Contribute to a group mind-map

Assessment:

Students contribute to a group mind-map, using words and illustrations to summarize what they have learned. There will be opportunity to discuss this within the group and reflect as a class. The teacher may ask questions related to emerging gaps in their knowledge. Written teacher comments will be in the form of questions to extend understanding for students to reflect on in the next session.

Sequence of activities:

Step 1: (5-7 minutes) – Introduction: True or false? (Appendix 1 – Quiz sheet and answers)

In pairs or small groups, students are given a series of statements about the oceans, seas and marine resources. Students discuss these in their groups and decide which are true and which are false. Answers are then displayed and briefly discussed.

Step 2: (5-7 minutes) – Finding More Information

Ask students where they might find out more facts and information about the oceans. Discuss printed and online resources. How might they discriminate between reliable and unreliable sources? *Teacher suggested books and websites, international organisations .org, .ac etc.* How might they refine their search? *Using key questions.*

Step 3: (30-35 minutes) – Research

In groups of 3 or 4, students use printed and online resources to research the ocean's resources, ecosystems and role in the environment. The essential questions will guide their research. Students will share out the keys questions and record their findings on a group mind-map using notes and illustrations. (Appendix 2 – Student prompt sheet)

Step 4: (10 minutes) – Sharing

In their groups, students complete the mind-map and share their findings. (Teachers may help the students by introducing the mind-map on the classroom board).

Step 5: (5 minutes) – Reflecting

Students come back together as a class and reflect on what they have learned.

Resources

For Students:

- True or False? [appendix 1]
- Life Below Water available from
  http://www.un.org/sustainabledevelopment/wp-content/uploads/2016/08/14_Why-it-Matters_Goal-14_Life-Below-Water_3p.pdf
- http://marinebio.org/oceans/ocean-resources/
- https://www.nationalgeographic.com/environment/oceans/critical-issues-ocean-acidification/
- https://oceanservice.noaa.gov/facts/
- https://vimeo.com/42619545
- Search engines – Look for .org, .gov, .ac.

For Teachers:

- https://sustainabledevelopment.un.org/sdg14
- https://unchronicle.un.org/article/goal-14-conserve-and-sustainably-use-oceans-seas-and-marine-resources-sustainable
- https://sustainabledevelopment.un.org/topics/oceanandseas
- http://overfishing.org/
- http://news.nationalgeographic.com/2017/07/plastic-produced-recycling-waste-ocean-trash-debris-environment/
- http://www.pbs.org/emptyoceans/fts

Lesson 2: What can the sea see: A view of the horizon

Grade: 6   Time Frame: 60 - 70 minutes

Summary and Rationale:

To identify and understand some of the threats to the oceans, seas and marine resources and understand what the impact of these threats may be. Students will make links with SDG 14 and begin to understand and discuss the significance of this on their own and others' lives.

Instructional Goal:

To encourage students to identify some of the threats to the oceans, seas and marine resources and begin to critically think about ocean sustainability and SDG 14 goals

Understanding Goals:

- Acidification, dead zones, waste and overfishing are some of the threats to the oceans, seas and marine resources and these threats have an adverse effect on the environment, climate, health, wealth and marine life.
- Conservation and sustainability are key concepts for protecting oceans, seas and marine resources from these threats.

Essential Questions:

- What is acidification and what are the effects of this?
- What are dead zones and what problems do they raise?
- What is waste pollution and where does it come from?
- What do we mean by overfishing?
- How could we begin to overcome these threats?

Student Learning Objectives:

Students will be able to:

- Understand what is meant by SDGs

- Research a threat to oceans, seas and marine resources using printed and online resources
- Explain the threat and how it is caused
- Describe the effect of the threat on the ocean and the wider implications for the planet
- Suggest some ways that the threat can be negated
- Present their findings to the class

Assessment:

Students will self-assess against the learning objectives. They will present their findings to a larger group. Other students and the teacher may ask questions in a short Q and A at the end of each presentation.

Sequence of activities:

Step 1 : (5 minutes) – Reflecting on Last Week

Students reflect on their group mind-maps from last week and discuss any questions set by the teacher with their group (assessment from session 1).

Step 2: (5 minutes) – Life Below Water

Show the video – Global Goal 14: Life below water (running time 1:03) https://www.youtube.com/watch?v=rXbEZzsWnOE. Students reflect and discuss the content of the video in the context of previous learning about the oceans, seas and marine resources (Session 1).

Step 3: (5 minutes) – Ocean Threats

Students work in mixed ability groups of 4. Each group is allocated a threat to the ocean to research: acidification, dead zones, pollution and waste or overfishing. (Depending on group size, more than one group may be allocated the same threat to research.)

Step 4: (20 - 25 minutes) – Research

Students research their issues using the Learning Objectives and recording under the following headings:

- Threat to the ocean: (name the threat)
- What is it? (describe the threat)
- How is it caused?
- What is the effect on the ocean?
- What can be done?

Step 5: (5 minutes) – Sharing in Small Groups

Groups that have researched the same threat come together to share work.

Step 6: (20 - 25 minutes) – Sharing with the Larger Group

Each (larger) group has up to 5 minutes to present their findings and hold a short Q and A for the whole class.

Resources

For Students

- https://www.nationalgeographic.com/environment/oceans/critical-issues-ocean-acidification/
- https://www.worldwildlife.org/threats/overfishing
- https://oceanservice.noaa.gov/ (use the search bar within the site)
- http://www.nationalgeographic.com/environment/oceans/critical-issues-overfishing/
- https://www.nytimes.com/2014/08/26/opinion/choking-the-oceans-with-plastic.html
- https://oceanservice.noaa.gov/facts/coralreef-climate.html

For Teachers

- Protect life below water (printable), available from http://cdn.worldslargestlesson.globalgoals.org/2016/06/23-Protect-Life-Below-Water.pdf
- https://www.conserve-energy-future.com/reduce-reuse-recycle.php
- http://www.recycling-guide.org.uk/rrr.html

- http://www.teachoceanscience.net/teaching_resources/education_ modules/coral_reefs_and_climate_change/how_does_climate_chan ge_affect_coral_reefs/
- http://www.gbrmpa.gov.au/managing-the-reef/threats-to-the-reef/climate-change/what-does-this-mean-for-habitats/coral-reefs
- http://www.npr.org/sections/thesalt/2013/12/12/250438904/how -plastic-in-the-ocean-is-contaminating-your-seafood

Lesson 3: What the see saw: A balancing act

Grade: 6   Time Frame: 60 - 70 minutes

Summary and Rationale:

Students have already learned about the effect of oceans, seas and marine resources on the planet. In the second session they had identified threats to the oceans and considered the impact that this has on the planet. They have begun to identify ways to prevent or slow down the damage to the oceans. This lesson builds on previous learning as students take part in a structured discussion designed to deepen understanding and encourage students to reflect on their own roles and responsibilities towards conservation and sustainability.

Instructional Goal:

Students will take part in a structured discussion designed to deepen understanding and encourage students to reflect on their own roles and responsibilities towards conservation and sustainability.

Understanding Goals:

- Conservation and sustainability are key concepts for protecting oceans, seas and marine resources and governments and other organisations have a role to play in this.
- We all have a contribution to make towards conservation and sustainability.

Essential Questions:

- What are the key issues affecting our oceans?
- What needs to be done?
- What do we mean by conservation and sustainability?
- Who is responsible?

Student Learning Objectives:

Students will be able to:

- Use prior learning to contribute to a structured discussion
- Discuss the issues that affect the oceans and what needs to be done
- Explain what is meant by conservation and sustainability
- Reflect on who is responsible for change towards SDGs

Assessment:

The teacher may guide the discussion where appropriate. The teacher will take notes of evidence of deeper learning and understanding. Students will have opportunity to reflect on their learning after the discussion and physically indicate their feelings about whose responsibility SDG 14 is. The teacher will invite some students to talk about what they have concluded and why.

Sequence of activities:

Step 1: (5 minutes) – Ground Rules

Students sit in a large circle. Ground rules for discussion are established: no wrong answers, one person talking at a time, be respectful etc.

Step 2: (10 minutes) – Stimulus

Students pass pictures related to acidification, dead zones, pollution and waste or overfishing, passed around the circle. They silently reflect on what they see and how it makes them feel. In pairs students discuss what they saw and how they felt.

Step 3: (10 minutes) – Life Below Water

Read the following sections of *Life Below Water* (resources for teacher below): 'What would it cost to correct this?' and 'So what can we do?' Establish vocabulary, sustainability and conservation. What do students understand by these things? Display the definitions (Appendix 3). Students reflect on their personal beliefs: *Who's responsibility is this?* (Governments, charities, individuals?)

Step 4: (30 - 40 minutes) – Discussion

Students take part in a structured discussion about where the responsibility lies. Display building blocks for structured discussions: Following on from what x said, I think.., I agree with x because.., I disagree with x because.., In addition to.., on the other hand.., another consideration would be…

Step 5: (10 minutes) – Final thoughts

A line is marked on the floor. At one end, 'Governments and organisations', on the other end, 'individuals.' Students place themselves somewhere on the line to represent their view about whose responsibility SGD 14 is. The teacher will ask some students to explain why they have placed themselves at a given point on the line.

Resources

For students:

- http://www.mdgmonitor.org/sdg14-conserve-and-sustain-the-oceans-seas-and-marine-resources/
- https://www.forbes.com/sites/ups/2013/03/14/how-a-company-recycles-ocean-plastic-twice-the-size-of-texas/#37e0a07e4e22
- https://corporate-citizenship.com/2015/09/08/sdg-number-14-conserve-and-sustainably-use-the-oceans/

For teachers:

- Life Below Water available from http://www.un.org/sustainabledevelopment/wp-

content/uploads/2016/08/14_Why-it-Matters_Goal-14_Life-Below-Water_3p.pdf
- https://www.iucn.org/theme/global-policy/our-work/sustainable-development-goals/iucn-and-sdgs/sdg-14

Lesson 4: A prescription for sea-sickness: Project design

Grade: 6   Time Frame: 60 - 70 minutes

Summary and Rationale

Students will design a project intended to highlight an issue related to oceans, seas and marine resources. They will use the research, knowledge and personal reflections to decide upon which issue they would like to highlight. They may produce a booklet, leaflet, PowerPoint or poster explaining the issue, how it is caused and what can be done about it. Students will write persuasively with the aim of causing change in their intended audience.

Instructional Goal

Students produce a booklet, leaflet, PowerPoint or poster (at the teacher's discretion) explaining the issue, how it is caused and what can be done about it.

Understanding Goals

Students will show their understanding and knowledge of the understanding goals in sessions 1-3.

Essential Questions

- What issue are you going to highlight?
- Who is your intended audience?
- What is the purpose of your project?
- How are you going to present your argument?

Student Learning Objectives

Students will be able to:

- Show their understanding of what is meant by SDGs and why they are important (Introduction)
- Identify a threat to oceans, seas and marine resources (Title)
- Explain the threat and how it is caused (What is it and how is it caused?)
- Describe the effect of the threat on the ocean and the wider implications for the planet (Why does it matter?)
- Persuade their chosen audience to make a change towards conservation and sustainability (What can we do?)

Assessment

Students will self-assess against the learning objectives. The teacher will provide structured feedback and each group should be given time between this session and session 5 to reflect and respond to the feedback.

Sequence of activities

Step 1: (5 minutes) – Describe the Task

Students will produce a booklet, leaflet, PowerPoint or poster (at the teacher's discretion – teachers may decide which model students will use, or give a choice of models to students to choose from) explaining the issue, how it is caused and what can be done about it.

Step 2: (5 minutes) – Example

Look at a worked example (headings linked to learning objectives which should be shared with students).

- Title
- Introduction
- What is it and how is it caused?
- Why does it matter?

- What can we do?

Step 3: (5 – 10 minutes) – Deciding on the Issue

In groups, students decide on an issue they would like to highlight and agree on their audience (e.g. governments, organisations, individuals).

Step 4: (40 - 45 minutes) – Group Work

Students work collaboratively in their groups on their project. (This time may be extended if timetabling allows).

Step 5: (5 - 10 minutes) – Presentations

Students practice presenting their work.

Lesson 5: A prescription for sea-sickness: Project implementation

Grade: 6   Time Frame: 60 - 70 minutes

Summary and Rationale

Students will present their projects to their intended audience. This may be to the rest of the class, or wider opportunities can be sought, for example a community event. If possible, interest groups such as NGOs or local government representatives should be encouraged to attend the lesson. The idea of practical application of their work should be instilled in the students. Local community leaders could therefore implement schemes or ideas based on the student's findings. Students will be empowered to spread the message about SDG 14 and know that they are taking a real role in affecting change.

Instructional Goal

Students present their project to an intended audience.

Understanding Goals

- Awareness about SGD 14 is essential for communities to recognize the importance of sustainable oceans and marine life.
- We all have a role to play in affecting change.

Essential Questions

- How will you communicate your knowledge and understanding?
- Why is this issue important?
- Is it important to you?
- How are you going to hook your audience in and keep your audience listening?

Student Learning Objectives

Students will be able to:

- Speak knowledgeably and persuasively about SDGs and the issue they have highlighted.
- Understand that their views matter and they change make a change.
- To be able to demonstrate to an outside audience that their opinions matter.
- Have the strength of conviction on their own views.
- Demonstrate both teamwork and presentation skills.
- Persuade their audience of the need for change and give realistic suggestions about how this could be done.

Assessment

Students will self-assess against the learning objectives. Presentations can be recorded, displayed or reproduced for a wider audience. Teachers will be able to check knowledge and understanding from watching the presentations and from the printed/electronic materials that students produced. In addition, students will be all be awarded a certificate of completion on "Student Awareness on Sustainable Development for Life Below Water."

Sequence of Activities

Step 1: (10 minutes) – Preparation

Groups prepare pictures, resources and/or electronic equipment needed to present their projects.

<u>Step 2: (60 minutes) – Presentations</u>

Groups present their projects to the audience. This could be:

- the rest of the class
- another class / whole school
- at a community event
- to guests including local councils, organisations or other influential people.

Questions and answers could be done formally at the end of each presentation, or informally at the end of all the presentations in a social context.

Appendix A: Quiz sheet and answers

True or False? (answers)
- Oceans cover three quarters of the Earth's surface.
- Oceans contain 97 % of the Earth's water, and represent 99 % of the living space on the planet by volume
- Oceans contain nearly 200,000 identified species, but actual numbers may lie in the millions
- Oceans absorb about 30 percent of carbon dioxide produced by humans, buffering the impacts of global warming
- Oceans serve as the world's largest source of protein, with more than 3 billion people depending on the oceans as their primary source of protein
- Marine fisheries directly or indirectly employ over 200 million people
- As much as 40 % of the world oceans are heavily affected by human activities, including pollution, depleted fisheries, and loss of coastal habitats

Source: United Nations

True or False?

- Oceans cover three quarters of the Earth's surface.
- Oceans contain 97 % of the Earth's water, and represent 99 % of the living space on the planet by volume
- Oceans contain nearly 100,000 identified species.

- Oceans absorb about 30 percent of carbon dioxide produced by humans, buffering the impacts of global warming
- Oceans provide a source of protein, producing almost as much protein as land animals
- Marine fisheries directly or indirectly employ over 5 million people
- As much as 25% of the world oceans are heavily affected by human activities, including pollution, depleted fisheries, and loss of coastal habitats

Appendix B: Student resource sheet

Research Questions
- What key natural resources do the oceans provide?
- How do oceans help with the breakdown and removal of waste and pollution?
- How do coastal ecosystems protect the coast?
- How do healthy oceans support the mitigation of climate change?
- How do Marine Protected Areas contribute to poverty reduction?
- What kinds of creatures and organisms live in the marine environment?

Resources
- Life Below Water [PDF] also available from http://www.un.org/sustainabledevelopment/wp-content/uploads/2016/08/14_Why-it-Matters_Goal-14_Life-Below-Water_3p.pdf
- http://marinebio.org/oceans/ocean-resources/
- https://www.nationalgeographic.com/environment/oceans/critical-issues-ocean-acidification/

Appendix C: Sustainability

Noun

1. the ability to be sustained, supported, upheld, or confirmed.

2. Environmental Science. the quality of not being harmful to the environment or depleting natural resources, and thereby supporting long-term ecological balance:

The committee is developing sustainability standards for products that use energy.
Dictionary.com

Conservation

Noun
1. the act of conserving; prevention of injury, decay, waste, or loss; preservation:
conservation of wildlife; conservation of human rights.
2. official supervision of rivers, forests, and other natural resources in order to preserve and protect them through prudent management.
3. a district, river, forest, etc., under such supervision.
4. the careful utilization of a natural resource in order to prevent depletion.
5. the restoration and preservation of works of art.
Dictionary.com

Learning to Collaborate for the Global Common Good

Debating the Best Approaches to Achieving the SDG Goals: A Global Curriculum

Tina Owen-Moore, Pilar Cuesta, Beatriz Giraldo and Florencia Mingo

The following curriculum is designed so that teachers can engage students in debating strategies to meet the Sustainable Development Goals (SDGs). The curriculum starts from the point of agreement that the SDGs are goals that have been agreed upon by nations and provides students with opportunities to debate the best approaches towards meeting those goals. It is designed to be a curriculum that is implemented progressively throughout the high school years, starting with local examples in the first year, looking at national problems and solutions in the second year, and examining global questions in the third year. This particular lesson focuses on SDG 16, *Promoting Peaceful and Inclusive Societies*, yet the lesson format can be used for each of the SDGs. The goal of this curriculum is to ensure that young people are aware of and committed to meeting the Sustainable Development Goals set by the United Nations.

The debates are best suited to be a schoolwide initiative, where students of other grades can observe, provide feedback, and register their positions before and after the debate, but the lessons can be used in a single classroom or amongst several classrooms. They may be part of a social studies or communications curriculum or can be used as a team teaching unit plan, engaging students in all subject areas over a four-month period. For example, students examine statistics and create visual representations in math classes, engage in research in humanities classes, study what other countries have done in social studies classes, etc. Or different grades or subject area teams can choose to focus on different SDGs. However, the lessons are used, there should be communication amongst teachers to ensure that there is not repetition of lessons.

Lessons Overview

Developing 21st century skills and community solutions to meet the agenda outlined in the Sustainable Development Goals (SDGs) identified through the *Transforming Our World: The 2030 Agenda for Sustainable Development*.

Debating the Best Approaches to Achieving the SDG Goals:
A Global Curriculum

Learning Goals

The purpose of this lesson plan is to use debate to support high school students in developing solutions to meet the Sustainable Development Goals (SDGs). Teachers should feel comfortable adapting the debate topics and lessons to their specific contexts. Specifically, this lesson is addressing the SDG 16: "Promote peaceful and inclusive societies for sustainable development, provide access to justice for all and build effective, accountable and inclusive institutions at all levels." It is also meant as a learning experience that involves practice, feedback and improvement through a peer mentoring system. Through these activities, the students will develop the following competencies:

- Knowledge of the Sustainable Development Goals and how they were developed;
- A sense of ownership of the goals and their own capacity to influence the outcomes;
- The ability to do critical research and basic comparative studies;
- Strong communication and debate skills;
- The ability to work in groups and to collaborate to solve problems.
- The ability to form an opinion based on evidence and to communicate that opinion in written and verbal forms.

Lesson 1: Creating Peace: Debating Effective Strategies for Meeting SDG 16

This lesson engages students in debating causes, effects, and possible solutions to global pressing situations threatening peaceful and inclusive societies around the world.

In this particular lesson plan students will approach the following SDG 16 targets:

- Significantly reduce all forms of violence and related death rates everywhere
- End abuse, exploitation, trafficking and all forms of violence against and torture of children
- Ensure responsive, inclusive, participatory and representative decision-making at all levels

- Strengthen relevant national institutions, including through international cooperation, for building capacity at all levels, in particular in developing countries, to prevent violence and combat terrorism and crime

Grade Level Debate Topics

Grade 9: Peacebuilding in our school. *How can we, as a school community, develop effective strategies to reduce violence and increase peace in our school?*

The teacher/ debate organizer identifies two potential strategies to be considered (for debate) based on the school context.

Examples:

1. Violence has been increasingly a problem in schools. Schools use different strategies to avoid violence, which one would be more effective to apply?
    a. Argument #1: Violence must be prevented through strict monitoring and enforcement of rules. In order to reduce violence in schools, we should invest in increased security measures, such as increasing the number of security guards in schools, installing metal detectors, and enacting harsher penalties for bullying and other violent acts.
    b. Argument #2: No amount of security measures can stop violence. It is best to teach young people about the impact of violence so that they don't want to cause harm and to help them to change behaviors through socio-emotional learning, restorative justice, and other community-building approaches. Our resources would be best used to train teachers in these practices.
    c. Schools have student organizations for the purpose of giving the student body voice on certain school issues. Some "student-student" and "student-teacher" conflicts are being solved at administrative levels, without student representation or participation.
2. Argument #1: Student organizations and bodies of governance, such as student council, should address certain types of "student-student"

61

and "student-teacher" conflicts to assure student participation in conflict resolution.

    a. Argument #2: In order to protect student identities, student-student and student-teacher conflicts should only be addressed by the administration.

The teacher can use the following questions to orientate student reflection prior to the debate:

- What issue threatens peace in the school?
- How can school communities reduce all forms of violence and abuse against students?
- How can schools ensure responsive, inclusive, participatory and representative decision-making among students and between students and teachers?

The teacher may also choose to show data from the OECD Programme for International Student Assessment (PISA) Student Well-being Survey to highlight rates of bullying in schools and nations.

- PISA: http://www.oecd.org/edu/pisa-2015-results-volume-iii-9789264273856-en.htm.

The following video may be used to provide an example of how students participate in resolving student conflicts in some schools:

- Student-led restorative practices:
https://www.youtube.com/watch?v=zgw7gY9fbz8

Grade 10: Peacebuilding at a national level. *How can countries develop effective strategies to resolve conflicts between social groups and increase peace nationally?*

Examples:

1. Social inequality within a country can lead to political instability and conflict. What should the national government do to address social inequality and prevent conflict?

    a. National government should raise taxes in order to re-distribute benefits equally among society.

     b. National government should strengthen capitalism and economic growth, ensuring unemployment is low and people activate local economy.

2. In many countries, divides between political parties erupt in violence. How can countries develop peaceful solutions to discontent between competing political parties?

     a. Argument #1: It is the government's responsibility to ensure differences in political parties don´t escalate into violent manifestations.

     b. Argument #2: Competition between political parties is essential for democracy.

3. Civilians have an important role to solve inequality within society, mostly because they personally live through it. How can they most effectively reach feasible, long-term solutions?

     a. Argument #1: Civilians should tackle inequality through the private sector, creating Foundations, NGO and nonprofits that address each cause.

     b. Argument #2: Civilians should tackle inequality through the public sector, engaging, participating and working for government initiatives.

The teacher can use the following questions to orientate student reflection prior to the debate:

- What issues threaten peace in our country and what are some solutions that have been proposed to address similar issues in other countries?

- How can countries reduce all forms of violence and related death rates at a national level?

- How can countries end abuse, exploitation, trafficking and all forms of violence against and torture of children?

- How can countries ensure responsive, inclusive, participatory and representative decision-making at all levels?

- Which institutions exist nationwide that can help building capacities at all levels to prevent violence and combat terrorism and crime?

Debating the Best Approaches to Achieving the SDG Goals:
A Global Curriculum

The teacher may also assign the following readings to help students to understand some of the problems that nations face when it comes to creating peace:

- The UN's role in maintaining peace:
  http://www.un.org/en/sections/what-we-do/maintain-international-peace-and-security/
- There are only ten countries that are free from conflict:
  http://www.independent.co.uk/news/world/politics/global-peace-index-2016-there-are-now-only-10-countries-in-the-world-that-are-not-at-war-a7069816.html
- What makes for a peaceful nation?
  https://wilpfact.wordpress.com/2013/10/03/what-makes-for-a-peaceful-nation/

Grade 11: Peacebuilding as a global community. *How can international organizations contribute to peacebuilding when conflicts arise between two or more countries worldwide? How can countries resolve conflicts with other countries in peaceful ways?*

Examples:

1. Some experts say that our next imminent World War will happen because water is a conflicting scarce resource. How to promote peace? How to avoid this possible third World War?
   a. Argument #1: Water used for farming contributes to water scarcity. We should invest resources in new technologies for farming and for education in farming communities to reduce overuse of water.
   b. Argument #2: Individuals must be the solution to water scarcity. We should invest resources in educating young people about water conservation.
2. Nuclear weapons are a huge threat for most countries around the world. How to promote peace and avoid these attacks?
   a. Argument #1: Safety is a matter of being prepared. We must invest in continuing to develop our nuclear strength in order to predict and prevent the possibility of any nuclear attack.

      b.   Argument #2: The use of nuclear energy creates a nuclear threat worldwide. The nation should invest its resources in eliminating nuclear power plants and turning to green energy sources.

3.   Religion is inherently controversial, because of the passion it inspires. These controversies can evolve into violence. How do you think governments should promote peace across different religions? How can you help to build a tolerant world?

      a.   Argument #1: We should invest resources in having leaders of different religious communities participate in activities designed to build understanding of the commonalities between the religions.

      b.   Argument #2: We should invest resources to ensure that there are world religions courses in schools.

The teacher can use the following questions to orientate student reflection prior to the debate:

- What issues threaten peace worldwide today? What are some solutions that have been implemented before to address similar worldwide issues?
- How can the world significantly reduce all forms of violence and related death rates everywhere?
- How can the world end abuse, exploitation, trafficking and all forms of violence against and torture of children?
- How can the world ensure responsive, inclusive, participatory and representative decision-making at all levels?

Summary and Rationale

While there may be agreement that creating peaceful and inclusive communities should be a goal of any community, there is much disagreement in communities around how best to meet this goal. The *Developing Community Solutions Curriculum* engages high school students in debates around possible solutions and engages them in developing community solutions to local problems.

Debating the Best Approaches to Achieving the SDG Goals:
A Global Curriculum

Overview of the Lesson

This lesson is designed to help high school students at three different grade levels think about how they can meet the goal of creating peaceful and inclusive communities at the local school level, the national level, and the global level. Moreover, it will include a mentoring process where older and more experienced students who have participated in these debates before will provide feedback to younger, less-experienced students.

Grades. 9th grade, 10th grade and 11th grade.

Time frame. Research and delivery of debates occurs over a four-month period.

Subjects

This lesson could easily be integrated into subjects like history, philosophy and ethics, or it could be a cross-curricular project amongst several teachers and subject areas.

Instructional goal

Through the debate activities students will develop 21st century knowledge and skills, which are skills identified as necessary for success in the 21st century work and citizenship environment. (See Appendix B).

Standards

This curriculum is based on the Core SEL Standards created by the Collaborative for Academic, Social, and Emotional Learning. The five standards are: self-awareness, self-management, social awareness, relationship skills, and responsible decision-making. This lesson helps to achieve SUSTAINABLE DEVELOPMENT GOAL 16: Promote peaceful and inclusive societies for sustainable development, provide access to justice for all and build effective, accountable and inclusive institutions at all levels. See Appendix A for detail on each target for this SDG.

Competencies

The activities outlined in this lesson plan help students to develop the following competencies:

- Understand ideas and concepts associated with the targets of the Sustainable Development Goals and how the goals were developed.
- The ability to question one's own and others' understandings of critical issues threatening peaceful and inclusive societies.
- Analyze and compare the effectiveness of current solutions adopted at the local, national, and international level to ensure peace and inclusiveness.
- Apply and interpret knowledge in order to come up with potential solutions to address the different targets.

Understanding Goals

Students should understand that there are many ways to approach achieving the SDG goals and that it takes research, collaboration, and critical thinking to determine the best solutions for any local context.

Essential Questions

The following questions can be used before and after the lesson to engage students in thinking about the concept of peace and discussing what it means to them as individuals and members of various communities.

- What does peace look like? Is it simply not fighting, or is there more to it than that?
- Why is peace in any one country important to the leaders and citizens of other countries?
- Why are some places more peaceful than others? What are the factors that contribute to peace?
- What are effective strategies for promoting peace? What actions or strategies have the potential to deter peace?
- What is my initial and final position according to the topic in debate? If there is any change in position, why did this happen?

Student Learning Objectives

The lesson will achieve the following objectives:

- Students will study various definitions of peace and inclusivity, and will examine how different nations, organizations, and individuals have defined and communicated the concept of peace. Through these studies, students will be able to develop their own definitions/ understandings of peace and inclusivity.
- Students will develop the skill of researching solutions to pressing community problems.
- Students will be able to communicate clearly and effectively.
- Students will learn how to collaborate with peers to develop persuasive arguments.
- Students will adjust their delivery according to feedback given by their mentors and peers.

Assessment

Students will be graded according to the quality and depth of their arguments. Consensus over either argument is not expected. Both the quality of the student's investigation and the final performance in the debate will be considered in the final grade. Students will receive a checklist with the details of the amount, depth and quality of research required and a rubric with the aspects that will be evaluated. Teachers should create these based on the grade level and curriculum requirements of the course.

Half of the grade is associated with content analysis:

- Information accurately and clearly presented, supported with facts or statistics
- Arguments and counterarguments are pertinent and strong. The students do not incur in fallacies in the construction of the argument.
- Arguments are coherently organized in order to contribute to a main argument
-

The other half of the grade involves the delivery of this content:

- Level in which the students keep the attention of the audience. Enthusiasm and use of nonverbal communication (gestures, tone of voice, eye contact)
- Students shows a deep understanding of their topic and are able to demonstrate their position in a persuasive and convincing way, using emotive language, quotes, anecdotes or metaphors to get the audience involved.
- Correct use of time in the arguments and counterarguments exposure.
- Contribute to the team, participate and perform the tasks assigned, and listen and give credit to the other members of the team

Sequence of Activities

Teachers may use the following sequence of activities or develop a sequence that meets the needs of their individual classrooms.

Step 1: Motivator

Goal: learn to express personal positions, contemplate difference, disagree/agree with an idea (not the person), promote tolerance and respect among classmates.

In preparation for the debate: the teacher will draw a line across the room and invite the students to stand freely on either side of it. The teacher will prompt the students with different questions that will invite them to take posture by staying away from the line or walking towards the line. After every prompt, each student will walk away from the line ready to act on the next prompt. See Appendix C for prompt examples. The teacher may choose to show this video to give students an example of this activity: https://www.youtube.com/watch?v=jD8tjhVO1Tc

In addition, students will register their initial position to the topic debated, before any research, preparation or discussion is conducted. Teachers may choose to use the online polling systems, Slido or Poll Everywhere, to register positions before and after the debate. If computers or phones are not available, students can stand on one side of the class or the other to votes. If the teacher desires to make the voting anonymous, students can put their heads down and put their thumbs up or down to register a position.

1. Core events

   o Students divide in minimum groups of four or maximum groups of 8. Each group will have a topic assigned, as well as a "for or against" posture. If the classes are large, the teacher can decide whether to have several groups work on similar positions, or to develop several positions or arguments for the question.

   o Two students lead the research in preparation for the debate, one other will structure and deliver the initial arguments, and another will structure and deliver the counterarguments.

   o The previous research includes paper, magazines, news, articles, interviews and the analysis of other sources, in order to gain understanding of the topic.

   o The teams will face each other and start debating by exposing a first argument that meets their position, the other team will respond with their own initial argument. Alternation of initial arguments will continue until at least three arguments per team are delivered.

   o Time is given to better prepare counterarguments. They are delivered in alternation for each team.

2. Conclusion

   o Use computers for this last session or allow the use of cellphones in class. Use Slido or Poll Everywhere to invite your students to an interactive voting activity. If computers or cell phones are not available, teachers can have students vote by moving to one side of the classroom or by putting their heads down and voting with a thumb up or down.

   o Students will vote for each of the issues discussed accordingly to their grade and themes of interest.

   o Once the results are gathered, the teacher should show the change in positions from the initial and final voting process, and should pose the following reflection questions along with the results: What differences do you notice comparing our initial and final voting? How do you explain this consistency or inconsistency? Is this an expected or unexpected situation?

o   Students will have a chance to share if they are for or against each of the discussed issues. Reflect on the influence others can have on your own opinion: polarization or shift of position over debated topics.

o   Students should write a final persuasive paper which argues a personal position with logical evidence and reasoning.

Student Activities

1.   Read SUSTAINABLE DEVELOPMENT GOAL 16: Promote peaceful and inclusive societies for sustainable development, provide access to justice for all and build effective, accountable and inclusive institutions at all levels.
2.   Read about a local issue or conflict.
3.   Read strategies that have been proposed for addressing the issue or conflict.
4.   Teams develop a set of arguments to support given solution based on research and comparable settings.
5.   Students participate in a structured debate defending their positions, with local community members and policy-makers as judges.
6.   Students reflect and write a final position paper based on their own beliefs about best potential solutions.

Resources for students	Resources for teachers:
The Sustainable Development Goals (SDGs): http://www.undp.org/content/undp/en/home/sustainable-development-goals.html	Debates in the Classroom, a resource from Education Week: http://www.educationworld.com/a_curr/strategy/strategy012.shtml Essential Tips for Conducting a Class Debate, a resource from Busy Teacher: http://busyteacher.org/7245-conducting-class-debate-essential-tips.html Design for Change curriculum. How to bring debated ideas, into action http://www.dfcworld.com/SITE/Join movement

Appendix A: SDG 16 targets to promote peace, justice, and strong institutions for sustainable development

http://www.un.org/sustainabledevelopment/peace-justice/

- Significantly reduce all forms of violence and related death rates everywhere

- End abuse, exploitation, trafficking and all forms of violence against and torture of children

- Promote the rule of law at the national and international levels and ensure equal access to justice for all

- By 2030, significantly reduce illicit financial and arms flows, strengthen the recovery and return of stolen assets and combat all forms of organized crime

- Substantially reduce corruption and bribery in all their forms

- Develop effective, accountable and transparent institutions at all levels

- Ensure responsive, inclusive, participatory and representative decision-making at all levels

- Broaden and strengthen the participation of developing countries in the institutions of global governance

- By 2030, provide legal identity for all, including birth registration

- Ensure public access to information and protect fundamental freedoms, in accordance with national legislation and international agreements

- Strengthen relevant national institutions, including through international cooperation, for building capacity at all levels, in particular in developing countries, to prevent violence and combat terrorism and crime

- Promote and enforce non-discriminatory laws and policies for sustainable development

Appendix B: 21st Century Skills addressed in this curriculum

Cognitive Skills	Interpersonal skills	Intrapersonal skills
Critical Thinking · Reason effectively, use systems thinking and evaluate evidence · Use various types of reasoning (inductive, deductive, etc.) as appropriate to the situation · Use systems thinking: Examine ideas, identify and analyze arguments · Synthesize and make connections between information and arguments · Effectively analyze and evaluate evidence, arguments, claims and beliefs · Evaluate. Assess claims and arguments · Infer. Query evidence, conjecture alternatives and draw conclusions · Explain. Stating results, justifying	· Communication: · Competency in language in mother tongue and additional languages · Ability to communicate, in written or oral form, and understand, or make others understand various messages · Ability to formulate one's arguments in a convincing manner and take full account of other viewpoints · Confidence when speaking in public · Collaboration: interact effectively with others · Know when it is appropriate to listen and when to speak · Speak with clarity and awareness of	· Curiosity about global affairs and world cultures · The ability to recognize and weigh diverse cultural perspectives · The ability to recognize and examine assumptions when engaging with cultural differences · Self-management · Identify personal biases

procedures and presenting arguments	audience and purpose	
· Problem solving: ask significant questions that clarify various points of view and lead to better solutions	· Empathy towards people from different cultures	
· Information skills: access and evaluate information	· Resolve culturally based disagreements through negotiation, mediation, and conflict resolution	
· Access information efficiently and effectively		
· Evaluate information critically and competently		
· Use technology as a tool to research, organize, evaluate and communicate information		

Appendix C: Prompt examples for the motivator activity

The prompts could be:

- Who has the new _____ album? (famous singer at that moment)
- Anyone who prefers day to night
- Who believes in climate change?
- Anyone that recycles at home?
- Anyone who has traveled in another country?
- Anyone who has participated in public protests?
- Are you part of a group or club of interest?
- Anyone who feels represented in any minority group?

Bibliography

Binkley, M. e. (2010). *ACTS Draft White Paper. Defining 21st Century Skills.* Melbourne: Assessment and Teaching of 21st Century Skills Project, University of Melbourne.

Reimers, F. a. (2016). *Teaching and Learning for the Twenty First Century.* Cambridge: Harvard Education Press.

Reimers, F. a.-R. (2014). Getting to the Core and Evolving the Education Movement to a System of Continuous Improvement. *New England Journal of Public Policy*, 186-205.

Reimers, F. C. (2016). *Empowering Global Citizens: A World Course.* Cambridge: CreateSpace Independent Publishing Platform.

The Collaborative for Academic, S. a. (2017, September 27). Core SEL Competencies. Retrieved from CASEL's Core SEL Competencies: http://www.casel.org/core-competencies/

UN Web Services Section, D. o. (2017, September 27). *Sustainable Development Goals: 17 Goals to Transfrom Our World.* Retrieved from A United Nations Website: http://www.un.org/sustainabledevelopment/sustainable-development-goals/

Debating the Best Approaches to Achieving the SDG Goals:
A Global Curriculum

Equity, Social Justice, and Sustainable Development: An Integrated Curriculum

Jessica Bergmann, Allison Casey, Ana Marcela Lozano, Victoria Gale Modesto, Michelle A. Ward, & Jesella Zambrano

The Sustainable Development Goals (SDGs) were established to coordinate international efforts toward the creation of prosperous, equitable societies inhabiting a healthy planet, which can continue to meet the needs of future generations (United Nations, 2015). Learning about the aims, challenges, and approaches of the SDGs enables students to develop essential skills and competencies that are needed to face the challenges of our continuously-evolving, interconnected world in the 21st century (Reimers et al., 2016). Many schools around the world are limited by available resources, time, money, and/or capacity, and as such, cannot afford to redesign and replace existing curricula. The Equity, Social Justice, and Sustainable Development Curriculum, outlined below, proposes a framework to efficiently integrate the SDGs into existing curriculum standards in schools with limited capacity and resources.

Overview

The SDGs, adopted by the United Nations in September 2015, are part of the global development agenda enacted to end poverty, fight inequality, and tackle climate change internationally. The seventeen goals are a call to action for countries to pursue sustainable measures in economic growth, environmental protection, and social needs (United Nations, 2015). In order for the SDGs to be met in the 15-year timeline, rich, middle-income, and poor countries around the world must mobilize ambitious efforts. However, it is not just the efforts of politicians and world leaders that matter. Governments, private institutions, civil society, and private citizens must also play an important role. Thus, an essential element of the SDGs is educating the world's population about these global needs for prosperity and sustainable development (United Nations, 2015).

Integrating the SDGs into education, is a very important element in developing responsible, engaged citizens with global perspectives (Reimers et al., 2016). Traditional curricula, which focus on numeracy, literacy, science, and history, do not typically include 21st century skills, such as critical thinking, leadership, creative problem solving, grit, collaboration, communication, and technological literacy, among others. Ambitious curricula that center around the SDGs and 21st century skills have already been created, however many schools and school systems around the world, and in the United States in particular, do not have sufficient resources to redesign existing curriculum. As facilitators of learning and bearers of knowledge, teachers have the capacity to deliver the most important, contextually relevant lessons for their students. The curriculum outlined below provides a framework for teachers who seek to develop students' 21st century skills through integrated lessons that combine existing curriculum standards with SDG learning objectives.

Curriculum Content: Competencies & Pedagogical Approaches

This curriculum focuses on quality education as defined by SDG Goal Four, which promotes sustainable development and sustainable lifestyles through education, aiming "by 2030, (to) ensure that all learners acquire the knowledge and skills needed to promote sustainable development...through education for ... sustainable lifestyles, human rights, gender equality, promotion of a culture of peace and non-violence, global citizenship, and appreciation of cultural diversity and of a culture's contribution to sustainable development needs" (United Nations, 2015). In order to engage students in topics of human rights, social justice, and equity, the curriculum presented includes content on SDGs one through five and SDGs 10, 12, and 16, including quality education. These include no poverty, zero hunger, good health and well-being, gender equality, reduced inequalities, responsible consumption and production, and peace, justice and strong institutions (United Nations, 2015).

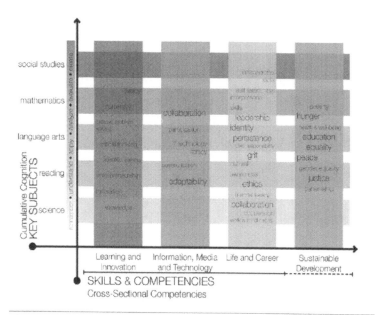

Figure 1. Cross-sectional competencies are embedded into lessons, assignments, and activities covered in core subject areas. The proposed Equity and Sustainable Development Curriculum uses this framework to integrate the SDGs into existing curriculum. Equity and Sustainable Development learning framework developed based on Bloom's Taxonomy (Bloom et al., 1956) and the Framework for 21st Century Learning (Partnership for 21st Century Learning, 2015).

This curriculum aims to develop 21st century skills including interpersonal skills, intrapersonal skills, ethics, knowledge and learning, and work and mind habits. These elements are crucial for the holistic development of students in the 21st century (Reimers & Chung, 2016). Existing curricula typically integrate cross-sectional competencies into core subject areas. Competencies such as learning and innovation, information, media, and technology, and life and career skills are embedded into lessons, assignments, and activities covered in core subjects (Partnership for 21st Century Learning, 2015). The proposed Equity, Social Justice, and Sustainable Development Curriculum uses this framework to integrate the SDGs into existing curriculum, as shown in Figure 1. Lessons, assignments, activities, and projects in core courses will not cover subject matter abstractly. Instead, courses will use the SDGs to frame core subject matter, enabling students to learn content through the lens of sustainable development issues.

Curriculum Prototypes

Lessons within this curriculum integrate cross-sectional skills and competencies into existing core content curriculum requirements. An example of this is included in the lesson plan prototype "Percent Change as a Tool to Analyze Progress" (see Appendix A for full lesson plan). This specific lesson plan example integrates SDG goals 5 and 10 into learning standards set forth by the Texas Essential Knowledge and Skills (TEKS) mathematics curriculum. The lesson, which introduces the concept of percent change, asks students to utilize this tool to analyze the political inclusion of marginalized groups. The lesson is split into four parts: launch, explore, practice, and summarize, further explained in Figure 2. During "Launch" students are introduced to the lesson through questions that enable critical thinking about the data. In "Explore" students use the percent change formula to calculate the change in African American representation from the 95th to the 105th United States Congress. During "Practice" students are asked to continue to use the percent change formula to calculate percent change for various other marginalized groups and are encouraged to think beyond the math to the human beings these figures represents. Finally, during "Summarize" the teacher leads a class discussion that critically analyzes the results of the exercise.

LAUNCH	PRACTICE
What stories does this data tell? What questions do you have about this data? The 111th Congress was the most diverse congress in the history of the US up to that time. Do you think it is diverse enough? What criteria would a congress need to meet in order to be "diverse enough?"	Calculate the percent change of political inclusion of various marginalized groups. As you're doing your calculations think beyond the math. What/who do these numbers represent?
	SUMMARIZE
EXPLORE	Why did the change of 14 seats mean a 467% increase for women and a 14% decrease for men? How do you think women feel about the change in their access to power? How do you think men feel about it? 467% change is HUGE! Does this mean we have hit our goal of equal opportunities for women? What useful information does percent change provide? How is this different from the information amount of change provides? Which calculation of change tells the best story of progress for women? What are the pros and cons of each? Do we need to tell both to get the full picture?
$$percent\ change = \frac{amount\ of\ change}{original\ amount} \times 100$$ How can we use this formula to calculate the percent change of African Americans in the House from the 95th Congress to the 105th Congress?	

Figure 2. The "Percent Change as a Tool to Analyze Progress" lesson, presented in a simplified version above, introduces the concept of percent change and asks students to utilize this tool to analyze the political inclusion of marginalized groups. The lesson is split into four parts: launch, explore, practice, and summarize.

Further examples of integrated lesson plans are included in Appendices B, C, D, and E, below. Lesson plans for a variety of grade levels spanning primary and secondary school are included in science, mathematics, history, and reading/language arts content areas.

Lesson Plan Framework

The following steps outline the process teachers can use to create a lesson plan that integrates SDG learning objectives with standard curriculum content learning objectives. Figure 3, below, provides a guiding framework for use during the development of lesson plans.

1. Choose your content standard
2. Create an objective for your content standard
3. Develop a way to assess the content objective
4. Choose a Sustainable Development Goal (SDG) that is related to your content standard
5. Create an objective for your SDG
6. Develop a way to assess the SDG objective

7. Combine the objective for your standard and the SDG into one learning objective for your lesson

8. Combine your content and SDG assessments to create your assessment of mastery at the end of the lesson

9. Design the elements of your lesson plan, keeping in mind the following question:

   a. How are you going to get your students interested in the topic?

   b. In what ways can your students use or challenge their prior knowledge and thinking?

   c. How will you address misconceptions?

STANDARD	OBJECTIVE	ASSESSMENT
Content Standard:	Content Objective:	Content Assessment:
	+	+
Sustainable Development Goal:	Sustainable Development Goal Objective:	Sustainable Development Goal Assessment:
	=	=
	Learning Objective for Lesson:	Lesson Assessment:

Figure 3. Lesson Planning Outline

In order to introduce equality, social needs, and human rights issues through the SDGs, a sequential process for creating inclusive classrooms and schools is essential. This process helps students deal with diversity through cognitive and affective learning and enables them to engage with the issues in a non-threatening way (Davidson & Shneidewind, 2006). The sequence includes four phases that allow teachers to lead students through the learning process. Lessons differ in complexity and content according to each of these phases. Phase one begins with creating an inclusive, trusting community where students appreciate diversity in the classroom. Phase two enables students to empathize with others' life experiences and explore why and how inequality and social needs based on differences exist. Phase three follows by helping students examine discrimination and human rights issues in the institutions in their lives, analyzing how it has impacted them and their peers. Finally, phase four empowers students to envision and create change to foster greater equality (Davidson & Shneidewind, 2006). The lesson plan prototype "Percent Change as a Tool to Analyze Progress" is part of phase three of the process to introduce equity issues. The additional sample lesson plans provided demonstrate other phases in this process.

Conclusion

In many schools, measures of high-stakes testing, accountability systems, threats of probation and closing, teacher evaluations based on student test scores, and top-down standards restrict teachers' ability to innovate in course content (Gutstein & Peterson, 2013). This, coupled with limited resources, time, and capacity can further constrain teachers. However, limiting education to traditional content knowledge is a great disservice to students as they prepare to become 21st century citizens. Teaching about equity and sustainable development is part of a larger and essential effort to develop responsible, engaged, and active citizens. It is essential for critical educators to embed humanity, responsibility, and equity into learning. No knowledge is neutral and it would be a wasted opportunity if the core content knowledge is not used to develop the skills expected of 21st century citizens (Gutstein & Peterson, 2013). Allowing content knowledge to respond to the aspirational competencies and skills students should develop is a natural evolution in the creation of curriculum. The aspirational purpose of education has always been to create human beings with the capacity for problem-solving, self-actualization, and lifelong learning. However, there has always been a gap between the skills and knowledge students develop in the classroom and the application of those skills and knowledge in the real world. The approach proposed by the Equity, Social Justice, and Sustainable Development Curriculum deepens student knowledge and empowers students to think beyond the classroom to solving real-world problems.

References

(1997). *Texas Essential Knowledge and Skills for Kindergarten-Grade 12*: 19 TAC Chapter 111, Mathematics. Austin, TX: Texas Education Agency.

Partnership for 21st Century Learning (P21). (2015). *Framework for 21st century learning*. Washington, DC. Retrieved from http://www.p21.org/storage/documents/docs/P21_framework_08 16.pdf

Bloom, B., Englehart, M., Furst, E., Hill, W., & Krathwohl, D. (1956). *Taxonomy of educational objectives: The classification of educational goals. Handbook I: Cognitive domain.* New York, Toronto: Longmans, Green.

Davidson, E., & Shneidewind, N. (2006). *Open minds to equality.* Retrieved from http://rethinkingschools.aidcvt.com/publication/omte/OmteIntro.s html

United Nations. (2015). *Sustainable development agenda.* Retrieved from http://www.un.org/ga/search/view_doc.asp?symbol=A/RES/70/1 &Lang=E

Gutstein, E., & Peterson, B. (Eds.). (2013). *Rethinking mathematics.* Milwaukee, WI: Rethinking Schools, Ltd.

Reimers, F., & Chung, C. (Eds.). (2016). *Teaching and learning for the twenty-first century.* Cambridge, MA: Harvard Education Press.

Reimers, F., Chopra, V., Chung, C., Higdon, J., & O'Donnell, E.B. (2016). *Empowering global citizens.* North Charleston, SC: CreateSpace Independent Publishing Platform.

Appendix A

	Lesson Title	Designers
	Teaching Percent Change as a Tool to Analyze Progress	Victoria Gale, adapted from a lesson by Flannery Denny
	Subject and Grade Level	Time Frame
	Mathematics Grade 8	50 minutes
Desired Results	Texas Essential Knowledge and Skills (TEKS)	Sustainable Development Goals
	8.3B (R) Students will estimate and find solutions to application problems involving percents and other proportional relationships such as similarity and rates.	**Reduced Inequality:** empower and promote the social, economic and political inclusion of all, irrespective of age, sex, disability, race, ethnicity, origin, religion or economic or other status **Gender Equality:** Ensure women's full and effective participation and equal opportunities for leadership at all levels of decision-making in political, economic and public life
	Content Learning Objectives (LO)	SDG Learning Objective
	Students will be able to calculate percent change.	Students will be able to analyze the political inclusion of marginalized groups.
	Lesson Learning Objective	
	· Students will be able to use percent change to analyze progress of political inclusion of marginalized groups. · Students will be able to analyze the progress made	

towards political inclusion for all using their knowledge of percent change.

Understandings	Essential Questions
What are the big ideas? What specific understandings about them are desired? What misunderstandings are predictable?	What provocative questions will foster inquiry, understanding, and transfer of learning?
· Mathematics is a tool to better understand injustice. · Amount of change and percent change tell different stories. · Percent change is a comparison of old values to new values.	1. Do our political representatives truly represent us? Should they? 2. How do we decide if progress towards equal representation is being made? 3. How have marginalized groups access to power changed over time? How do you think they feel about it? 4. How have non-marginalized groups access to power changed over time? How do you think they feel about it? 5. What useful information can percent change provide? How is this different from the information amount of change provides?

Demonstration of Learning (DOL) and Corresponding Exemplar Student Response

Performance Task

Through what authentic performance tasks will students

demonstrate the desired understandings? By what criteria will performances of understanding be judged?

Given data for the Dallas ISD School Board of 1975 and 2016, students will be able to calculate the percent change of political representation for Men, Women, African Americans, and Latinx with 100% accuracy. Students will be asked to explain each part of the percent change equation as it relates to the context. Students will be asked to use the result of their calculations to analyze progress made towards political inclusion for all in their community.

Students will know… "What" key points	Students will be able to… "How" key points
· Amount of change is the difference between the original value and the new value · Percent change is a comparison between the original value and the new value. · Many groups of people are not equitably represented in Congress. · Progress towards equitable political inclusion/representation has been made.	We can calculate amount of change by subtracting the new value from the original value We can calculate percent change by dividing the amount of change by the original amount and then multiplying by 100. We can use our knowledge of percent change to analyze progress made towards achieving the Sustainable Development Goals.

Learning Plan	**LAUNCH** (8 minutes):	
	Purpose for teachers:	Purpose for students:
	· *Set the purpose of the day* · *Present a learning activity or experience that prepares students to engage in the explore portion of the lesson*	·*Make initial connections to key points necessary for engaging in the explore portion of the lesson*
	Teacher Actions	Student Actions

Distribute the data handout to students.	Scholars read the data handout, reflect, and discuss with their partner.
Say: In front of you are three sets of data. One from the 95th US Congress which was from 1977-1979, another from the 105th US Congress from 1997-1999, and the last is the 111th US Congress from 2009-2011. Independently, you have 1 minute to read the data and take note of what you notice. What stories does this data tell? What do these stories mean for you? What do they mean for your community? Country? You will then have 2 minutes to discuss your reflections with a partner.	Anticipated responses: · Why aren't men listed? · Why is there so much more information in the 111th congress? · More racial/ethnic, gender, and religious minorities are included in congress in 2011 compared to 1977.*** · The racial/ethnic, gender, and religious diversity in congress isn't representative of the diversity of the people in our country.***
Give scholars 1 minute to read silently and then direct them to spend the next 2 minutes discussing their thoughts with their partner. Tell them to justify their thinking using the data.	
	*** Exemplar responses.
Say: Let's come back together as a group and discuss what we're noticing.	Students share out what they discussed with their partners.

Say: We know that statistics and data tell us stories about the world we live in. What stories do you see in this data? What do these stories mean for you/your community/your country? How does this make you feel?	Students discuss whole group.
Listen and engage with students as they contextualize this data to themselves and their lives.	Anticipated responses:
Questions to pose to push discussion:	· It's not diverse enough because there still are more men than women and more white people than people of color.
· The 111th Congress was the most diverse congress in the history of the US up to that time. Do you think it is diverse enough?	· There would need to be equal number of men and women. There would need to be equitable number of seats for each race/ethnicity.
· What criteria would a congress need to meet in order to be "diverse enough?"	
· Do you notice different amounts of progress in the House vs the Senate? Why do you think that is?	· There are more seats in the House than in the Senate.
· (Briefly explain gerrymandering) How do you think the way our voting districts are set up affect elections?	· Communities of color should have a fair chance to elect representatives that are people of color and who come from their own community. Gerrymandering
· (Briefly explain The	

Voting Rights Act) Why is it important to set up voting districts fairly?	and other racist laws/policies make it difficult for people of color to gain representation in politics.
Say: We are now going to learn an important tool called percent change. This tool can help us better understand this data. As we work through the lesson today, I challenge you to think through the following questions: 1. What progress has our country made towards political inclusion for all? How do we know? 2. What would it take for our country to achieve equitable political inclusion for all racial/ethnic, gender, and religious minorities? Why is this so important to us?	

EXPLORE (5 minutes)

Purpose for teachers:	Purpose for students:
· *Facilitate students' thinking toward understanding the key points through questioning (without providing answers or explanations)*	· *Deeply explore concepts and come up with theories and conjectures (e.g., making observations, identifying patterns)*

Teacher Actions	Student Actions
Write the formula for percent change on the board. Say: How can we use this formula to calculate the percent change of African Americans in the House from the 95th Congress to the 105th Congress? Go through the example whole-group. Discuss the meaning of original amount as it pertains to this context. Discuss how to calculate amount of change. Push students to think about what these numbers mean contextually. [Check for students' understanding before moving on]	Exemplar response: Find the amount of change by subtracting the original number of African Americans in the House (17) from the new number of African Americans in the House (41). Then, divide that amount of change (24), by the original amount (17). Then, multiply that (1.41) by 100. The percent change is 141%. Scholars continue to respond to teacher questioning.
Practice (10):	
Purpose for teachers:	**Purpose for students:**

· Guide student practice where students get immediate feedback · Coach and provide feedback during independent practice · Assess student understanding	· Apply understanding by practicing in groups, pairs, and independently · Reflect and self-assess on learning
Teacher Actions	**Student Actions**

Say: *Look at the chart on the board. Each of you is going to calculate the percent change of different groups' representation in Congress over time. Once our chart is complete, we will be able to make comparisons. Remember as you're doing your calculations to think beyond the math, push your partner to do the same. What/who do these numbers represent?*

During practice, make sure all students are on task and narrate positive behavior. Check in with struggling students and walk around the room to gather trends in misconceptions. Check student work as you walk around. Put checks on correct answers and circle the parts of incorrect answers students need to correct.

Direct students to add their calculations to the chart on the board.

Transition to Summarize where we will synthesize the information.

Scholars use the percent change formula to independently calculate the percent change of political inclusion of various minority groups over time.

Scholars think beyond the numbers and make sense of their calculations in the context of political inclusion.

Scholars push their partners to describe their calculations - what each number represents, what these numbers mean in regards to the SDG goal of political inclusion, what these findings mean for themselves and their community.

Anticipated responses:

· The original amount is the number of men that used to have seats in the Senate. In the 95th senate there were 97 men so the original amount is 97.

· The amount of change is the difference between the original amount and new amount of men in the Senate. There used to be 97 and now there are 83. The amount of change is 14.

	· Using the percent change formula, there was a 14.4% change. Since the number of men is less than before, this is a percent decrease. · The representation of men in the Senate has decreased over time but this is a positive thing for progress towards the SDG of equitable political inclusion for all. Men are only half of the population and should have only half the Senate seats. Scholars add their calculations to the chart on the board until the chart is complete.
SUMMARIZE (20 minutes)	
Purpose for teachers: · *Facilitate a whole-group conversation about the exploration* · *Synthesize student ideas: clarify key points and address misunderstandings* · *Connect key points from exploration to understandings and*	**Purpose for students:** · *Solidify key points from practice and exploration* · *Connect their ideas to classmates' ideas*

essential questions

Teacher Actions	Student Actions
Teacher facilitates a discussion about the percent change experienced by different groups of people. Questions to use to facilitate discussion: · What do you notice when you compare the percent change of men and the percent change of women? · Between the 95th and the 111th Congress, 14 seats changed from men to women. Why did the change of 14 seats mean a 467% increase for women and a 14% decrease for men? · How do you think women feel about the change in their access to power? How do you think men feel about it? · What does this mean for our progress towards achieving the Sustainable Development Goal of Gender Equality? · 467% change is HUGE! Does this mean we have hit our	Scholars actively participate in the summary discussion by: · respond to teacher questions · pose questions to the group · clarify their understandings · make connections between contexts · make connections between the math and the real world · push themselves and their peers to think critically about progress towards equitable political inclusion · apply their understandings of percent change to justify their claims about progress towards equitable political inclusion

goal of equal opportunities for women? Why or why not? What will it take for us to achieve that goal?

·   Using this example, what useful information does *percent change* provide? How is this different from the information *amount of change* provides?

·   Which calculation of change tells the best story of progress for women? What are the pros and cons of each? Do we need to tell both to get the full picture?

Assessment (7 minutes)	
Purpose for teachers: · *Assess student understanding*	**Purpose for students:** · *Reflect and self-assess on learning*
Teacher Actions	**Student Actions**

Say: *We are now going to apply our new tool of percent change to analyze the progress our own community has made towards the SDG of political inclusion for all. Silently and independently, read the prompt, analyze the data, make your calculations, and justify your responses.*	Students silently and independently complete the DOL.
Pass out DOL. Monitor students behavior and redirect off-task behaviors. Answer questions only about the instructions. Do not provide help with the calculations or analysis, only direct students to consider how they can apply their learnings and discussions from the lesson.	Students check their responses against the answer key. Students write a short reflection of their demonstration of learning.
After 5 minutes, reveal the answer key and exemplar responses. Instruct students to write a short reflection self-assessing their demonstration of learning.	

Optional	**Extension:**
	Purpose for students: · *Use content skills to better understand the world around them* · *Encourage curiosity*

Student Actions
Students use their new tool of percent change to analyze progress made towards any of the SDGs that most interests them. Possible examples: Percent change of: ·   Female representation in main characters of children's books ·   LGBTQ representation on the Disney Channel ·   Plastics floating in the ocean ·   Children experiencing poverty ·   Communities with access to clean drinking water ·   Children from low-income communities enrolled in early childhood education programs

Appendix B

	Lesson Title	Designer
	Basic Human Needs	Michelle A. Ward
	Subject and Grade Level	**Time Frame**
	Social Studies Grade 1	60 minutes
Desired	Texas Essential Knowledge	Sustainable Development

Results	and Skills (TEKS)	Goals
	1.7B: Economics: The student understands how families meet basic human needs. The student is expected to: (B) describe similarities and differences in ways families meet basic human needs	**Zero Hunger:** End all forms of hunger and malnutrition by 2030, making sure all people—especially children—have access to sufficient and nutritious food all year round. This involves promoting sustainable agricultural practices: supporting small scale farmers and allowing equal access to land, technology and markets. It also requires international cooperation to ensure investment in infrastructure and technology to improve agricultural productivity.
	Content Learning Objectives (LO)	**SDG Learning Objective**
	Students will be able to identify basic human needs and explain how their families meet their needs.	Students will be able to identify and describe the problem of hunger in the world.
	Lesson Learning Objective	

Students will be able to identify basic human needs and analyze how their families meet those needs in comparison to families living in other countries around the world.

Background Knowledge

Prior to this lesson, students should have engaged in an introductory lesson about the difference between wants and needs and between goods and services. An in-depth understanding of these concepts is not necessary, but students should be familiar with the vocabulary words and their meanings. Additionally, students should have some experience identifying similarities and differences.

Understandings	Essential Questions
What are the big ideas?	What provocative questions will foster inquiry, understanding, and transfer of learning?
What specific understandings about them are desired?	
What misunderstandings are predictable?	

- All humans need to meet basic needs in order to survive.
- Humans make choices in order to meet their needs.
- Families meet their basic human needs in different ways.

- Why do people need to meet basic human needs?
- Why do you think families meet their basic human needs in different ways?
- Why is it important to ensure that families are able to meet their basic needs?
- What happens if basic human needs are not met?
- What are the consequences of experiencing hunger?

Demonstration of Learning (DOL) and Corresponding Exemplar Student Response

Performance Task

Through what authentic performance tasks will students demonstrate the desired understandings?

By what criteria will performances of understanding be judged?

Students will draw a picture and write a sentence about the basic human needs. The drawing and sentence should include a description of what the basic human needs are, how they are met, and why they are important. Then the student will draw a picture of his or her family meeting their basic needs and a picture of a family in a county experiencing hunger meeting their basic needs. Last, students will write two sentences comparing how his or her family meets their basic needs versus how a family experiencing hunger meets their basic needs. These sentences should provide one similarity and one difference.

Students will know...	Students will be able to...
"What" key points	"How" key points

· Basic human needs are water, food, air, and shelter. · All humans need to meet their basic human needs in order to survive. · Human have to make choices in order to meet their basic human needs. · Families meet their basic human needs in different ways. · People experience hunger when they do not have enough food to eat. · People around the world experience hunger because they do not have enough food to eat.	· Reflect and discuss how their families meet their basic human needs. · Analyze videos about how families experiencing hunger meet their basic human needs. · Compare and contrast how students' families meet their basic human needs with how families in the videos meet their basic human needs.

Learni	**ENGAGE (10 minutes):**

ng Plan	Purpose for teachers:	Purpose for students:
	· *Set the purpose of the day* · *Present a learning activity or experience that prepares students to engage in the explore portion of the lesson*	*· Make initial connections to key points necessary for engaging in the explore portion of the lesson*
	Teacher Actions	**Student Actions**

Say: *In our previous lesson, we learned the difference between wants and needs. Turn and discuss with a partner the difference between wants and needs.*

Give students time to discuss with a partner and then call on one or two students to share out their responses. Briefly discuss the difference between wants and needs.

Say: *In our lesson today, we will be thinking about our basic human needs. We are going to work together to determine what we think the basic human needs are and how people meet those needs.*

Divide the students into small groups of three or four. Provide magazines and/or newspaper ad circulars. If that is not available, print out pictures from the internet. Ask students to cut out pictures of goods they think are basic human needs.

Provide students with three or four minutes to complete this activity. Then ask students to share out some of the basic needs they found. Ask students to share why they thought each of the items they chose are examples of basic human needs. Discuss student responses and what the basic human needs are: water, air,

Students discuss with a partner the difference between wants and needs.

Exemplar Responses:

. Wants are things we would like to have but do not need in order to survive. Needs are things that we must have in order to live.

. Wants are goods and services that are nice to have and needs are

food, and shelter.	goods we need to survive.
After discussing as a class, ask students to think about their selections and whether any items should be removed, because they are not examples of basic needs.	Students work together in small groups to find pictures of basic human needs.
	Students will share examples of the basic needs they found.
	Exemplar responses:
	.
	Pictures and answers involving food, especially healthy food

	• Pictures and answers involving shelter
	• Pictures and answers involving water
	• Pictures and answers involving air
	Students analyze the pictures they have chosen and decide if any should be removed because they are not examples of basic needs.
EXPLORE (20 minutes)	

Purpose for teachers:	Purpose for students:
· *Facilitate students' thinking toward understanding the key points through questioning (without providing answers or explanations)*	· *Deeply explore concepts and come up with theories and conjectures (e.g., making observations, identifying patterns)*
Teacher Actions	**Student Actions**

Say: *Now that we know more about the four basic human needs, we're going to explore how we meet these needs. Think silently about how you and your family meet your basic needs.*

Now turn and talk to a partner about how you and your family meet your basic human needs.

Call on students or ask for volunteers to share out their responses about how they and their families meet their basic human needs. Discuss with students using the following questions as prompts:

- When you are thirsty, where do you get water?

- How does the water get there?

- When you are hungry, where do you get food?

- Where does your family get food?

- How does your family get food?

- Where do you sleep at night?

- Why do you need air?

- What does your family do in order to meet your basic human needs?

- Why do you need to have your basic needs met?

Students silently think about how they meet their basic human needs.

Students turn and talk to a partner and discuss how they and their families meet their basic human needs.

Students share out their responses with the class.

Anticipated

Say: *In our discussion just now, we learned that families meet their basic human needs in different ways. Our families buy food in different places and live in different types of shelters. Families make choices in order to meet their basic needs. We talked about how many of our moms and dads choose to work so they can earn money to pay for food and homes. Families also make choices about where they buy their food and what type of food to buy.*

However, children and families in many places around the world are not able to meet their basic human needs. Hunger is a big problem for many families around the world.

What do you think it means to be hungry? Turn and tell a partner.

Call on students to share out their ideas with the class. Discuss what hunger means, focusing on hunger that happens to everyone when they're ready to eat again and then on the hunger that people experience when they don't have enough food to eat.

Say: *We're going to do an activity to help us learn more about hunger around the world.*

(activity adapted from http://www.actionagainsthunger.org/sites/default

/files/publications/race-hunger-guide-

Student Responses:

· When I'm thirsty I get water from the refrigerator in the kitchen or from the water fountain at school.

· My family goes to the grocery store to buy food and we eat that food at home. I also eat food from the cafeteria at school. My mom has to work so she can buy us food.

· I sleep in my bedroom in

115

burundi.pdf)

Divide students into four groups and instruct each group to go to a different corner of the room. Explain that these different groups represent the global community and that you will be providing each group with their food supply for the entire day. Tell students they can't eat their food supply yet though!

Give group 1 enough cookies (or a healthy treat) so that each person has two cookies.

For groups 2, 3, and 4, give each group unequal amounts at your discretion, ensuring that there is not enough for each member of the group.

Provide each group with a poster or sheet of chart paper and ask them to answer the following questions in their groups:

· How are you going to distribute the cookies and why?

· Will anyone in your group be without food? If so, what will they do for food?

· Why do you think your group got the amount of food that it got?

my apartment at night with my little brother.

.

We need air so that we can breathe and we have to breathe in order to live.

.

My mom and dad have jobs where they work and earn money so they can pay for our food and our house.

· I need to meet my basic needs so that I can live and be healthy.

During this time, circulate between the groups, listening in to their discussions. After groups have had a chance to answer all the questions, bring the students together to discuss their experience and answers to the questions.

After the discussion, redistribute the cookies (or healthy treat) so that each student has one to eat.

Students share with a partner what they think it means to be hungry.

Students share out their answer with the class.

Anticipated student responses:

· You're hungry when you're ready to eat and your stomach starts growling.

· I get hungry when I haven't had enough

		food to eat.
		.
		Hunger is when you don't have food to eat.
		Note: Be mindful that some students in class may have experienced hunger and food insecurity.
		Students move to their assigned groups in different corners of

the room.

Students discuss the questions as a group and write their answers on the poster or chart paper provided.

Students discuss their answers to the questions and their experience with the class.

Students eat their cookies (or healthy

treat).

PRACTICE (20):	
Purpose for teachers: · *Guide student practice where students get immediate feedback* · *Coach and provide feedback during independent practice* · *Assess student understanding*	**Purpose for students:** · *Apply understanding by practicing in groups, pairs, and independently* · *Reflect and self-assess on learning*
Teacher Actions	**Student Actions**

Show students the world hunger map.

(Retrieve from https://www.wfp.org/content/hunger-map-2015)

Say: *This map shows where people around the world are experiencing hunger. People experience hunger when they don't have enough food to be healthy and survive.*

Explain the map key and help students interpret what is shown on the map. Have students discuss with a partner and then with the whole class what they notice from the map.

Discuss with the students the reasons that people in the world don't have enough food, including:

· People don't have enough money to buy food.

· Food is really expensive at certain times and people don't have enough money to buy it.

· When there is war and fighting, people often have to move and they have a difficult time getting food.

· Some places don't get enough rain so it's hard to grow food.

· Sometimes there are floods and

Students analyze the map and discuss with a partner what they notice. Students share their reflections about the map whole class.

Anticipated student responses:

· A lot of people in the world are hungry.

· People in lots of different countries don't have

other types of natural disasters that destroy food.	enough food.
· There aren't good roads for people to travel on to go to work or buy food.	· People in Asia and Africa don't have enough food.
Say: *We are going to watch a short video about a woman named Jacqueline and how she works to help her family meet their basic human need of food.*	· People in South America are hungry.
(Retrieve from http://gideonmendel.com/four-stories-about-hunger/) Note: The video has English subtitles so you will likely need to read the subtitles aloud to students during the video. Make sure to stop the video about Jacqueline's story ends.	
Say: *Now we are going to watch a video about another family in Kenya and how they work to meet their family's needs.*	
(Retrieve from https://www.youtube.com/watch?v=pm15Q2 2Sdlw)	
Note: This video is too long to watch the entire video, preview ahead of time and choose a few clips to use with students.	
Ask students to silently reflect on what they saw and compare it to how their family meets their needs.	
	Students

Tell students to share their thoughts with a partner.	watch video about Jacqueline.
Give students paper and instruct them to write a sentence and draw a picture about how their family meets their basic needs and how it is similar and different from how the families in the videos met their basic human needs.	
	Students watch video about family in Kenya.
	Students think about how the

families in the videos helps their families meet their basic needs and how that is similar and different from how their family meets their basic needs.

Students share their thoughts with a partner.

Students write a sentence and draw a picture comparing and contrasting how their families meet their basic needs and how the families

		in the videos met theirs.

SUMMARIZE (5 minutes)	
Purpose for teachers: · *Facilitate a whole-group conversation about the exploration* · *Synthesize student ideas: clarify key points and address misunderstandings* · *Connect key points from exploration to understandings and essential questions*	Purpose for students: · *Solidify key points from practice and exploration* · *Connect their ideas to classmates' ideas*

Teacher Actions	Student Actions

Say: *Today we have learned about the basic human needs we need in order to survive. We've talked about why those needs are important. Turn and tell your partner what the basic human needs are and why they are important.*

Call on students to briefly share their answers whole group.

Say: *We talked about the different ways that our families meet their basic human needs and we learned about two families in Africa who meet their needs in ways that are similar and different from the way we meet our needs. What basic need did the families in these videos struggle to meet and why? Turn and talk to your partner.*

Call on students to briefly share their answers with the whole class.

Say: *We've learned that hunger is a problem in lots of places around the world and that people struggle to meet their basic needs. Why do you think it is important that families are able to meet their basic human needs? Discuss with your partner.*

Call on students to briefly share their thoughts

Students discuss with a partner the basic human needs and why they are important. Then they share out answers with the class.

Exemplar responses:

. The basic human needs are food, water, air, and shelter.

. These basic human needs are important because we need them

129

with the class.	to live.
	.
	If people can't meet their basic human needs then they can't survive and be healthy.
	Students talk with a partner about the families in the videos and how they struggled to meet their basic need of food. Then they share out answers with the class.
	Exemplar responses:
	.

| | | Both families didn't have enough food so they were hungry and their children got sick because they didn't have enough to eat.

. The families didn't have enough to eat because they didn't have enough money to buy food.

. The family couldn't get enough food to meet their needs.

Students |

| | discuss with a partner why it is important that families are able to meet their basic needs. Then they share out answers with the whole group.

Exemplar responses:

. Families need to be able to meet their basic human needs so they can be happy and healthy.

. All people should have the things they need in order to survive. |
| --- | --- |

Assessment (5 minutes)	
Purpose for teachers: · *Assess student understanding*	Purpose for students: · *Reflect and self-assess on learning*
Teacher Actions	**Student Actions**

Say: *Now you are going to have a chance to show what you have learned about basic human needs. First, you will draw a picture and write a sentence about what basic human needs are and how families meet them. Then you are going to draw two pictures: one of your family meeting their basic human needs and one of a family experiencing hunger meeting their basic human needs. Finally, you will write two sentences comparing how the way your family meets basic human needs and the way a family experiencing hunger meets basic human needs are the same and different.*

Pass out DOL. Monitor students' behavior and redirect off-task behaviors. Answer questions only about the instructions. Repeat directions as necessary and break down into manageable chunks for students.

After 5 minutes, collect DOL responses and ask students to share their responses with a partner. Then call on a few students or ask for student volunteers to share their DOL responses with the class. Discuss their answers and provide exemplar response.

Students silently and independently complete the DOL.

Students

	share their DOL responses with a partner. Then, a few students share their DOL responses with the class. Students discuss exemplar response in comparison to their responses with a partner.

Optional	**Extension:**
	Purpose for students: · *Use content skills to better understand the world around them* · *Encourage curiosity*
	Student Actions

Students explore the ways that families in different countries meet their basic human needs. This can be accomplished through books or through conversations with people who have experiences in other countries (including students). This can be extended by having students explore the specific reasons that families experience hunger in some countries, such as lack of land.

Additionally, students can learn more about how different families in the United States meet their basic needs and consider how they might be able to help people meet their basic needs.

Additional Resources:

http://www.actionagainsthunger.org/sites/default/files/publications/race-hunger-guide-burundi.pdf

http://hunger.generationon.org/sites/default/files/hunger/genOn-Lesson_Plan-MYMH.pdf

http://www.foodspanlearning.org/_pdf/lesson-plan/unit3/lesson14-hunger-lessonplan.pdf

https://kidworldcitizen.org/great-lessons-teach-kids-about-hunger-food-insecurity/

http://www.fao.org/home/en/

Appendix C

	Lesson Title	Designers
	Empowerment through Poetry	Jesella Zambrano
	Subject and Grade Level	Time Frame
	Reading, Grades 5-6	60 minutes
Desired Results	Common Core State Standards	Sustainable Development Goals

CCSS.ELA-LITERACY.RL.5.2: Determine a theme of a story, drama, or poem from details in the text, including how characters in a story or drama respond to challenges or how the speaker in a poem reflects upon a topic; summarize the text.	Promoting Just, Peaceful, and Inclusive Societies: Promote and enforce non-discriminatory laws and policies for sustainable development.
CCSS.ELA-LITERACY.RL.5.4: Determine the meaning of words and phrases as they are used in a text, including figurative language such as metaphors and similes.	
CCSS.ELA-LITERACY.RL.5.6: Describe how a narrator's or speaker's point of view influences how events are described.	
Content Learning Objectives (LO)	SDG Learning Objective
Students will be able to identify figurative language and explain how it functions to convey ideas in support of a larger theme.	Students will be able to discuss how activists have used poetry to celebrate empowerment and the fight for equality.
Lesson Learning Objective	

- Students will be able to identify and explain the meaning of figurative language (e.g.., similes and metaphors) in a poem.

- Students will be able to analyze poetry as a form of advocacy and describe how a poet uses figurative language to promote

Understandings	Essential Questions
What are the big ideas? What specific understandings about them are desired? What misunderstandings are predictable?	What provocative questions will foster inquiry, understanding, and transfer of learning?
• Authors and poets use figurative language to paint vivid pictures and convey complex ideas to their readers. • The fight for equality by African Americans during the civil rights movement continued after the movement and is evident in literary works.	11. What is empowerment? What does it feel like? 12. What does it feel like to be marginalized? 13. In what historical contexts has a group been suppressed. 14. How can individuals use literature to advocate for empowerment and justice?
Demonstration of Learning (DOL) and Corresponding Exemplar Student Response	

Performance Task

Through what authentic performance tasks will students demonstrate the desired understandings?

By what criteria will performances of understanding be judged?

Through the analysis of Maya Angelou's poem "Still I Rise" students will be able to describe how a poet conveys her experiences as an activist through the theme of empowerment, using figurative language, namely metaphors and similes. Students will be tasked with individually identifying the different forms of figurative language utilized by Angelou, discuss the meaning of these literary techniques in the context of the poem, and engage in a class discussion focused on how the figurative language relays the theme of empowerment.

Students will know... "What" key points	**Students will be able to...** "How" key points
· Authors and poets use figurative language to highlight specific themes and motifs. Similes and metaphors make comparisons between two ideas. · The fight for equality in the United States has spanned many generations and continues today.	· Identify figurative language in texts, specifically similes and metaphors. · Describe the major themes of a poem.

Learning Plan	MOTIVATOR (15 minutes):	
	Purpose for teachers · *Set the purpose of the lesson* · *Present a learning activity or experience that prepares students to engage in the next portion of the lesson*	**Purpose for students:** ·*Make initial connections to key points necessary for engaging in the next portion of the lesson*
	Teacher Actions	Student Actions

Learning Plan	MOTIVATOR (15 minutes):	
	Distribute to students a printed copy of the poem "Still I Rise" (1978) by Maya Angelou (accessible at: https://www.poetryfoundation.org/poems/46446/still-i-rise).	Students spend 2 minutes discussing their knowledge of the United States civil rights movement with a peer.
	Say: I am passing out a copy of the poem "Still I Rise" written by Maya Angelou, a writer and civil rights activist. Before reading the poem, please turn to your partner and discuss what you know about the civil rights movement in the United States.	
	After 2 minutes begin calling on students to share what they discussed with their peers. As a class, spend 5 minutes creating a concept map on the board with the student responses.	Students work together to create a concept map of their prior knowledge of the civil rights movement.
	Say: Today we are going to explore the theme of empowerment through poetry. Before we read today's poem, I want us to quickly review what we have learned about figurative language. Please turn to your partner and answer the following questions: · What is figurative language? Name a few examples.	Students review various figurative language techniques with a partner— focusing on similes and

Learning Plan	MOTIVATOR (15 minutes):	
	· What do similes and metaphors do? · What is the difference between the two? How can you tell similes and metaphors apart? · Come up with 2 examples of each (2 similes and two metaphors) and be ready to present them to the class. After 3 minutes, call the class together again and ask for a few student examples of metaphors and similes. Spend 5 minutes creating a list of the board.	metaphors. Students practice writing their own similes and metaphors.
	CORE ACTIVITY (20 minutes)	

Learni ng Plan	MOTIVATOR (15 minutes):	
	Purpose for teachers: · *Facilitate students' thinking toward understanding the key points through guided questioning*	Purpose for students: · *Generate questions they are seeking to answer through the study of several texts*
	Teacher Actions	**Student Actions**

Learni ng Plan	MOTIVATOR (15 minutes):	
	Say: Now that we have refreshed our memories about metaphors and similes, we will read and analyze Maya Angelou's poem "Still I Rise". Please take out your yellow and orange highlighters. Read the poem individually. Highlight all the similes you find in yellow and the metaphors in orange. While you read, I will pass out a worksheet you will use to analyze the figurative language Angelou utilizes in her poem.	Students individually practice identifying similes and metaphors, and understanding how to distinguish the two.
	Give students 5 minutes to read the poem and identify the figurative language.	Students engage in a discussion with a peer about the figurative meaning behind the similes and metaphors identified.
	Say: Now turn to your partner and compare what you found. If your partner identified a metaphor or simile that you missed, highlight it on your own page. Then list all the similes and metaphors identified in the first column of your worksheet (Appendix A).	
	Give students 5 minutes to fill out the first portion of the worksheet.	Students reflect on how literary themes reflect the experiences of a civil rights activist.
	Say: Now that you have all the similes and metaphors, consider what each might mean. What tone and mood does each image evoke? What feelings? Discuss with your partner and	

Learni ng Plan	MOTIVATOR (15 minutes):	
	fill out the second column of the worksheet.	
	Give students 3 minutes to fill out the second column.	
	Say: Now think back to what you discussed with your partner at the very beginning of the lesson regarding the civil rights movement. How do the similes and metaphors reflect the thoughts, feelings, and experiences of an African American woman who lived during that time? What does Angelou allude to her own empowerment?	
	SUMMARIZE (10 minutes)	

Learning Plan	MOTIVATOR (15 minutes):	
	Purpose for teachers: · *Facilitate a class conversation about the poem.* · *Push students to think deeper about poetry as a form of advocacy for empowerment.*	**Purpose for students:** · *Solidify understanding of figurative language* · *Make connections between a literary text and historical contexts.*

Learning Plan	MOTIVATOR (15 minutes):	
	Teacher Actions	**Student Actions**
	Teacher engages the class in a discussion that summarizes the key themes in the poem and their connection to activism. Questions to use to facilitate discussion: · How did people fight for justice and empower themselves during the civil rights movement? · What forms of discrimination did African Americans face during and after the civil rights movement? · How does Maya Angelou allude to her struggles as an African American woman in her poetry? · How does Maya Angelou convey a sense empowerment? · What actions can an individual take or attitudes can they adopt to empower themselves?	Students engage in a class-wide discussion: · Responding to teacher questions · Responding to peer responses · Make connections between literature and a specific historical context. · Apply understanding of the different forms that empowerment

Learni ng Plan	MOTIVATOR (15 minutes):	
		can take.
	Assessment (15 minutes)	
	Purpose for teachers: · *Assess student understanding*	**Purpose for students:** · *Practice the skills acquired during the lesson*
	Teacher Actions	**Student Actions**

Learning Plan	MOTIVATOR (15 minutes):	
	Say: Now that we have analyzed and discussed how one poet relayed her empowerment story through the use of figurative language, you will practice doing the same. Each of you will write one 4-line stanza of poetry in which you describe a time you felt empowered, having fought for something you felt was just. You must include at least one simile and one metaphor in your poem. Give students 15 minutes to write their poem and then collect for grading.	Students silently and independently write a poem that allows them practice using figurative language to relay ideas related to empowerment and justice.

"Still I Rise" Figurative Language Worksheet

	Figurative Language	Feeling Evoked	Meaning / Connection to Author
Example 1			
Example 2			
Example 3			
Example 4			
Example 5			

Appendix D

	Lesson Title	Designers
	Teaching concepts of Energy Efficiency and Conservation to understand Sustainable Consumption	Allison Casey
	Subject and Grade Level	**Time Frame**
	Biology Grade 9	50 minutes
Desired Results	**Georgia Performance Science Standards**	**Sustainable Development Goal**
	SB4. Students will assess the dependence of all organisms on one another and the flow of energy and matter within their ecosystems. · SB4d. Students will assess and explain human activities that influence and modify the environment such as global warming, population growth, pesticide use, and water and power consumption.	**Responsible Consumption and Production:** Ensure sustainable consumption and production patterns
	Content Learning Objectives (LO)	**SDG Learning Objective**

· Students will revisit the concept of renewable and nonrenewable energy. · Students will analyze how the environment is impacted by the energy consumption patterns of humans. · Students will understand concepts of energy efficiency and energy conservation.	· Students will analyze the sustainability of human consumptions patterns. · Students will strategize how to make their own energy consumption patterns more sustainable.

Lesson Learning Objective

Students will be able to apply their understanding of human energy consumption, energy efficiency, and energy conservation to assess the sustainability of human consumptions patterns.

Understandings	**Essential Questions**
What are the big ideas? What specific understandings about them are desired? What misunderstandings are predictable?	What provocative questions will foster inquiry, understanding, and transfer of learning?

· Biology is a tool to better understand sustainable consumption.	· How does human energy consumption impact the availability of energy sources in our environment?
· Energy is either renewable or nonrenewable.	
· Human energy consumption impacts the environment.	· How does energy conservation and efficiency impact the availability of these resources?
· Energy efficiency and conservation can contribute to sustainable consumption.	· How can the human race make progress towards the SDG of Responsible Consumption and Production?

Demonstration of Learning (DOL) and Corresponding Exemplar Student Response

Performance Task

Through what authentic performance tasks will students demonstrate the desired understandings?

By what criteria will performances of understanding be judged?

Using data from the U.S. Energy Information Administration, students will assess how much renewable and nonrenewable energy the nation consumes. Students will then learn the concepts of energy efficiency and energy conservation. With partners and as a class, students will strategize how these concepts can be applied to human practices to reduce the amount of nonrenewable energy consumed in everyday life.

Lastly, students will independently demonstrate their understanding of the concepts, as well as to think critically about how they personally can become more responsible consumers.

Students will know... "What" key points	Students will be able to... "How" key points
· Humans can consume both nonrenewable and renewable energy sources. · The U.S. consumes far more nonrenewable energy than renewable energy; this is not sustainable in the long term because nonrenewable energy cannot be replenished easily or quickly. · Energy conservation and efficiency can help reduce the amount of nonrenewable energy sources consumed by humans.	· We can differentiate between the concepts of energy efficiency and conservation. · We can apply both concepts of energy efficiency and energy conservation in our daily lives to become more responsible energy consumers.

Learning	**LAUNCH (10 minutes):**

Plan	Purpose for teachers:	Purpose for students:
	· *Set the purpose of the day* · *Present a learning activity or experience that prepares students to engage in the explore portion of the lesson*	·*Make initial connections to key points necessary for engaging in the explore portion of the lesson*
	Teacher Actions	**Student Actions**

Handout the "U.S. Energy Consumption by Source, 2014" worksheet (see appendix).	Students read the handout, reflect, and create estimates with their partner.
Say: Recall from our earlier lesson that there are two types of energy—renewable and nonrenewable. In front of you is the list of energy sources used in the U.S. to meet everyday energy needs. Next to each resource, estimate what percent of the nation's energy is fueled by that resource.	
Give students 2 minutes with the person next to them to estimate the percentages for each resource.	Students share out the numbers they estimated with their partners.
Say: Let's come back together as a class and share our estimates.	
Write on the board of some of the estimates from the class.	Students calculate the actual percent of resources used that are non-renewable, and the percent of resources used

Say: Now, let's take a look at what the numbers actually are.	that are renewable
Write the actual values next to the estimates (found in answer key in appendix). Give the students a minute to total the actual percent of resources used that are non-renewable, and the percent of resources used that are renewable.	Students discuss as a group.
	Anticipated responses:
Say: We know that energy sources are called nonrenewable because they are limited. For example, petroleum cannot be reproduced in a short time and is therefore considered to be of limited supply. We also know that renewable resources are called renewable because they can be easily replenished. For example, sunlight and wind are thought to be available long term. As you see, 90.3% of the nation's energy is provided by nonrenewable sources, while 9.6% of the nation's energy is provided by renewable sources. Why do you think this is?	· Government officials, citizens, and business owners may be unaware of the environmental impact of nonrenewable energy sources, or may not know about alternatives.

· Nonrenewable energy may be convenient to use, while switching to renewable energy may be costly or inconvenient.

· As profitable industries, producers of nonrenewable energy may advocate for their continued use. |

Questions to pose to push discussion:

· Sustainable Development Goal 12 is "Responsible Consumption and Production." How do you think our country is doing in achieving this goal?

· Do you notice certain nonrenewable sources that are used more than others? How about for renewable sources?

Say: We are now going to learn about two important concepts: energy conservation and energy efficiency. This can help us better understand how we can become more responsible consumers of energy. Throughout the lesson, I encourage you to keep the following questions top of mind:

3. In what ways can I conserve energy, or use energy more efficiently, in my daily life?

4. In what ways can I encourage my community to conserve energy or use energy more efficiently?

EXPLORE (5 minutes)	
Purpose for teachers:	Purpose for students:
· *Facilitate students' thinking toward understanding the key points through questioning (without providing answers or explanations)*	· *Deeply explore concepts and come up with theories and conjectures (e.g., making observations, identifying patterns)*
Teacher Actions	**Student Actions**

Write on the board the definitions of "Energy Conservation" and "Energy Efficiency"

Energy Conservation: any behavior that results in the use of less energy

Energy Efficiency: the use of technology that requires less energy to perform the same function

Give students a moment to read through the definitions.

Exemplar response:

Say: Now, let's take a closer look at one of the sources from the "U.S. Energy Consumption by Source" handout. We will look at Petroleum for now. Notice the "uses" listed as transportation and manufacturing. With either of these uses in mind, can someone provide an example of energy conservation for petroleum? How about an example of energy efficiency for petroleum?

· An example of energy conservation for petroleum would be to drive my car less. This change in behavior would reduce the amount of energy consumed.

· An example of energy efficiency for petroleum would be to use biomass to fuel my car, rather than petroleum. This would reduce the consumption of nonrenewable energy, but

	perform the same function.
Clarifying points: · Conservation of energy helps to slow down the use non-renewable resources by changing behavior · Through the use of technology, energy efficiency helps to slow down the use of nonrenewable without changing consumption patterns [Check for students' understanding before moving on]	.

Practice (10 minutes):	
Purpose for teachers: · *Guide student practice where students get immediate feedback* · *Coach and provide feedback during independent practice*	Purpose for students: · *Apply understanding by practicing in groups, pairs, and independently* · *Reflect and self-assess on*

· *Assess student understanding*	*learning*
Teacher Actions	**Student Actions**
Pair students into groups of 2 and assign each group a "Nonrenewable" energy source from the handout. Note that depending on class size, some groups may be assigned the same source. **Say:** As with our prior example, your group's task is to address one of the "uses" of your non-renewable resource (i.e. transportation) and identify one way you could apply the concept of energy conservation, and one way you could apply the concept of energy efficiency, to that function. During practice, check in with students and assist those who are struggling. Engage students who may not be contributing sufficiently to their group's	Students strategize ways to conserve energy and use energy more efficiently given their chosen "use" of their nonrenewable energy. When considering energy efficiency, students should think beyond swapping their current energy source with a renewable one. For example, students may pose the idea of repairing rather than replacing electronic devices as a way consume less nonrenewable energy. Exemplar response: · Nonrenewable

discussion.	Energy Source: Natural Gas
	Use: heating
Transition to Summarize where we will synthesize the information.	Efficiency Example: Replace drafty windows with newer windows to better insulate my house and avoid unnecessarily overheating the home.
	Conservation Example: Avoid heating my house when no one is home.
SUMMARIZE (15 minutes)	
Purpose for teachers:	Purpose for students:
· *Facilitate a whole-group conversation about the exploration*	· *Solidify key points from practice and exploration*
· *Synthesize student ideas: clarify key points and address misunderstandings*	· *Connect their ideas to classmates' ideas*
· *Connect key points from exploration to understandings and essential questions*	
Teacher Actions	**Student Actions**

Have students share out their examples with the rest of the class.	Students share out their examples with the rest of the class.
Facilitate a discussion about the different examples identified by various groups.	Students actively participate in the summary discussion by:
Questions to facilitate discussion:	
· Did you find it challenging to identify ways to conserve energy and ways to use energy more efficiently?	· responding to teacher questions
	· posing questions to the group
· Did anyone identify a practice from his or her own experience?	· clarifying their understandings
	· making connections between biology and their own behavior
· After hearing these ideas, how would you rank your own household and community for responsible and sustainable consumption?	· pushing themselves and their peers to think critically about progress towards responsible consumption using their understanding of energy conservation and efficiency

Assessment (10 minutes)

Purpose for teachers: · *Assess student understanding*	Purpose for students: · *Reflect and self-assess on learning*
Teacher Actions	**Student Actions**
Write on the board: · What is getting in the way of you and/or your community becoming more responsible consumers of energy? · What will it take for us to overcome these barriers to achieve the SDG of responsible consumption and production? Include one example of energy efficiency and one example of energy conservation. **Say:** We are now going to apply our new understandings of energy efficiency and conservation to our own households and community. Please silently and independently write out your answers to the prompts. Monitor students and redirect	Students silently and independently complete the assessment.

off-task behaviors. Do not provide help with answers; only direct students to consider how they can apply their learnings and discussions from the lesson. After 10 minutes, collect written responses. Assess written responses and returned to students with feedback in the following days. Responses should demonstrate a clear understanding of the difference between energy conservation and energy efficiency, as well as critical reflection on how to overcome barriers in order to apply these concepts to their daily lives.	Students receive feedback on their understanding of concepts, as well as on their plans to work towards progress.

Handout (to be printed as half-sheets):

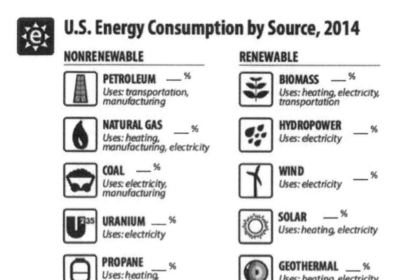

Data: Energy Information Administration

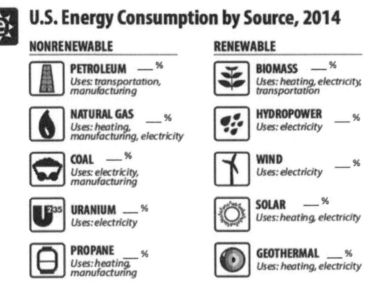

Data: Energy Information Administration

Handout Answer Key:

U.S. Energy Consumption by Source, 2014

NONRENEWABLE	RENEWABLE

 PETROLEUM 34.9%
Uses: transportation, manufacturing

 BIOMASS 4.8%
Uses: heating, electricity, transportation

 NATURAL GAS 27.5%
Uses: heating, manufacturing, electricity

 HYDROPOWER 2.5%
Uses: electricity

 COAL 18.0%
Uses: electricity, manufacturing

 WIND 1.7%
Uses: electricity

 URANIUM 8.3%
Uses: electricity

 SOLAR 0.4%
Uses: heating, electricity

 PROPANE 1.6%
Uses: heating, manufacturing

 GEOTHERMAL 0.2%
Uses: heating, electricity

Data: Energy Information Administration

169

Appendix E

Lesson Title	Designers
Inequality in the Criminal Justice System: Racial Profiling	Jessica Bergmann
Subject and Grade Level	**Time Frame**
Humanities, Grades 9-10	60 minutes

Desired Results	**Common Core State Standards**	**Sustainable Development Goals**
	CCSS.ELA-Literacy.CCRA.R.9: Read closely to determine what the text says explicitly and to make logical inferences from it; cite specific textual evidence when writing or speaking to support conclusions drawn from the text. **CCSS.ELA-Literacy.SL.9-10.1.D:** Respond thoughtfully to diverse perspectives, summarize points of agreement and disagreement, and, when warranted, qualify or justify their own views and understanding and make new connections in light of the	**Promoting Just, Peaceful, and Inclusive Societies:** Promote the rule of law at the national and international levels and ensure equal access to justice for all; ensure public access to information and protect fundamental freedoms; develop effective, accountable and transparent institutions at all levels.

evidence and reasoning presented.	
Content Learning Objectives (LO)	**SDG Learning Objective**
Students will be able to produce an argument and support their argument by citing specific textual evidence from multiple sources of information.	Students will be able to analyze the criminal justice system in the United States.
Lesson Learning Objective	

· Students will be able to analyze diverse perspectives of the criminal justice system presented in multiple sources.

· Students will be able to produce an argument on whether the criminal justice system in the United States ensures equal access to justice for all.

Understandings	Essential Questions
• What are the big ideas? • What specific understandings about them are desired? • What misunderstandings are predictable?	• What provocative questions will foster inquiry, understanding, and transfer of learning?
·　Multiple sources of information can present conflicting opinions/viewpoints of the same issue ·　Marginalized groups do not always have equal protections under the law	1. What is justice for all? 2. What fundamental freedoms should be guaranteed to all individuals? 3. Is it ever justified to limit the freedoms of certain individuals/groups in service of the greater good? 4. What actions should be taken when justice for all is not being achieved? Are these actions justified? 5. What responsibility do non-marginalized groups have to developing more accountable

	institutions?

Demonstration of Learning (DOL) and Corresponding Exemplar Student Response

Performance Task

Through what authentic performance tasks will students demonstrate the desired understandings?

By what criteria will performances of understanding be judged?

Given a diverse selection of texts on current practices of the United States' criminal justice system, students will be able to formulate an argument of whether the criminal justice system ensures equal access to justice for all. Students will be asked to engage with multiple sources on the topic of racial profiling (news articles, op-eds, podcasts, and/or videos) and gather evidence that supports their argument. Students will be asked to engage in a whole-class discussion, responding to diverse perspectives and justifying their viewpoints while understanding how their viewpoints may have changed in light of evidence and reasoning presented by their peers.

Students will know… "What" key points	Students will be able to… "How" key points
· Formulating a strong argument includes using relevant evidence from a text or multiple texts to support a claim · Many groups of people do not have equal access to justice in the United States · Progress towards more accountable and fair institutions has not been sufficient	· Define racial profiling practices in the United States · Synthesize multiple viewpoints on racial profiling and use evidence to support their own viewpoint · Engage in constructive dialogue with peers who may have differing viewpoints

Learning Plan	MOTIVATOR (15 minutes):	
	Purpose for teachers: · *Set the purpose of the lesson* · *Present a learning activity or experience that prepares students to engage in the next portion of the lesson*	**Purpose for students:** *·Make initial connections to key points necessary for engaging in the next portion of the lesson*
	Teacher Actions	**Student Actions**

Learning Plan	**MOTIVATOR (15 minutes):**	
	Distribute to students a printed copy or have students access a digital copy of the article "Issue Overview: Racial Profiling" (accessible at: newsela.com/read/overview-racial-profiling/id/21199).	Students spend 2 minutes discussing with their partner any prior knowledge they have of racial profiling.
	Say: In front of you is a reading that will help us to frame our conversation today. As I distribute the reading, turn to a partner to discuss what you know about racial profiling. What is it? What are some examples of racial profiling? We will come back together in 2 minutes to discuss.	Students share out what they discussed with their partners. Students read the opening article and annotate the text.
	Give students time to discuss briefly with their partner. Then come back together as a class to solicit ideas from groups. Write these ideas on the board as students share.	Students engage in the preliminary discussion of racial profiling practices in the United States.
	Say: Today we are going to engage with the topic of racial profiling. Before we dive deeper, let's start by making sure we have a common understanding of racial profiling practices in the United States. We are going to read this article as a whole	

Learning Plan	MOTIVATOR (15 minutes):	
	class. As we read, I would like for you to annotate the text with Thinking Notes (examples include + for agree, - for disagree, ! for this surprises me, A for argument/claim, EV for evidence/reasoning author uses to support claim, MI for main idea, etc.).

The teacher may choose to read the text aloud or have students take turns reading portions of the text aloud.

Questions after reading:

· What is racial profiling? What are some examples of racial profiling cited in the text?

· What is the history of racial profiling as a practice? What role has the criminal justice system played in racial profiling?

· What tensions exist around the use of racial profiling? | |
| | CORE ACTIVITY (25 minutes) | |

Learning Plan	MOTIVATOR (15 minutes):	
	Purpose for teachers: · *Facilitate students' thinking toward understanding the key points through guided questioning*	**Purpose for students:** · *Generate questions they are seeking to answer through the study of several texts*
	Teacher Actions	**Student Actions**

Learning Plan	**MOTIVATOR (15 minutes):**	
	Say: We are now going to learn more about the use of racial profiling by reading texts that present multiple perspectives and generating our own argument for how racial profiling assists or prevents us from being able to achieve justice for all. As we work through the texts, I challenge you to think about the following questions: 1. How does racial profiling fit into the larger conversations occurring on race relations in our society? 2. Is it ever justified to limit an individual's rights or freedoms in service of the greater good? During the activity, make sure all students are on task and engaging with one another and the texts. Students should work in groups of 2-3. The teacher can choose whether to assign texts to the group, or whether the group can select the texts they wish to read. Each group should read at least one text from the "Pro" column and one text from the "Against" column. The teacher should provide groups with questions to complete while engaging in a close reading of the texts. Questions could include:	Students engage with 1-2 peers to closely read 2-3 texts and use the guiding questions provided by the teacher to analyze arguments made and evidence provided. Students work with their group to think beyond the texts and make sense of how racial profiling fits into the larger criminal justice system. Students push their partners to back their own arguments using evidence from the texts. Students prepare to share their arguments with the larger class in the next portion of the lesson.

Learning Plan	**MOTIVATOR (15 minutes):**	
	1. What argument does this text make? What evidence does the author use to support their argument? 2. To what extent do you agree or disagree with the argument being made? Why? 3. What role does opinion/bias play in the writing, if any? How does this inform the way you engage with the text and the information it presents? 4. Generate 1-2 questions you would like to bring to the larger discussion. 5. Based on the texts you read, what is your argument for or against racial profiling? Provide 2-3 pieces of evidence that support your claim. Check student work and dialogue as you walk around. Redirect students to examine parts of the text closer where further evaluation or consideration may be needed. Monitor the timing of this portion of the lesson. With 5 minutes remaining, direct students to ensure they come to the larger discussion prepared with their arguments and evidence.	

Learning Plan	**MOTIVATOR (15 minutes):**	
	Suggested Resources	
	Pro	**Against**
	· "This Study Found Race Matters in Police Shootings, but the Results May Surprise You" by Tom Jackman · "What Looks Like Profiling Might Just Be Good Policing" by Heather MacDonald · "Can Stereotyping, and Profiling, Ever Be Good Things?" by Matt Herrington · "Ray Kelly Defends Stop and Frisk and Racial Profiling – NYPD is Guilty of Saving 7,383 Lives" via YouTube · "Positive Results of 'Stop and Frisk' Can't Be Ignored" by Greg Molinda McDonald · "The Argument for Stop-And-Frisk" via NPR's Tell Me More · "Stop and Frisk Doesn't Target Minorities, It Protects Them" by Michael Barone	· "Racial Profiling Raises Its Ugly Head (Again): A Night in the Life of a Black Man in Milwaukee" by Caleb Roberts · "The Disproportionate Risks of Driving While Black" by Sharon LaFraniere and Andrew W. Lehren · "What the Data Really Says About Police and Racial Bias" by Kia Makarechi · "New Mexico Sheriff's Office Pulls Over the Same Black Federal Agent – Three Times in a Month" by Micah McCoy · "Mother of Eric Garner: The Recurring Nightmare

Learning Plan	**MOTIVATOR (15 minutes):**	
		of My Son's Death" by Gwen Carr · "Questions and Answers About Racial Profiling" via Amnesty USA · "A Look at Racial Profiling" by Evan Horowitz
	SUMMARIZE (20 minutes)	
	Purpose for teachers: · *Facilitate whole-group conversation on the readings* · *Synthesize student ideas: clarify key points and address misunderstandings*	**Purpose for students:** · *Solidify key arguments and evidence from exploration and activity* · *Connect their ideas to classmates' ideas*

Learning Plan	MOTIVATOR (15 minutes):	
	Teacher Actions	**Student Actions**
	Teacher facilitates a discussion about the multiple sources that students have read or viewed about racial profiling.	Scholars actively participate in the discussion by:
	Questions to use to facilitate discussion: · Does racial profiling as a practice promote justice? Prevent justice? Explain. · How does racial profiling affect relationships between individuals? Relationships between individuals and institutions? · The article we read at the beginning of the class stated that "supporters of profiling say it works when it's based on solid evidence that certain traits are linked to higher rates of crime." To what extent do you agree or disagree with this statement? At what point does profiling go too far? · Is racial profiling ever justified? Why or why not? · Can racial profiling be justified if it limits an individual's freedoms? · What would it take for our country to achieve justice for all	· responding to teacher questions · responding to other students' responses · posing their own questions to the group · make connections between texts · make connections between the texts and the real world · push themselves and their peers to think critically about injustices in society · apply their understandings of

Learning Plan	**MOTIVATOR (15 minutes):**	
	racial/ethnic, gender, and religious minorities? Why is this so important to us?	racial profiling to justify their claims about equal access to justice
	Assessment: Exit Ticket (10 minutes)	
	Purpose for teachers: · *Assess student understanding*	**Purpose for students:** · *Reflect and self-assess on learning*
	Teacher Actions	**Student Actions**

Learning Plan	**MOTIVATOR (15 minutes):**	
	Say: *We are now going to synthesize our understandings of racial profiling in light of our original question at the beginning of class: does the criminal justice system in the United States ensure equal access to justice for all? Silently and independently, read the prompt, produce your argument, and justify your responses using evidence from the text and today's discussion.*	Students silently and independently complete the exit ticket.
		Students share a short reflection on their learning in class or for homework.
	Display the writing task on the board. Monitor students behavior and redirect off-task behaviors. Students may use any of the texts provided to include direct quotations if desired by the teacher.	
	After 10 minutes, have students submit their writing to be reviewed by the teacher. If time allows, have students share their reflections on their learning with a partner or with the whole class. This could be completed using an online discussion board, with a potential homework assignment asking students to respond to 2-3 peers' reflections.	
Optional	**Extension:**	
	Purpose for students:	
	· *Use content skills to better understand historical and current*	

Learning Plan	**MOTIVATOR (15 minutes):**
	events • *Encourage students to engage critical dialogue surrounding issues of race*
	Student Actions
	Students use text analysis and argumentative writing and speaking/listening skills to further understand the inequalities present in the United States' criminal justice system, the origins of these inequalities, and how they have evolved over time. Possible examples of additional topics to be included in the curriculum: • Jim Crow laws • The war on drugs • Mass incarceration • Police brutality Possible anchor texts: • *The Hate U Give* by Angie Thomas • *How It Went Down* by Kekla Magoon • *To Kill a Mockingbird* by Harper Lee • *The New Jim Crow* by Michelle Alexander

Oath to the Ocean

Veena Wulfekuhle

Grade Level: 5th   Time Frame: Two Weeks

Summary and Rationale

"Through the Eyes of an Orca"

In this lesson plan the goal of the student is to show why caring about Sustainable Development Goal (SDG) 14 is important. The ocean has been a resource for transportation and nourishment for humanity for centuries. Due to the neglect of those two items, the waters have also changed, affecting the marine life within it. Although humans do not live in these seas, we are dependent on them. The outcome to be learned in this lesson is to make us want to achieve STG 14, since what is happening firsthand to marine life within the ocean will eventually affect our race.

This outcome will be obtained by having one see life below water through the eyes of a whale over the past century. Each student will choose to represent a specific endangered orca from a pod in the Salish Sea and write a narrative story of the number of pollutants, and marine population in this time span while swimming in these waters. The student will then take a three-pillar pledge and promise to protect the "mind body and spirit" of the sea falling within the lesson plan of Oath to the Ocean. Their paper will tie the three-pillar pledge with three targets of Sustainable Goal 14 within a framework. The linkage will show how taking this pledge prior to writing this paper will make those in power, want to meet those targets in this personal journey. Each student will present their story to class and then vote on their favorite. The winner's article will be submitted to the whale museum for publication and awarded an Orca to be adopted by the class. After the presentation of the adopted Orca, the classmates will meet as "superpod" to talk about why they chose the story they liked best. Teaching this goal is important because it will help students see and show how one of the oldest members of an orca pod, "Granny", who lived over a century, started as common, and turned into an endangered soul of the Salish sea species.

GRANNY (J-2)
ESTIMATED BIRTH YEAR 1911
YEAR OF DEATH 2016

A LONG LIFE WELL LIVED.
SHE TOUCHED THE HEARTS OF MANY.
IT IS WITH GREAT SADNESS WE SAY GOODBYE TO GRANNY.
SHE WILL ALWAYS HAVE
OUR RESPECT AND APPRECIATION.

THIS IMAGE IS TO KEEP THE CONNECTION OF GRANNY (J-2)
TO THE SOUTHERN RESIDENT COMMUNITY OF J, K, AND L PODS.
SHE WAS THEIR LEADER FOR MORE YEARS THAN WE KNOW.

Subjects

Marine Biology, Geography, Science, Food Sciences, Health

Instructional Goal

In this lesson plan, students are expected to obtain the below to evaluate the last century in the Salish Sea and take a three-tier pledge to make a change with that knowledge through the eyes of an orca by writing a narrative story. The three-tier pledge will specifically tie to three targets to meet Sustainable Development Goal 14 through the framework of the lesson plan being Oath to the Ocean.

1. Knowledge and Skills
   a. Number of marine life now in the Salish Sea from 100 years ago?
   b. Number of seafood now in the Salish Sea from 100 years ago?
   c. Number of pollutants in the Salish Sea from 100 years ago?
2. Work and Mind Habits
   a. Pledge - "I promise to protect the Mind, Body and Spirit of the Sea".
   b. Oath To The Ocean Framework

Standards

Sustainable Development Goal 14: Conserve and sustainably use the oceans, seas and marine resources for sustainable development.

Targets to Tie with Three Tier Pledge in Framework:

1. 14.1 = Mind: By 2025, prevent and significantly reduce marine pollution of all kinds, in particular from land-based activities, including marine debris and nutrient pollution.

2. 14.6.1 = Body: By 2020, prohibit certain forms of fisheries subsidies which contribute to overcapacity and overfishing, eliminate subsidies that contribute to illegal, unreported and unregulated fishing and refrain from introducing new such subsidies, recognizing that appropriate and effective special and differential treatment for developing and least developed countries should be an integral part of the World Trade Organization fisheries subsidies negotiation.

3. 14.C.1 = Spirit: Enhance the conservation and sustainable use of oceans and their resources by implementing international law as reflected in UNCLOS, which provides the legal framework for the conservation and sustainable use of oceans and their resources, as recalled in paragraph 158 of The Future We Want.

Essential Questions

- What happens if we do nothing?
- What happens if we do something?
- How can we develop the competencies in school that make the achievement of the goals more likely?
- What are some of the learning outcomes and competencies needed that would help achieve the SDG's by those that have the Power of Positive Change? Make this part of your story.

Student Learning Objectives

Your story should show how your pledge of "I promise to protect the Mind, Body and Spirit of the Sea" is relevant for the orcas and links with the lesson plan's framework of Oath to the Ocean:

1. Mind - You are what you know.
2. Body - You are what you eat.

3. <u>Spirit</u> - You know you should do about the Sea.

The thoughts in your story should tie with the three targets of SDG 14 and show why they need to be met.

1. 14.1.1 = <u>Mind</u>: Think of what will happen to the whales if they continue to swim in polluted waters?
2. 14.6.1 = <u>Body</u>: What will happen to the orcas if measurements are not taken to control overfishing?
3. 14.C.1 = <u>Spirit</u>: Why is it our responsibility to help protect the food and waters for these orcas and how and why does that affect humans?

Assessment

- Each student will be asked to read their story aloud in front of the class and have a picture of the orca they choose to represent and the pod it came from.
- Each student will be asked to vote on their favorite story which cannot be their own. After the award, the class meets as a "superpod" to discuss why they chose each story.
- Student's goal: Convince your classmates to care about these targets to help keep your pledge and show the power of positive change.
- Winner gets an adopted orca to follow for a year and article submission to the Whale Museum.

Sequence of Activities

Step 1: Opener

Pretend you are a whale swimming through the Salish Sea!

Step 2: Core

Pick an Orca to represent from the endangered J, K, and L pods of the Southern residents. Write a narrative about you as a whale describing your and other pods' diet, population, and environment over the last 100 years. Think of how Granny would feel as she hears these stories of her family whales as she lived over a century in these waters. The students will be given two weeks for this one-off activity.

Step 3: Conclusion

Use the essential questions as guidance using data to support from research in the narrative. After answering the essential questions, plan your story. Your story in narrative should answer and meet the student objectives.

Resources

- http://www.undp.org/content/undp/en/home/sustainable-development-goals.html
- http://www.killer-whale.org/killer-whales-endangered/
- https://whalemuseum.org/

Lesson Framework Introduction: Addressing Injustice: Identity, Perspective-Taking, and Empathy

Lauralee Y. Rodd

The ability to successfully engage in perspective-taking behavior and practice empathy is the foundation for a more accepting society; one that can seek commonalities and accept differences of those in the global and diverse global community in which we all live. These skills--perspective taking and empathy--are critical to addressing injustice in the many places it rears its head in our daily world. Injustice so often comes from lack of understanding, from the inability to see, understand, or accept the differences of others or other's situations, and from a lack of challenging of one's one perceptions and biases.

This lesson sequence is designed to encourage children to better understand themselves and others as well as question common misconceptions, misrepresentations, bias or injustices they will encounter in daily life, and empower them to address it in daily conversation, in the interpretation and critical analysis of media they consume, in the voting booth, and as decision makers, employers, and leaders of tomorrow. It is hoped that students leave this lesson sequence with a better understanding of the roots of injustice and the skills that are needed for the everyday citizen to think critically and identify, speak up for, and address injustice in their daily lives.

Addressing Injustice: Identity, Perspective-Taking, and Empathy
Overview:
Learning Goal
This lesson sequence is focused on student's ability to address inequities by better understanding their identity and the identity of others. They learn to appreciate differences of others and engage in perspective taking about the impact of those differences in others' lives. They confront misrepresentations, stereotypes and bias—their own and that of others, captured in media or other content. They then take action to share what they

have learned and/ or address bias they have encountered.

Please note, these lessons are encouraged to be performed in sequence, however, consider spacing them according to the needs and maturity of your classes. Due to the depth and density of the subject matter, it may be better to provide students some time between these activities instead of doing them all back-to-back.

Lesson Sequence

Lesson 1	Understanding Self: Exploring Identity
Lesson 2	Identity of Self and Others: Seeing Similarities, Appreciating Differences
Lesson 3	Confronting Misrepresentations, Stereotypes and Bias
Lesson 4	Confronting Our Own Biases
Lesson 5	Taking Action: Capstone Project

Learning Objectives

- Students will better understand one's own identity and heritage connections they have to other cultures, nations, ethnicities, etc. They will understand how identity impacts their view of the world.
- Students will better understand other's identities and appreciate differences. They will better see how different aspects of identity impact us all differently.
- Students will engage in critical reading/ thinking to identify misrepresentations, stereotypes and bias in external content. They will understand how these challenges impact different groups.
- Students will become aware of their own unconscious bias, and discuss how to address those biases. They will understand how bias in all forms compromises the goal of reduced inequity and affects perceptions of social justice.
- Students will take action to share learnings about identity and connection or to address identified misrepresentations, stereotypes and bias.

**Please note, this was designed with an American-school population in mind, however adaptations to local contexts is encouraged. In parts of the world where personal identities,

misperceptions, or biases are less commonly discussed or explored, consider adapting the lessons here by focusing less on identity and more on experiences or cultures, as this may reduce the level of resistance in case some students are not culturally familiar with this kind of topic.

Lesson 1: Understanding Self: Exploring Identity,

Grades: 8 or 9,   Time: 3-6 hours in-class time + take home work time
Summary and Rationale

Help students understand the important aspects of their identity and their connections to other nationalities or cultures as a lead in to Lesson 2, where they learn to connect with and appreciate the similarities and differences to others' identities.

Subjects

Potential ties to Geography, History, Civics, as well as, Art, Performing Arts or Speech (project)

Instructional Goals

- Students will better understand their unique identity and the impact it has on their worldview.
- Students will broaden their view of self as a global citizen by understanding their connections to other cultures, nationalities, ethnicities, communities, or populations other than those they commonly identify with.
- Students will consider what the elements of their identity mean to them and consider what it feels like to be misunderstood or misrepresented.

Standards

Sustainable Development Goals (SDGs): Goal 5: Gender Equality, Goal 10: Reduced Inequalities, Goal 16: Peace, Justice, and Strong Institutions

Competencies: *(Defined where needed upon first use, subsequent usages will not be defined).*

- Intercultural competence: "the ability to interact successfully with people from different cultural identities and origins" (Reimers, Chopra, Chung, Higdon & O'Donnell, 2016, p. lvii).
  - Intrapersonal skills: "ability to recognize and weigh diverse cultural perspectives... to recognize and examine assumptions" (Reimers et al, 2016, p. lx).
- Self-awareness and connection as a global citizen: Understanding of self, personal identity and its context within the communities, nations and world (Reimers et al, 2016).
- Ethical orientation: "recognition of common values and common humanity... appreciation of every person regardless of socio-economic origin... ability to interact with people of diverse cultural backgrounds while demonstrating humility, respect, reciprocity, and integrity... understanding of the role of trust in sustaining human interaction" (Reimers et al, 2016, p. lviii)
  - Explore and develop an understanding of personal identity
  - Develop appreciation of other's identities
- Empathy and perspective taking: understanding and sympathy for the feelings of others, ability and willingness to consider others viewpoints, or put oneself in another's shoes (Reimers et al, 2016).

Understanding Goals

- We all have identities made up of a unique combination of factors
- Our identities influence who we are and how we see the world
- Developing self-awareness prepares us to better appreciate other's unique identities and the impact those identities have on how they see the world.

Essential Questions

- What is identity? Why is it important?
- What characteristics, traits and values shape your identity?
- What perceptions, assumptions, world views do you have that are influenced by your identity?
- How are you connected to other members of the global community?

Student Learning Objectives

- Students will demonstrate thoughtful reflection of self and others in class discussion; show developing awareness of connection to others within the global village.
- Students will demonstrate understanding of heritage as evidenced in thoughtful and thorough one-page summary of results of "Explore Your Heritage" activity.
- Students will demonstrate thoughtful consideration and self-evaluation in development of Mind Map project.

Assessment

- Engaged and thoughtful input during class discussion
- One-page summary of results of "Explore Your Heritage" activity (sufficient detail to show that research was done).
- Completed Mind Map project (should represent high level of thoughtful effort, descriptions and creativity).

Sequence of Activities

Opening: Guided Discussion:

- What is identity? Why is it important?
- What are elements of identity?
  - o Potential answers: culture, religion, ethnicity, nationality, gender, disability, age, personal traits, etc.
- Do all elements of identity that are personal to you fall into easy categories? What elements of your identity are not common categories of identity?
  - o Potential answers: family values, personal values, defining experiences, roles we play (brother, sister, friend, etc.)
  - o Discuss the concept of intersectionality or the idea that multiple facets of identity can interact in meaningful ways (for example being BOTH a woman and a person of color can be important aspects of identity for a person).
- Why is identity important? What does your identity mean to you?
  - o Potential answers: connection to others, to community, to a purpose or cause

Lesson Framework Introduction: Addressing Injustice: Identity, Perspective-Taking, and Empathy

Activity: Understanding Self Project

Note: Before the activity begins, discuss vulnerability and the importance of respecting others as we share parts of ourselves and our identity that are important and personal. Discuss the importance of respect and trust as we acknowledge differences.

Project Background

Our identities are made up of a combination of many factors. Even if elements are shared, no two identities are the same. Identity impacts how we take in and react to the world around us.

- Discuss: Ask the class to think about and provide examples of the uniqueness of identity and how we use our identity to perceive the world.

Think about the important elements of your identity. What are they? How do they impact you? What misunderstandings do you face? Might a common trait you have with others be a more important aspect of your identity than it is for them?

Project Part 1: Explore Your Heritage

Note: Depending on characteristics and needs of your class, this can be a take-home project or one you do in class or in a computer lab depending on your school resources.

Students will explore their background and heritage as parts of their identity. Students can register for free access to FamilySearch.org and use the data and information there to build a family tree or research ancestors. *Note: Students may have varying degrees of ancestry information available—this is a non-for-profit website largely built by volunteer contributors—thus while the data is robust, it is not all-inclusive.* (If costs are feasible or if a student's family already has access, ancestry.com will offer similar information/ services). If students do not have much information available online, or if they prefer, encourage them to interview family members to understand their background and heritage.

Assessment

Students should bring a one-page summary of their findings (a family tree, a summary of results, a basic mind-map, etc.) that captures what cultural, national, or other heritages they have.

In-Class Discussion

- What connections did you find? Did you find anything that surprised you?

- In addition to your current nationality, how does your heritage make you feel connected to the global community?

- What does it mean to you that you have ancestry from other places that you may have never been to/ know much about?

- For those who did know the heritage of your family (and perhaps have even visited your family's ancestral lands), what do those connections mean to you? How do they impact your sense of identity and your perspective as a global citizen?

Project Part 2: My Unique Identity and Inter-cultural Connections

Note: Depending on characteristics and needs of your class, this can be a take-home project or one you do in class. If in-class, recommend that students have a variety of supplies and materials to be able to explore and creatively represent themselves.

Instruct students that they are to create a piece that represents them. It will highlight an Identity Mind Map, but can take any form (art, mobile, diorama, digital, etc.). Encourage the students to be creative. [See example in teacher resources]. For their Identity Mind Map, students will start with themselves at the center. Each branch should represent an important element of their identity. The next level of branches should capture what that trait means to them, how it impacts them or how it makes them feel. If the project is being completed outside of class, have students do some brainstorming on traits, characteristics and elements of identity that they would like to share in class before starting. This will allow them to ask questions they may need before beginning the project.

Note: Make sure students understand in advance that the intention is for them to be able to share (at least part of) their pieces during the next class discussion, so they do not have to include any element of identity that would be uncomfortable to share.

Closing

Instruct each student to think about the below questions to set the stage for discussion in Lesson 2:

- What elements of identity are most important to me and why?
- What connections do I have to cultures, nationalities, ethnicities, or religions different than those I might most commonly identify with? How am I connected to the communities and world around me?
- How might my identity affect my unique view of the world?
- What elements of my identity are misunderstood by others?
- How does it feel to be misrepresented or misunderstood?

Resources for students:

- Free Mind Map Maker (by Canva): https://www.canva.com/graphs/mind-maps/
- Mind Map Example Worksheet (attached)

Resources for teachers:

- FamilySearch.org or ancestry.com

Lesson 2: Identity of Self and Others: Seeing Similarities, Appreciating Differences,

Grades: 8 or 9,   Time: 2-4 hours in-class time

Summary and Rationale

Help students understand their identities in the context of a larger peer group and class group. Empower students to appreciate and respect differences and make connections to others. Help students confront assumptions they may have had about different aspects of others' identity and to realize that no one is defined by only one aspect of their identity (in preparation for later discussions on generalizations, bias and stereotypes.)

Subjects

Potential ties to Math or Speech/Presentations (charts, graphs and visualizations)

Instructional Goals

- Students will consider their identities in relation to those around them.
- Students will appreciate others' identities and how they influence their worldviews differently.
- Students will appreciate the uniqueness of each person's identity, understand that one feature of identity does not define a person, and that people may experience the same element of identity differently.
- Students will be more empathetic and open to the differences and values of others.

Standards

Sustainable Development Goals (SDGs): Goal 5: Gender Equality, Goal 10: Reduced Inequalities, Goal 16: Peace, Justice, and Strong Institutions

Competencies

- Intercultural competency
- Intrapersonal skills
- Self-awareness and connection as a global citizen
- Ethical orientation
- Empathy and perspective taking
- Valuing differences

Understanding Goals

- Similar elements of identity impact us differently or mean different things to us
- We are alike and different
- Our differences are special and should be respected
-

Essential Questions

- How are we alike and how are we different?
- What do our differences mean to us? How do they impact us?

- Does one characteristic define all others? Why is this a dangerous assumption? (i.e. Does having one or some characteristics in common mean having the same identity)?

Student Learning Objectives

- Students will provide engaged and thoughtful input during table and class discussions completing form and group Venn diagram.
- Students will demonstrate maturity, curiosity, and empathy about others' identities.
- Students will actively participate in the work on the Class Mind Map.
- Students will thoughtfully reflect on learning and submit a short write-up.

Assessment

- Engaged and thoughtful input during table and class discussions.
- Completes form during table discussion. Table's Venn diagram completed.
- Contributes to the Class Mind Map.
- Completes a short paragraph write-up reflecting learning.

Sequence of Activities

Note: Again, remind students again of the importance of understanding and respect. What is being shared is vulnerable information for some, it is brave to share, and we should treat everyone with respect.

Beginning: Discussion/ Teaching

Review identity from prior lesson. Ask for student reactions to building their maps. Was it difficult to define what elements of identity were most important to you? Why might that be?

- Potential answers: Sometimes the traits others use to define us are not ones we identify with. Sometimes the traits valued or important to others close to us are not as important to us as they are to them. Sometimes we may face fear in sharing parts of ourselves that are sensitive or special.

Remind students that this should remain a safe place. Students should strive to make everyone feel welcome, safe and comfortable.

Understanding Oneself in Relation to Peers

Have students share their Identity Mind Maps in small groups. If a student is uncomfortable with sharing detail on any part of their map they may choose to only share a specific branch. Give the student time to not only share their different characteristics but also how that plays out in their lives, what it means to them, and how it affects them. Allow time for other students to ask respectful questions that can help them learn more about differences.

After each student presents, have each person around the table share:

- One thing they most admired about what the presenter shared.
- One element where you are the same?
- One element where you are different?

Assessment and Reflection

- Have each student turn in a form (see resources) with each presenter from their table on it:
  - o Select one identity element:
  - o What did I learn about this element of identity?
  - o What assumptions might I have had that were different?
  - o What did that identifying element mean to the person presenting?

How are We Alike and Different: Venn diagram Table Activity

- As a table fill in a large Venn Diagram by writing directly on it, using small post-its or post-it flags. Worksheets with pre-made Venn Diagrams for printing are included in the resources, however students could work together to draw theirs on large sheets of butcher paper).
- Discuss: The value of the differences and similarities.

How Are We Alike and Different: Classroom Identity Mapping

Note: This activity can happen on the same day or a different day than the above depending on time and class focus.

On a chalkboard, whiteboard, or large paper make a class Identity Mind Map:

- Start with class name at the map's center.
- Each student should have 1-2 post-its showing a characteristic or trait of their identity.
- Students must work together to identify common groupings among them (recognizing that everyone may not label a particular trait or characteristic in the same way).
- The student's groupings of similar characteristics of students' post-its will form each branch of the mind map.

Note: Depending on time and objectives, students could be more creative and illustrative with their branches or post-its. Developing creative representations or artistic interpretations may allow some students to better express their feelings about certain aspects of identity. It can also encourage creativity and engagement.

Discuss

- What is surprising when we look at our class identity map?
- Are there any characteristic groupings that surprised you?
- What can we learn about our differences?

What Does it Mean to Each of Us?

- Group students who share a common characteristic/trait branch, and give them chalk. Ask them to discuss as a group and add a second layer of branches to the map representing at minimum: (a) the impact of this characteristic on their life (or how it looks in their life), (b) what it means to them, and (c) what others do not know or understand. *Note: Students should capture all the different answers for each point (some may be the same, but some may be different).* Make sure to give students plenty of time to discuss and explore with other students who share similar characteristics.
- Repeat for other like groupings until the map has two layers filled in.

Discuss (as a class)

- What was surprising when you discussed similarities?
  - Did it help you feel connected or better connected to someone?
  - What did the impact to your life have in common?
  - What was different?
- How did people who shared a characteristic or trait with you, experience it differently in their life?

Discussion Extension: Broader Impacts

Note: Use this extension as needed, based on the time, desired depth into topic, and maturity of class.

- Just because two people have the same characteristics, does it mean the same thing to their identity? Why or why not?
- Does one characteristic define all others (i.e. does being a girl mean that you have the same identity as all other girls?), why or why not? Why might it be dangerous or hurtful to assume this?
  - Discuss generalizations and stereotypes, and the problems they present. Encourage students to discuss (if comfortable) how generalizations or stereotypes they have faced, made them feel.
- Ask students to reflect and share (if comfortable): Of the elements that are the strongest parts of your identity, why are these elements of your identity most important to you? How did they become important to you?

Closing: Assessment and Reflection

- Have each student write a short paragraph personally reflecting and identifying:
  - What did I learn today about myself and others?
  - Why is identity important? Why is respect for and understanding of others' identities important?
  - How do our identities influence our lives? Our worldviews?

205

Lesson Framework Introduction: Addressing Injustice: Identity, Perspective-Taking, and Empathy

Resources for teachers:

- Mind Map Example Worksheet (attached)
- Table Discussion Form (attached)
- Venn Diagram Example Forms (attached)
- Facilitating Effective Group Discussions: https://www.brown.edu/about/administration/sheridan-center/teaching-learning/effective-classroom-practices/discussions-seminars/facilitating

Lesson 3: Confronting Misrepresentations, Stereotypes and Bias

Grades: 8 or 9,   Time: 2-4 hours in-class time + take home work time
Summary and Rationale

After learning about their own identities and how to appreciate the differences of others, students are encouraged to understand the impact of misrepresentation, bias, or stereotypes. They will understand the impact they have on themselves and others. They will have improved empathy and better ability to engage in perspective taking. They will become better at identifying misrepresentation, bias, or stereotypes in content they consume and develop skills in articulating and addressing these misrepresentations, etc. to others.

Subjects

Potential ties to: History, Civics, Government, or Current Events

Instructional Goals

- Students will understand the impact of misrepresentation, bias, or stereotypes.
- They will apply critical thinking skills to the content they consume and become better at identifying misrepresentation, bias, or stereotypes. They will learn to question what they read or watch.
- Students will be empowered to articulate or advocate against incorrect information they encounter.

Standards

Sustainable Development Goals (SDGs): Goal 5. Gender Equality, Goal 10. Reduced Inequalities, Goal 16. Peace, Justice, and Strong Institutions

Competencies

- Empathy and perspective taking
- Intrapersonal skills
- Self-awareness and connection as a global citizen
- Ethical orientation

Understanding Goals

- Misrepresentation, bias, or stereotypes exist all around us. They can affect our and others' view of the world and certain groups of people. They all undermine the goals of "Reduced Inequalities" and "Peace, Justice, and Strong Institutions."
- We should be aware of the potential biases in what we read and watch and be able to identify them when we encounter them.
- We should feel comfortable expressing what we know to be incorrect about the content encountered.
- Through our own experiences with misrepresentation, bias, or stereotypes, we can better empathize with others.

Essential questions

- How have I and others experienced misrepresentations, stereotypes and bias?
- What impact does it have?
- How do we identify misunderstandings, misrepresentations, stereotypes and bias in what we read and watch?
- How do misunderstandings, misrepresentations, stereotypes and bias affect our ability to address inequality and social justice?

Student Learning Objectives

- Students will understand how others experience misrepresentations, stereotypes and bias through participation in class discussion, self-reflection and community interviews.
- Students will learn that they can be overt or covert.

207

- Students will develop awareness and apply critical reading skills to evaluate the underlying biases inherent in what we read or watch, demonstrated by identifying content reflecting this.
- Students will gain empathy for others' feelings from or experiences with these challenges through class discussion, self-assessment and community interviews.

Assessment

- Provides engaged and thoughtful input during class discussions.
- Completes identification of a misrepresentative piece and articulately presents how it misrepresents an element of their identity.
- Completes interview of a community member and submits one-page summary of findings.
- Identifies a misrepresentative piece based on the interview and articulately presents how it misrepresents an element of the community member's identity.

Sequence of Activities

Opening: Discussion, Teaching

- What are misrepresentations, stereotypes and bias? Are they all the same?
  - o Misrepresentations: information or content that represents things or people incorrectly, improperly, or falsely or to represent them in an unsatisfactory manner (Oxford Dictionaries, 2017).
  - o Stereotype: a widely held but fixed and oversimplified image or idea of a particular type of person or thing (Oxford Dictionaries, 2017).
  - o Bias: Inclination or prejudice for or against one person or group, especially in a way considered to be unfair (Oxford Dictionaries, 2017).

Small Group Work and Discussion

- After reviewing the definitions with the class, have each small group brainstorm and select an example of each of the three: misrepresentations, stereotypes and bias.

Class Discussion:

- Why is it important to identify misunderstandings, misrepresentations, stereotypes and bias?
- How can misrepresentations, stereotypes or bias in the media we consume affect our views of social justice?
- Where do we find bias? Why is it sometimes hard to identify misunderstandings, misrepresentations, stereotypes and bias?
  - o Explain that bias can be overt or covert, sometimes it is not obvious to us if we are not paying attention.
- How can we identify them?
  Note: Students should have covered this skill in prior curricular coursework, however, it can be valuable to review at a high level here.
  - o Potential answers: critical thinking/ reading, not taking all information at face value, evaluating the source of content and the intention, being aware that these things exist in all people and thus can be found in many places.
  - o Use the following as an example if needed: http://minorjive.typepad.com/hungryblues/2005/09/in_ne w_orleans_.html

Activity Part 1: Identifying Misrepresentations, Stereotypes and Bias Affecting Oneself

Select a characteristic of your identity: culture, religion, ethnicity, nationality, gender, disability, age, socioeconomic status etc. that you are comfortable sharing and identify a piece of literature, a news story, an article, media piece, speech or any form of content that misrepresents that characteristic, it can be overt or covert.

- Explain how your piece misrepresents the elements of identity selected.
    - o What specific words or phrases in the content indicate overt or covert forms of bias?
- Explain, what you know from personal experience that makes this representation incorrect.
- Share how it feels to have an aspect of your identity misrepresented.

Activity Part 2: Identifying Misrepresentations, Stereotypes and Bias Affecting Others

Select and interview someone from your community, and ask them about different aspects of their identity that are important to them (culture, religion, ethnicity, nationality, gender, disability, age, socioeconomic status etc.). Turn in a one-page summary of your findings. Then, identify a piece of literature, a news story, an article, media piece, a speech, a tweet, or any form of content that misrepresents that characteristic, it can be overt or covert.

- Explain how your piece misrepresents the elements of identity selected.
    - o What specific words or phrases in the content indicate overt or covert forms of bias
- Explain what you have learned from your interview that makes this representation incorrect.
- Where applicable, share how discrimination or bias impacted your interviewee.

Closing Discussion

- Were there misrepresentations that surprised you? Were there impacts to classmates or interviewees that you hadn't considered?
- What does what you have heard make you think about the ideas and worldview you may have? What does it make you think about the content and media we consume?
- What challenges did we see with discrimination and bias even when not overt nor designed to discriminate?

- What can, and should we do to think critically about what we consume?
- What can we and what should we do when we encounter discrimination or bias in what we consume?

Interdisciplinary Connection: History (Optional Lesson Expansion)

- Complete the same task above but using an historical example.
- Find a piece of literature or content that misrepresented a group. What was the impact?

Discussion

- In what different ways were groups misrepresented historically? What was the impact of this misrepresentation?

Resources for teachers:

- Media Literacy: https://www.literacyworldwide.org/blog/literacy-daily/2016/12/16/media-literacy-is-critical

- List of Videos on the Topic of Stereotyping and Cultural Representation in the Media and Popular Culture. Must have log-in to access from the site, but many of the titles can be found elsewhere: http://subjectguides.library.american.edu/c.php?g=175267&p=2788 310

- Example of news source racial bias: http://minorjive.typepad.com/hungryblues/2005/09/in_new_orlea ns_.html

Lesson 4: Confronting Our Own Biases,

Grades: 8 or 9, Time: 1-2 hours, in-class time

Summary and Rationale

After developing an understanding of misrepresentation, stereotypes and bias, and identifying each in outside sources, students must now take the next step of confronting bias within themselves. To better address inequality, students gain self-awareness of their own implicit biases and learn tactics to address them.

Subjects

Science (if opening experiment tie-in is utilized)

Instructional Goals

- Become aware of our own unconscious/ implicit biases and attempt to address them.
- Become more open minded, accepting, self-aware individuals.
-

Standards

Sustainable Development Goals (SDGs): Goal 5: Gender Equality, Goal 10: Reduced Inequalities, Goal 16: Peace, Justice, and Strong Institutions

Competencies:

- Self-awareness and connection as a global citizen
- Sense of responsibility for one's own biases
- Empathy and perspective taking
- Intrapersonal skills
- Intercultural competency
- Ethical orientation

Understanding Goals

- We all have unconscious biases that we should be aware of and try to address. No one is a bad person for having bias.

- Bias can affect our view of social justice and our perception of other peoples and groups.
- By being more self-aware, we gain better intercultural competency and become more accepting.

Essential questions

- What is unconscious/ implicit bias and who has it?
- How does unconscious bias affect us and others and what can we do to address it?

Student Learning Objectives

- Students will take IAT Tests and reflect on results in a short write up.
- Students will thoughtfully participate in group and class discussions.

Assessment

- Thoughtful consideration of impact of bias in post IAT test write up.
- Thoughtful and respectful input in discussions.

Sequence of Activities

Beginning: Establishing Activity

- Execute the following experiment, "See the World Through Color-Filtering Lenses": https://www.sciencefriday.com/educational-resources/see-the-world-through-color-filtering-lenses/

Discussion: How might we liken this to our world view?

Explain we all wear our own glasses that color or impact how we see the world. This affects what we naturally see or don't see. But we can learn to better see beyond our own lenses. This is known as unconscious or implicit bias.

Definition: "An explicit stereotype is the kind that you deliberately think about and report. An implicit stereotype is one that is relatively inaccessible to conscious awareness and/or control. Even if you say that men and women are equally good at math, it is possible that you associate math more strongly with men without being actively aware of it" (Greenwald, Banaji & Nosek, 2011).

Discussion, Teaching: Provide Background

- We all have inherent biases, many we may not even be aware of. Having biases does not make someone a bad person, but we can become more aware of them and try to address them. These affect how we perceive the world and those around us—what we believe is possible for ourselves and others.
- How might bias affect our view of social justice and our ability to be open minded, inclusive, global citizens?
    - o Potential answers (Thiederman, 2015):
        - ▪ Reduced ability to build and maintain diverse, inclusive groups or teams
        - ▪ An inability to relate effectively to people of diverse backgrounds
        - ▪ Reduced ability to see people accurately and, thereby, treat or judge them fairly
        - ▪ Diminished trust or feelings of exclusion and diminished status

Activity: Before class, have each student take three Implicit Association Tests (IAT), available here: https://implicit.harvard.edu/implicit/takeatest.html

After completing have the student write two short paragraphs answering each of the following

1. What biases were shown that surprised you?
2. What was shown that bothered you? Why?

Discussion

Note: It is important that we do not shame students or allow other students to shame each other because of biases they share. We all have inherent biases, many we may not even be aware of. Having biases does not make someone a bad person. This discussion must be handled with care. You may need to customize the group work according to the climate and maturity of your classroom.

- In a safe discussion environment, in small groups, have students discuss what surprised and/or bothered them. Students don't have to discuss specifics but are encouraged if they feel safe and comfortable in doing so.
- What are the impacts of some inherent biases (one from the table or others)?
- For example: If we tend to believe that certain roles are male associated, it might affect what a girl believes is possible for her to achieve. It may impact the way we write job descriptions and fill roles.
  - You can share the following example if desired/ appropriate for your class: In 2003, Harvard Business School conducted an experiment, providing the same case study to students changing only the name, in one instance using a female-associated name "Heidi" and the other using a male-associated name, "Howard." Students rated them as equally competent but agreed that they would like to work with Howard more than Heidi. Howard was seen as more likeable, Heidi more "difficult" even though they were the same. This study was highlighted in Sheryl Sandberg's book, *Lean In.*

Another example: If we tend to have biases we are unaware of we might unconsciously discriminate against a candidate with a name that is associated with a certain race.

- You can share the following example if desired/ appropriate for your class: A 2004 study sent identical resumes for jobs, changing only the names. Some had Anglo-sounding names, others had names identified to be black-sounding. Resumes from the first group of names were 50% more likely to get calls for interviews than the resumes with black-sounding names. Read more here: https://www.povertyactionlab.org/sites/default/files/publicatio ns/3%20A%20Field%20Experiment%20on%20Labor%20Mark et%20Discrimination%20Sep%2004.pdf

- How can being aware of our biases help us?

Closing Discussion: How do we address our own Biases?

Allow students to make suggestions or share things that they have done. Other potential answers and discussion points:

- Avoid the opportunity to let your bias impact your decision. For example, removing potential indicators of race, gender, etc. from a resume prevents us from evaluating someone on other factors and focuses the decision on the factors that matter (Greenwald, Banaji & Nosek, 2011).
- Involve others in a decision to limit any one person's bias to significantly impact the result.
- Ask ourselves: Would I feel the same way about the significance of this person's behavior if he or she were of a different group (Thiederman, 2015)?
- Take a pause before making an emotional reaction. Be leery of making purely "gut" decisions without passing it through a logic test first (Thiederman, 2015).
- Adjust according to our known biases by, for example, being friendlier to a group you may be biased against or taking care to consume content that portrays groups you may be biased against in positive, non-stereotypical ways (Greenwald, Banaji & Nosek, 2011).

Assessment and reflection

Encourage students to select one bias that bothered them and try one of the tactics identified to help address it. Have them report back in a later class session.

Resources for teachers:

- Science   Experiment   Object   Lesson: https://www.sciencefriday.com/educational-resources/see-the-world-through-color-filtering-lenses/
- Book: 3 Keys to Defeating Unconscious Bias: Watch, Think, Act Paperback – June 30, 2015

- Implicit   Association   Tests: https://implicit.harvard.edu/implicit/takeatest.html

Lesson 5: Taking Action- Capstone Project

Grades 8 or 9,   Time: Variable

Summary and Rationale

Provide students the opportunity to apply and share what they have learned and to address the challenges identified.

Subjects

Potential Ties: Art, Speech, Current Events, or Writing

Instructional Goals

- We can take action to address our bias or other instances of misrepresentation, stereotypes or prejudice.
- We can share what we have learned about identity and our connections to the global community.

Standards

Sustainable Development Goals (SDGs): Goal 5: Gender Equality, Goal 10: Reduced Inequalities, Goal 16: Peace, Justice, and Strong Institutions

Competencies

- Self-awareness and connection as a global citizen
- Sense of ownership for one's own biases
- Empathy and perspective taking
- Intrapersonal skills
- Intercultural competency
- Ethical orientation

Understanding

- We can all take action to improve our sense of interconnectedness and understanding of our identity in the context of our communities and the world in which we live.

217

- We can take action to address misrepresentation, bias and stereotypes.

Essential questions

- How will I make others more aware of our personal and shared identities?
- How can I help others to understand our interconnectedness despite the uniqueness of our identities?
- How can I address misrepresentation, stereotypes and biases?

Student Learning Objectives

- Students have an evolved sense of self and their interconnectedness to others, sufficient that they can share it with others in a meaningful and coherent way.
- Students have the skills and feel empowered to take action against misrepresentation, stereotypes and biases.

Assessment

Use a rubric to measure student's projects based on:

- Demonstrated understanding of concepts taught: 25%
- Accuracy of concepts shared: 25%
- Effectiveness of project in communicating and teaching others the concepts: 25%
- Effectiveness and/or creativity of project: 25%

Sequence of Activities

Beginning: Discuss, Teach

We can all address misrepresentation, stereotypes and biases. We are all responsible for standing up for social justice. We can address and confront our own biases as well as help be a voice for others. We should understand the influence of our own identities and backgrounds, be respectful and interested in the identities of others, and see our interconnectedness to those around us.

Activity: Student Project

Students can work independently or in groups to create a project addressing and applying what they learned about identity, differences and similarities, or bias.

- Based on your IAT results or your own self-awareness, select an identity characteristic or group you may have bias toward, and research ways that bias is present in media, or socio- political practices or movements (for example, diction difference in newspaper articles regarding people of color vs others, or analyzing wrongful termination court cases for women or people with disabilities). Write a paper on ways that biases might affect this particular group and what you might suggest to help address it.
- Develop a speech, presentation or artistic representation (dance, video, painting, etc.) and share with your class, others in your grade or the school about identity, differences and similarities we have, or biases we face.
- Develop a speech, presentation or artistic representation (dance, video, painting, etc.) to share with your class, others in your grade or the school, insights you gained about another culture, nationality, race, religion, etc. in your class discussions.
- Write to editor(s) or news source(s) of some of the identified biased content. Outline your points and request it be addressed. Write an article countering the previous representations made. Share the responses and results with the class.
- Create a school-wide identity map, allow others to contribute to where they share similarities and what impact characteristics have on their lives. Students could facilitate a school-wide discussion on respecting similarities and differences.
- Create your own project, teacher must approve.

Closing

Students share projects with school, community, family, class, or peers.

References:

Bias | Definition of bias in English by Oxford Dictionaries. (n.d.). Retrieved October 01, 2017, from https://en.oxforddictionaries.com/definition/bias

Stereotype | Definition of stereotype in English by Oxford Dictionaries. (n.d.). Retrieved October 01, 2017, from https://en.oxforddictionaries.com/definition/stereotype

Misrepresent | Definition of misrepresent in English by Oxford Dictionaries. (n.d.). Retrieved October 01, 2017, from https://en.oxforddictionaries.com/definition/ misrepresent

Greenwald, T., Banaji, M., & Nosek, B. (n.d.). ProjectImplicit. (2011) Retrieved October 01, 2017, from https://implicit.harvard.edu/implicit/faqs.html#faq1,

Reimers, F., Chopra, V., Chung, C. K., Higdon, J., & O'Donnell, E. B. (2016). *Empowering Global Citizens: A World Course*. North Charleston, SC: CreateSpace Independent Publishing Platform.

Thiederman, S. B. (2015). 3 keys to defeating unconscious bias: watch, think, act. San Diego, CA: Cross-Cultural Communications.

Example: Identity "Mind Map"

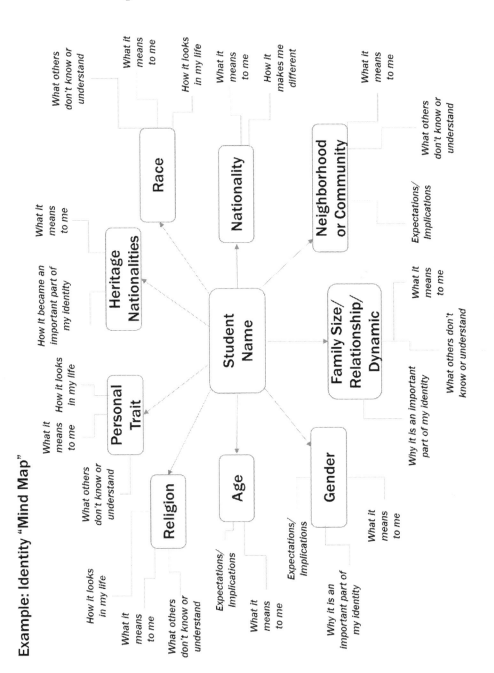

The Student Name is at the center, connected to: Heritage Nationalities, Race, Nationality, Neighborhood or Community, Family Size/Relationship/Dynamic, Gender, Age, Religion, Personal Trait.

Race: What others don't know or understand; What it means to me; How it looks in my life

Nationality: What it means to me; How it makes me different

Neighborhood or Community: What it means to me; What others don't know or understand; Expectations/Implications

Heritage Nationalities: How it became an important part of my identity; What it means to me

Personal Trait: What it means to me; How it looks in my life; What others don't know or understand

Religion: How it looks in my life; What it means to me; What others don't know or understand; Expectations/Implications; What it means to me

Age: Expectations/Implications; Why it is an important part of my identity

Gender: What it means to me; Why it is an important part of my identity

Family Size/Relationship/Dynamic: What it means to me; What others don't know or understand; Why it is an important part of my identity

Name: _____

Date: _____

Small Group Exercise: Understanding Ours and Other's Identities

Presenter:	Element of Identity:	What did I learn about it?	What assumptions had that were different?	What did it mean to the person presenting?

Venn Diagram Template-
3-Person Group

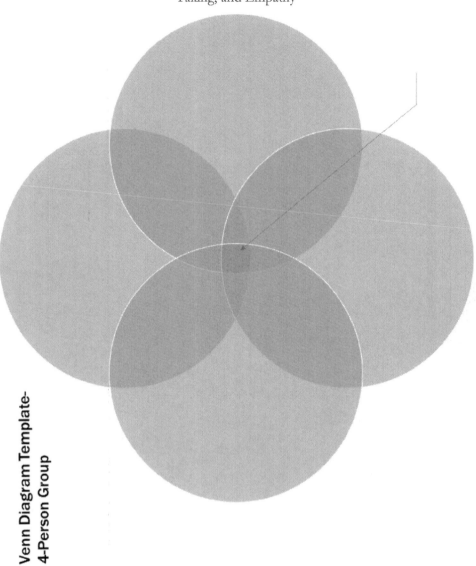

Venn Diagram Template-4-Person Group

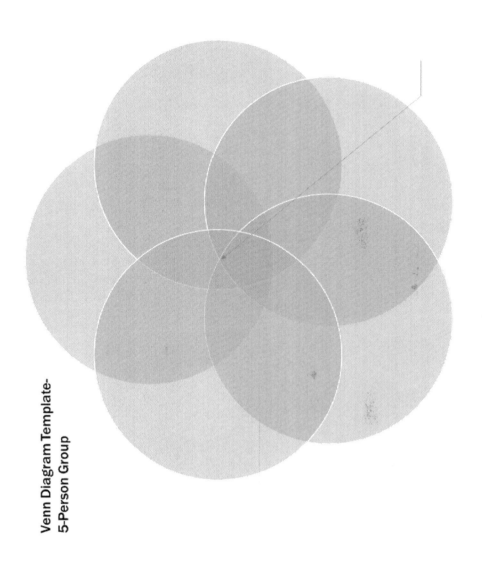

Venn Diagram Template-
5-Person Group

Learning to Collaborate for the Global Common Good

A Framework for Integrating Sustainability across the Curriculum

Katy Bullard, Jennifer Kuang, Sarah Thang

Introduction

Global citizenship in the 21st century demands an awareness of how individual actions and broader policies impact collective well-being, today and in the future. Environmental sustainability lies at the heart of global citizenship because it is closely tied to so many facets of individual and shared well-being, and so dependent on collective action. Global citizens in the 21st century must be knowledgeable about issues of justice and equity related to the natural environment and be equipped with the intrapersonal and social-emotional competencies to change their own behaviors and advocate for broader collective change around sustainability issues. While global citizenship is not limited to environmental wellness, sustainability is a prerequisite for a peaceful and just world.

Environmental sustainability is crucial for ensuring human health, safety, and wellbeing, now and in the future. A changing climate has expanded disease vectors, shifted rain patterns, altered crop yields, creating new risks to health, food security, and livelihoods (World Bank, 2015; WPRO, 2017). Increasingly intense climate events, such as floods and hurricanes, as well as gradual but sustained changes to climate, like droughts, have already led to displacement in many parts of the world as "climate migrants" seek safety or livelihoods; this phenomenon is expected to increase substantially in coming years (UNU-EHS, 2015). Given these extensive risks posed by climate change, the attainment of many other SDGs – including SDGs 2[1], 3[2], and 6[3] will require progress on environmental sustainability. Furthermore, given that the consequences of climate change tend to most severely affect the most marginalized (Patel, 2016), environmental

---

[1] "End hunger, achieve food security and improved nutrition and promote sustainable agriculture" (United Nations, 2015).

[2] "Ensure healthy lives and promote well-being for all at all ages" (United Nations, 2015).

[3] "Ensure availability and sustainable management of water and sanitation for all" (United Nations, 2015).

sustainability will be critical for the realization of SDG 10.[4] With growing recognition of the role that climate change can play in inciting instability and conflict (Popovski, 2017), promoting sustainability will be critical for realizing SDG 16.[5] A firm understanding of sustainability issues among today's students will also be essential for the realization of SDGs 8[6] and 9.[7], with their focus on preventing environmental degradation and ensuring sustainable growth.

Reflective of the wide-ranging effects of climate change, this framework presents recommendations for cross-disciplinary exploration of environmental sustainability. Often, study of sustainability (if it happens at all) is confined to natural science classes, focused mostly on the physical *causes* of climate change and much less on the extensive physical, social, political, economic, cultural, and emotional *impacts*. With this in mind, rather than limiting sustainability studies to a single discipline, this framework provides guidance and examples for integrating sustainability across subjects, from Grades 1 to 12. In this way, the framework aims to help students develop a more holistic understanding of sustainability and its impacts on many dimensions of our present and future lives. To this end, the framework aims to help teachers build student knowledge of: the (inequitable distribution of) impacts of climate change on human life; sustainable practices and policies; and major actors working on sustainability issues. Beyond this content knowledge, this framework aims to help teachers develop students' critical and creative thinking skills to: question narratives that minimize or disregard climate change and its impacts; critically examine the gap between those contributing most to climate change and those most impacted by its effects; and evaluate the relationship between the social, scientific, political, and economic dimensions of climate change and sustainability.

---

[4] "Reduce inequities between and within countries" (United Nations, 2015).

[5] "Promote peaceful and inclusive societies for sustainable development, provide access to justice for all and build effective, accountable and inclusive institutions at all levels" (United Nations, 2015).

[6] "Promote sustained, inclusive and sustainable economic growth, full and productive employment and decent work for all" (United Nations, 2015).

[7] "Build resilient infrastructure, promote inclusive and sustainable industrialization and foster innovation" (United Nations, 2015).

With environmental studies usually confined to the natural sciences, sustainability studies rarely prepare students to act and advocate. This framework, however, emphasizes students' own ability (and need) to contribute to sustainability through personal behavior changes and broader advocacy and activism in their communities. The framework emphasizes the need to scaffold students into developing the social-emotional and reflective thinking skills (along with the previously discussed critical thinking skills) to critically evaluate their own behavior and examine how they could act more sustainably, translating the knowledge they build into practices of sustainability. Action items are built into the examples to encourage and guide students through sustainability activism work. As reflected in the sample lessons, the framework relies on active pedagogies that engage students in critical dialogue and reflection about sustainability issues and their own roles and contributions. Collaborative and project-based learning are emphasized to prepare students with the experience and interpersonal skills to engage in the partnerships necessary to work for environmental wellness.

The framework is intended for teachers, school leaders, and teacher trainers in well-resourced countries to guide professional development and practice for teachers, schools, and districts interested in promoting sustainability. Recognizing that certain countries, such as the U.S., contribute disproportionately to climate change (for instance, in energy consumption and emissions), this framework especially targets schools in middle- and high-income countries that contribute heavily to climate change. Because contexts can vary substantially (in terms of school resources, students' and teachers' experiences, regional climate concerns, and so on), the framework is intended to be generally applicable in these high-emitting countries, but adaptable to the specific needs and circumstances of individual classrooms. The example lessons are also intended to provide enough flexibility to be integrated into a range of existing curricula that may approach a given content area at different times.

This framework outlines six examples (three of which are detailed in full lesson plans) of sustainability integrated in different subjects at different levels. The intention of showcasing these lessons is to highlight the wide range of disciplines in which issues related to sustainability can be incorporated with a focus on student action, and the varying levels of complexity with which these topics can be addressed according to student age and level. The lessons are intended to be flexible enough to be adapted to fit different grade levels; the primary school arts example, for instance, could be revised to work with more complexity in a middle or high school art class. The first two examples are lessons intended for a single class period, while the third includes several lessons and a capstone, demonstrating the diversity of ways in which sustainability can be integrated into existing subjects. In this way, the framework acts as a guide to help teachers recognize the many avenues for integrating sustainability issues into their teaching. Finally, we provide several brief examples of additional ways that sustainability topics can be integrated across five subject areas to provide additional starting points for teachers.

Example Lessons: The Framework in Action

This framework is comprised of several lesson plan overviews, two each for elementary, middle, and high school in the table below. Those with sample lesson plans following the table are indicated with an asterisk. Additional suggestions for topics to incorporate sustainability into various subjects at different grade levels are provided at the end as well.

Competencies and Learning Objectives:

Students should be able to:

- Recognize how humans live in harmony with the earth.
- Understand how their own behavior has an impact on the environment.
- Name and evaluate sustainable practices and processes.
- Understand the roles that governmental and non-governmental organizations play in the climate movement at a local, national, and international level.
- Consider the relationship between social, scientific, economic, and political implications of climate change and sustainability work.
- Question narratives that minimize or disregard climate change and its impacts
- Critically examine the gap between those contributing most to climate change and those most impacted by its effects.

230

- Work individually and in teams to translate knowledge about the environment into advocacy and activism.
- Take action to positively impact environmental concerns in their community.

Grade Level	Related Subjects	Standards	Instructional Goal - *Students will be able to...*
* Primary (Grades 1-5)	Art, Music	Responsible production and consumption (SDG 12) Climate Action (SDG 13) Life on Land (SDG 15)	Understand the concepts of recycle, reuse, and environmental conservation. Creatively recycle and reuse materials.
Primary (Grades 1-5)	English	Responsible production and consumption (SDG 12) Climate Action (SDG 13) *Teacher's choice:* Clean Water and Sanitation (SDG 6) Life below Water (SDG 14)	Explain the importance of one or more aspects of sustainability and environmental conservation (teacher's choice). Analyze the consequences for life on earth if issues of conservation and sustainability are not addressed. Create a picture book or story explaining one or more consequences arising from a lack of environmental consciousness. (For older grades, this story will also examine what actions they

Grade Level	Related Subjects	Standards	Instructional Goal - *Students will be able to...*
		Life on Land (SDG 15)	can take to mitigate environmental impact.)
* Middle (Grades 6-8)	Math	*Teacher's choice:* Affordable and Clean Energy (SDG 7) Responsible Consumption and Production (SDG 12) Sustainable Cities and Communities (SDG 11) Climate Action (SDG 13) Life Below Water (SDG 14) Life on Land (SDG 15)	Use simple quantitative data to analyze an environmental issue. Translate quantitative data into visual graphical displays. Draw conclusions based on quantitative data.
Middle (Grades 6-8)	History	*Teacher's choice:* Sustainable Cities and Communities (SDG 11) Responsible	Analyze a time in history when a community or country failed to be environmentally conscious and the direct negative impact on its people (e.g. through landslides). Evaluate the long and short term

Grade Level	Related Subjects	Standards	Instructional Goal - *Students will be able to...*
		Consumption and Production (SDG 12) Climate Action (SDG 13) Life Below Water (SDG 14) Life on Land (SDG 15)	effects of these consequences. Compare and contrast the above situation with a parallel, current situation. Synthesize learnings by creating recommendations for the people and/or the government in the current situation based on lessons from the historical context. Utilize technology to present information e.g. in a series of blog posts, website, or other form of technology.
* High School (Grades 9-12)	Geography Social Studies Civic Education	Good Health and Well Being (SDG 3) Clean Water and Sanitation (SDG 6) Responsible Consumption and Production (SDG 12)	Analyze and synthesize complex issues relating to clean water, health, and the environment. They will develop a broad understanding of these issues, and closely analyze a specific country or context. Make interdisciplinary connections between subjects such as geography, social studies, and civic education. Consider the influence they have in educating their community about these issues, and how they

Grade Level	Related Subjects	Standards	Instructional Goal - *Students will be able to...*
			might utilize personal agency to advocate for the marginalized and under-resourced.
High School (Grades 9-12)	Physical Education, Math, Science	Affordable and Clean Energy (SDG 7) Sustainable Cities and Communities (SDG 11) Responsible Consumption and Production (SDG 12) Climate Action (SDG 13)	Analyze some of the challenges, benefits, and barriers to affordable and clean energy. Synthesize and apply knowledge of math and physics to create a bicycle generator (or any type of generator that requires human exertion to function). Record and analyze data from conducting experiments on input (effort) and output (energy) using the bicycle generator. Create a visual representation of the amount of effort needed to generate a certain amount of energy, and extrapolate findings to make conclusions about energy conservation and reliable energy.

Sample Lesson Plans

Lesson Plan Title: Recycling as an Art

Designer(s) Names: Katy Bullard, Jennifer Kuang, Sarah Thang

Grade Level: Elementary/primary school students

Time Frame: 2-4 hours

Summary and Rationale: Students will play an active role in environmental conservation by learning to recycle and reuse products. Students will explore creative ways to recycle and gain information on sustainable patterns of consumption. Through this activity, students will learn about actions as a form of individual activism to contribute to the goal to "substantially reduce waste generation through prevention, reduction, recycling, reuse" (United Nations, 2015).

Subjects: Art, music

Instructional Goal:

- Students will understand the concepts of recycle, reuse, and environmental conservation.
- Students will create new products by creatively recycling and reusing materials.

Standards:

- SDG 12: Responsible production and consumption
- SDG 13: Climate Action
- SDG 15: Life on Land

Enduring Understandings:

- Students can play a role every day in combating climate change.
- Sustainable practices are important to the well-being of the planet and to humans.
- There are multiple ways in which one can help reduce waste.
- Goal-driven individual action is a form of activism.

Essential questions:

- Where does waste go?
- What are ways to reduce waste?
- What can I personally do to help prevent waste?

- How do we show appreciation for the planet and all the species that live within it?

Student Learning Objectives: *Students Will Be Able To (SWBAT)...*

- Define what recyclable materials are and identify examples of recyclable goods.
- Determine sustainable choices that people can make in their everyday lives to help the environment (e.g. recycle, compost, etc.).
- Examine and identify resources in their own community where one can practice sustainable choices (e.g. recycling center, etc.).
- Design creative ways to reuse materials.
- Learn to work in a team.

Assessment: The debriefing discussion at the end of the lesson will allow the teacher to perform informal checks on students' understanding of the activity. Teachers can also test students' understanding by having students list recyclable materials, why they are recyclable, and activities students can do with their families to help with environmental conservation.

Sequence of Activities:

Students will collect recyclable goods from their households and bring them to class (e.g. plastic water bottles, egg cartons, cardboard boxes, newspapers, etc.). On the day of the lesson, students will be asked to discuss which materials are recyclable. Students can also discuss whether they practice sustainability at home or are aware of sustainability activities in their communities.

Teachers can integrate this activity into an existing art or music curriculum. The guiding question for this lesson is, "What can you do with recycled material?" For art class, students can break into small groups of 3-4 and pool their collection of recycled materials to create an art project. If desired, the project can address an environmental problem (e.g. pollution, endangered species, etc.) by using art as a way to showcase the issue. Students also have the option of creating an object with utility. Students will present their project to the rest of the class, explaining the materials that make up the art. Students should also explain how the topic of their art project relates to protecting the environment.

In music class, students are instructed to create instruments from the recycled material they collected. Students can break into small "bands" of 3-4. The students can then present their instruments, and perhaps play a song as a band, to the class.

Teachers should conclude the lesson by asking what the students learned and how students plan on practicing environmentally sustainable habits in the future. For example, if students are using a lot of water bottles, one step could be to use reusable water bottles instead. Teachers can provide resources to learn more about where students can practice sustainable actions in their community. For older students, teachers can also facilitate a brief discussion on why taking individual action to protect the environment is important and how that can be translated into social justice activism in the future.

Resources for Students:	Resources for Teachers
• https://kids.niehs.nih.gov/topics/reduce/index.htm • https://www.earthday.org/take-action/	• https://www.weareteachers.com/earth-day-crafts-classroom-activities/ • http://files.eric.ed.gov/fulltext/EJ1102965.pdf • https://www.teachervision.com/recycling/recycled-art

Lesson Plan Title: *Using Math for Environmental Understanding*

Designer(s) Names: Katy Bullard, Jennifer Kuang, Sarah Thang

Grade Level: Middle school, grades 6-8

Time Frame: 1-2 hours

Summary and Rationale: This lesson aims to utilize and apply students' knowledge of mathematical concepts to real issues in the world. Students will produce a brief research paper with graphs and mathematical reasoning on an environmental topic of their choosing. Through this integrative and interdisciplinary lesson, students will gain a better understanding of environmental impact. Students will realize the importance of quantitative data in telling a story. Students will also foster 21st century skills in critical reasoning based on data, conducting research, and developing an evidence-based report.

Subjects: Mathematics

Instructional Goal:

- Students will be able to use simple quantitative data to analyze an environmental issue.
- Students will be able to translate quantitative data into visual graphical displays.
- Students will be able to draw conclusions based on quantitative data.

Standards:

- SDG 7: Affordable and Clean Energy
- SDG 12: Responsible Consumption and Production
- SDG 11: Sustainable Cities and Communities
- SDG 13: Climate Action
- SDG 14: Life Below Water
- SDG 15: Life on Land

Enduring Understandings:

- Math can be used to analyze environmental issues.
- Quantitative data is useful to show evidence of environmental issues.
- Understand how to draw conclusions from quantitative data.
- Using quantitative data can help strengthen an argument.

Essential questions:

- How can you use math to analyze environmental issues?
- What kind of data should you use to make your point?
- How have environmental issues changed over time?
- Are there multiple ways to interpret your data? What are they? Why did you decide to interpret the data in the way that you chose?

Student Learning Objectives: *Students Will Be Able To (SWBAT)...*

- Conduct simple research to find quantitative data.
- Identify what kind of data is appropriate for the research topic.
- Identify the different types of graphs and how to use and read them.
- Generate a graph using real-world data.
- Critically analyze mathematical data to draw a conclusion.

Assessment: Teachers should closely examine the graph(s) generated by the student to ensure student understanding of translating quantitative data to visual representations. Along with the student presentations, the paper will also allow teachers to assess students' critical thinking and ability to interpret and draw conclusions from quantitative data. A rubric for the paper can include a scale to evaluate the strength of the student's argument or conclusion derived from their quantitative data analysis.

Sequence of Activities:

Students will write a short research paper (about 2 pages) on an environmental issue of their choosing. Some examples include:

- Climate migrant movements
- Gas emissions
- Energy consumption
- Renewable energy trends
- Availability of drinking water
- Frequency of natural disasters
- Consumption of tuna
- Average annual temperature of the local state/region over time

Students will be instructed to research simple statistics on their chosen topic, either from the internet or by gathering data from book sources. Students should include a table of those statistics in their paper (e.g. energy consumption in the U.S. by year), and generate a graph for those statistics. Students should then identify data points of interest (average, range, outliers, etc.) and describe the general trend of their graph(s). Students should draw inferences from their research and answer the questions: What does your data say about your topic? What are the implications of your data? What does your data mean for the environment? In addition, students should address whether there are any solutions or ways to address the issue.

Students will then be asked to give a poster presentation on their papers, displaying the graph(s) they generated and discussing their findings. Teachers can wrap up the student presentations with a debriefing session in which all students synthesize what they learned through this exercise, both in terms of using mathematical data and the environmental issue they chose. Students can also discuss challenges that they had with finding and interpreting data, the decisions they made for the type of graphs they produced, and how mathematical concepts can help explain issues in the real world.

Resources for Students	Resources for Teachers
· https://www.factmonster.com/science/environment · https://www.sciencenewsforstudents.org/ · https://www.mathsisfun.com/data/index.html	· https://www.maa.org/press/periodicals/loci/joma/classroom-ready-data-sets-in-environmental-math-introduction · http://www.neok12.com/Statistics.htm

Lesson Plan Title: Water in the Developing World

Designer: Katy Bullard, Jennifer Kuang, Sarah Thang

Summary and Rationale: This lesson integrates issues of health, water, and pollution across existing subjects and courses. Students are challenged to build 21st Century Competencies of global awareness, social agency, and higher order thinking as they synthesize these issues and create a personal response.

In addition to identifying causes and effects of the global water crisis, students also learn about the global response to these issues. In higher grades, they are required to analyze the challenges and successes of these responses. Finally, students are provided with the space to consider how they can be agents of change in their communities.

Grade: High school, grades 9-12

Time Frame: It is recommended that this project be done over the course of the semester. Teachers of younger students might find it useful to schedule either more class time, or time outside the classroom in order to provide additional support.

Subjects: Geography, Social Studies, Civic Education.

Instructional Goal:

- Students will analyze and synthesize complex issues relating to clean water, health, and the environment. They will identify and analyze causes and effects, develop a broad understanding of these issues, and closely analyze a specific country or context.
- Students will also be able to make interdisciplinary connections between subjects such as geography, social studies, and civic education.
- Students will consider their influence in raising awareness in their community, and how they might utilize personal agency to advocate for the marginalized and under-resourced.

Standards:

- SDG 3: Good Health and Well Being
- SDG 6: Clean Water and Sanitation
- SDG 12: Responsible Consumption and Production

Enduring Understandings:

- Access to clean water is necessary for survival and is a human right.

- Individual and societal choices have wider social – and sometimes global – implications.
- We have a greater responsibility in ensuring that everyone can meet their basic needs.

Essential questions:

- Globally, who are some of the people who lack access to clean water? What are some barriers certain countries or communities might have to accessing clean water?
- What are some consequences when people do not have such access? These might be negative impacts on the individual, community, or country.
- What role might pollution or environmentally unsound practices play in preventing access to clean water? (For older grades only) Why can people or companies get away with these practices (assuming they can), and if not, what holds them accountable?
- What can external organizations do to help bring access? What can you do?
- (For older grades only) Is external help always welcome or helpful? Why or why not? What are some considerations that could be critical to keep in mind?

Student Learning Objectives: *Students Will Be Able To (SWBAT)...*

- Broadly explain the water crisis in developing countries and understand why access to clean water is crucial to life.
- Analyze the reasons access to clean water might be a challenge, including the role environmentally unsound practices might have in limiting this access.
- Evaluate the personal and social consequences when access to clean water is unavailable.
- Synthesize the above ideas and use it as a framework to analyze the water crisis in one specific country.
- Design a final project that will both serve as a tool students can use to educate their neighbors, and create a space for them to raise awareness for and/or advocate for the need for clean water around the world.

- (11th and 12th grade only) Evaluate the successes and challenges external organizations face in helping to bring clean water to developing countries. What are some ways they have done more harm than good, and vice versa? What are some challenges and considerations?

Assessment: In the final project, students demonstrate mastery of the material by synthesizing and applying the information learned. Turn-and-talks-then-share, reflection pieces, essays, and presentations, and will serve throughout as formal and informal checks for understanding.

Sequence of Activities:

Lesson 1: Broadly explain the water crisis in developing countries and understand why access to clean water is crucial to life.

- Opener: watch a video about the water crisis, reflect by sharing thoughts
- Core: Students should be broken in groups of 2-3, each read and synthesize an article about an issue related to the water crisis, and then share their findings with the class.
- Close: Students write a short personal reflection explaining why access to water is crucial to life, and how their lives would be different if clean water was not easily accessible.

Lesson 2: Analyze the reasons access to clean water might be a challenge, including the role environmentally unsound practices might have in limiting this access.

- Opener: In groups, students brainstorm reasons they think access to clean water might be a challenge, categorize these reasons, and share their thoughts with the class.
- Core: Using some of the online resources provided below and building off lesson 1, students conduct deeper, more specific research into the water crisis, and the reasons access to clean water is a challenge in developing countries. Students should also identify 2-3 countries and record specific data or examples for those countries, keeping an eye out of a country of interest they would like to further explore. In particular, students should look into the ways individual or societal actions have limited access to clean water (such as

through pollution). These activities should be conducted in pairs or trios.

- Older students should also conduct research into the corporate choices that impact access to clean water, and who/what bodies hold them accountable for their actions.
- Close: In their groups, students give a mini-presentation of their findings.

Lesson 3: Evaluate the personal and social consequences when access to clean water is unavailable.

- Opener: In pairs, create a visual representation summarizing key points from Lesson 2
- Core: Students should be asked to take some time to reflect on the personal and social consequences when people do not have access to clean water, after which they will do a pair-and-share activity of the teacher's choice.
- Close: Individual mini-essay analyzing and evaluating the water crisis.

Lesson 4: Explain the role of nonprofits, NGOs, or inter-governmental agencies in bringing access to clean water to developing countries.

- Opener: Students share knowledge they have or NGOs, inter-governmental agencies, and nonprofits. The teacher will then present information about these organizations, and students summarize in a chart their role and function.
- Core: Each group will research a type of organization or a specific organization that is actively involved in helping to provide access to clean water.
- Close: Present findings to class.

Lesson 5: Synthesize the above ideas and use it as a framework to analyze the water crisis in one specific country.

- Opener: Students identify a country of interest to delve more deeply into. The teacher might decide to limit their choices to one of 3-5 countries s/he is more familiar with.

- Core 1: Create a framework synthesizing the ideas from the above lessons.
  - Younger grades will need a more scaffolded process, such as completing a partially-filled table in pairs.
  - Older grades might be asked to design the framework and come up with a visual representation reflecting their analysis.
  - The class could create a "class framework" based on the discussion.
- Core 2: Students research one specific country and map the challenges in the framework onto what they learn about this country. To facilitate this process, teachers might also provide articles or reports for students to reference. Also, the research work is done in pairs, students should write a 1-2 page summary comparing and contrasting some of these general issues and reasons with their specific context.
- Close: On post-its, students add questions to two "walls" (butcher paper) - learnings that were surprising and impactful, as well as outstanding questions/curiosities.

Lesson 6: Design a final project that will both serve as a tool students can use to educate their neighbors, and create a space for them to raise awareness for and/or advocate for the need for clean water around the world.

- Opener: Teacher uses a video of a person/group exercising agency to affect change as a springboard for students to consider what it means for them to influence their community.
- Core: Final project design.
  - Students brainstorm in groups the ways in which they might raise awareness for one or more of these issues in their community, and what advocacy might look like.
  - In small groups or individually, students design an executable plan to influence their community and bring awareness to the topic at hand.
- Close: Students discuss some barriers or challenges they might foresee, and ways they might overcome it. Students are also encouraged to execute their plans and share with the class their experiences.

Extension (optional): Teachers invite a Program Manager or Executive Director of a local NGO/nonprofit organization dealing with international or local water issues to speak to the class about their work. Teachers might also consider a Skype call if no local organizations are available. Students should compile a list of questions to ask the guest speaker, and complete a short reflective paper describing points that resonated with or challenged them.

Resources for Students	Resources for Teachers
· https://water.org/ · https://www.humanium.org/en/water/ · https://gcc.concernusa.org/content/uploads/2014/08/Water.pdf · http://www.engineeringchallenges.org/challenges/water.aspx · https://www.worldvision.org/our-work/clean-water · https://businessconnectworld.com/2016/08/11/5-stunning-facts-clean-water-must-know/ · https://www.worldwildlife.org/threats/water-scarcity · https://www.theguardian.com/global-development-professionals-network/2017/jun/02/china-water-dangerous-	· http://www.un.org/sustainabledevelopment/water-and-sanitation/ · https://thewaterproject.org/resources/ · https://gcc.concernusa.org/content/uploads/2014/08/Water.pdf · http://www.un.org/waterforlifedecade/human_right_to_water.shtml · https://www.usaid.gov/what-we-do/water-and-sanitation · https://www.wateraid.org/uk/get-involved/all/schools-and-teachers · http://resources4rethinking.ca/en/resource/life-expectancy-and-access-to-clean-drinking-water · http://pulitzercenter.org/education/lesson-plan-global-

pollution-greenpeace · https://www.conserve-energy-future.com/causes-effects-solutions-of-water-scarcity.php	water-crisis · http://www.who.int/water_sanitation_health/publications/wash_standards_school.pdf

Further Lesson Plan Ideas

The objective of the sustainability framework is to provide ideas for how sustainability issues can be integrated into everyday schoolwork across disciplines. The key idea is to start with the core competencies students are to master during a certain lesson, and integrate sustainability topics into practice with an emphasis on activities that lead to actionable steps students may take take towards environmental sustainability. Teachers are able to decide which lessons or subject competencies are most suitable for incorporating sustainability issues, and the extent to which the topic is explored, though we suspect there are many diverse and creative ways this might be done. As a starting point, we have provided below samples of how to integrate sustainability topics into different subject areas as well as example topics, though the list is by no means exhaustive. The ultimate goal is for teachers to be able to integrate real-life sustainability issues into their teaching without overhauling their curriculum, thus creating a more enriching and relevant experience for their students while ensuring that their lesson planning workloads remain manageable.

Mathematics	
Primary (Grades 1-5)	Teachers incorporate real-life sustainability issues in word problems or while practicing concepts. For instance, students might practice the concept of averages by each determining the number of plastic bottles their family uses a week, and then calculating the average number of plastic bottles the class

Mathematics	
	consumes.
Middle (Grades 6-8)	Teachers select a sustainability topic as a theme for a unit on graphs. Students learn to create and analyze these graphs while utilizing real-life data on e.g. pollution.
High (Grades 9-12)	Students pick a sustainability topic and work on a long-term project researching this area of interest. For instance, they might research how issues of overfishing are affecting particular types of wildlife in a specific region of the world. Students will demonstrate not only a topical understanding of the sustainability topic of choice, but also mastery of math standards such as statistics. Teachers will designate which math competencies students should practice in completing this project.

Resources:

http://datatopics.worldbank.org/consumption/

http://oceana.org/

http://www.ams.org/samplings/feature-column/fcarc-climate

http://www.worldwatch.org/node/810

English	
Primary	Students read a story related to sustainability, then write a

English	
(Grades 1-5)	short story personifying one element studied. For instance, students write a short story in first-person depicting the "life" of a plastic bag from manufacture to the dump.
Middle (Grades 6-8)	As part of a unit on poetry, teachers select several sustainability-related poems for student to read and analyze. At the completion of the unit, students pick an area on which to write a poem, with sustainability as one of the options.
High (Grades 9-12)	Teachers select several sustainability-related current affairs topics for the unit on expository writing. As one of the practices, students one of these topics, then write an expository essay arguing their position.

Resources:

https://www.sciencerhymes.com.au/environmental-poetry

https://hellopoetry.com/words/sustainability/

https://hbr.org/2016/12/9-sustainable-business-stories-that-shaped-2016
https://www.scientificamerican.com/

Sciences	
Primary (Grades 1-5)	Students might study what it takes to grow a garden, then have the opportunity to create a community garden of their own. If there is no room available for a community garden,

Sciences	
	students could also bring to class self-propagating plants such as celery that could easily be "planted" in class.
Middle (Grades 6-8)	In a unit on biodiversity, students split into groups and research threats to biodiversity, such as habitat destruction or over-harvesting. Students will analyze the root causes, attempts to mitigate these threats, evaluate the successes of these interventions, and propose an intervention of their own. Alternatively, students create a brochure summarizing and explaining a sustainability topic e.g. the importance of bees and threats to their survival, the benefits and how-tos of composting, as well as the organisms involved in the composting process, etc. Older children might complete this as the final stage of an independent or group research project.
High (Grades 9-12)	Students research and present to the class a type of green technology. Components of the presentation could include an analysis of the movement towards green technology, an explanation of the technology of their choice, an evaluation of its effectiveness and/or shortcomings, as well as possible proposals to improve the technology, or considerations for those who choose to utilize green technology. Alternatively, students could research modifications individuals could make to their homes if they were interested in being more environmentally friendly. For instance, they could explain the process and options for putting in better insulated windows or roof-top solar panels, the associated cost, and calculate the energy and/or financial savings from

Sciences	
	employing these "technologies."

Resources
https://thewaterproject.org/community/student-resources/grades-3-4/
https://www.epa.gov/ground-water-and-drinking-water/drinking-water-activities-students-and-teachers
https://www.teachengineering.org/lessons/view/cub_environ_lesson06
https://www.green-technology.org/what.htm
https://www.huffingtonpost.com/2015/05/07/green-technology_n_7208264.html

History/Geography/Social Studies/Government	
Primary (Grades 1-5)	In groups or independently, students create and present a simple diorama of a sustainability topic studied in class.
Middle (Grades 6-8)	In a unit on human impact, students study how human actions might change the geographical landscape. In groups, students select a particular area to analyze the degree and type of impact, evaluate current actions (if any) being taken to discourage these actions and the rationale behind these actions, and synthesize this information to decide if they think these actions need to be addressed. Students present their findings

History/Geography/Social Studies/Government	
	and conclusions to the class.
High (Grades 9-12)	Students read and analyze a variety of news sources with differing points of views on a particular topic of sustainability. Higher order thinking skills employed could include comparing and contrasting points of view, evaluating the credibility of these sources e.g. biases or news source, analyzing the role of different players and their role in this issue, and synthesizing various pieces of information to develop their own argument.

Resources

http://www.sciencemag.org/

https://www.scientificamerican.com/

https://www.nationalgeographic.com/

https://climate.nasa.gov/

Performing Arts/Electives	
Primary (Grades 1-5)	Students take on different roles in an ecosystem of the teachers' choice, such as the rainforest, ocean, or savannah. Students learn different forms of dramatic movement while also understanding basic relationships within an ecosystem.
Middle	Teachers pick a theme such as farming or agriculture and provide students with several images related to the theme.

Performing Arts/Electives	
(Grades 6-8)	Teachers could also include a short background related to these images. Students use these images to practice a range of techniques such as sketching or watercolor, depending on the unit objective.
High (Grades 9-12)	Students synthesize a variety of art techniques mastered by creating a piece of art that is sustainability-themed. This could include artworks or art installations depicting the destructive effects to planet or man if sustainability is not prioritized, or the "reusing" of elements typically thrown away (such as candy wrappers or packaging material) to create a work of art.

Resources

https://agsci.oregonstate.edu/art-about-agriculture/art-about-agriculture

https://fineartamerica.com/art/agriculture

https://fineartamerica.com/art/farming

http://scholarworks.rit.edu/cgi/viewcontent.cgi?article=1033&context=jes

http://www.thedramatoolbox.com.au/primary-school/drama-workshops/

Sustainability topics

Agriculture

Biodiversity

Carbon footprint

Community gardens

Compost

Conservation

Electricity

Energy efficiency

Environment

Externalities (economic)

Farming

Food chains

Green Technology

Hydroelectric power

National parks

Nature

Organic produce

Plant ecology

Pollution

Power Generation

Recycling

Transportation

Waste

Water

For more topics, these resources could be helpful:

http://guides.library.ucla.edu/c.php?g=180477&p=1191364

http://www.ecoca.ro/meteo/tutorial/Sustainability/sustainability.html

http://www.neaq.org/learn/for-teachers/classroom-resources-activities/

https://www.worldwildlife.org/teaching-resources/

References

Popovski, V. (2017). Foresight Africa viewpoint: Does climate change cause conflict? *Brookings*. Retrieved from https://www.brookings.edu/blog/africa-in-focus/2017/01/20/does-climate-change-cause-conflict/

Patel, P. (2016). Climate injustice: Those who emit the least pay the most. Anthropocene. Retrieved from http://www.anthropocenemagazine.org/2016/02/those-who-emit-least-pay-most/

United Nations. (2015). Sustainable Development Goals. *United Nations*. Retrieved from https://sustainabledevelopment.un.org/sdgs

UNU-EHS [United Nations University Institute for Environment and Human Security]. (2015) *5 facts on climate migrants*. United Nations University. Retrieved from https://ehs.unu.edu/blog/5-facts/5-facts-on-climate-migrants.html

World Bank. (2015). Climate change complicates efforts to end poverty. *World Bank*. Retrieved from http://www.worldbank.org/en/news/feature/2015/02/06/climate-change-complicates-efforts-end-poverty

WPRO [World Health Organization in the Western Pacific Region]. (2017). All about climate change and vectorborne diseases. *World Health Organization*. Retrieved from http://www.wpro.who.int/mvp/climate_change/about/en/

Do You Know? Lesson Series

Mitsuko Peters

Target audience: Teachers

The *Do You Know?* series of educational lessons aims to promote knowledge, critical thinking, and cultural empathy in order to develop students into global citizens with twenty-first century competencies that enables them to achieve the targets for the Sustainable Development Goals (SDGs), specifically quality education (SDG 4) and gender equality (SDG 5).

- The *Do You Know?* series contains four lesson plans tailored for grade two students. Lessons may be integrated into existing courses, in particular social studies and language arts either as a unit or split across disciplines. However, lessons build upon each other and would be most effective if introduced in sequence. To highlight the students' efforts and encourage further curiosity, students will record their reflections on the issues presented in class in a *Do You Know?* journal. Journals may be any bound notebook.

- The *Do You Know?* lessons are applicable to a variety of contexts— developed and developing countries, urban and rural schools, rich and poor students, girl and boy students. However, the educational lessons aimed at creating global citizens would be most impactful in developed nations, such as the U.S., Germany, and Chile; and emerging country, such as Russia. A 2016 study conducted by GlobeScan for BBC World Service polled over 20,000 citizens from 18 developed and emerging economies to find out their level of identification as global citizens; i.e. strongly agree, somewhat agree, strongly disagreed or somewhat disagree, or do not know (globescan.com). Results showed that 43% of citizens among the 18 countries surveyed identified more as national citizens. However, over half of the populations in the noted countries above did not identify first as global citizens (globescan.com). Citizens in the U.S., Germany, Chile, and Russia identified more as national citizens, specifically, 56%, 57%, 65%, and 74%, respectively (globescan.com).

- The *Do You Know?* lesson series highlights quality education through gender equality. Quality education encompasses *effective learning*, i.e. gaining "relevant knowledge, skills, and competencies" (p. 11) and *relevance of learning* "for both work and 'global citizenship'" (unesco.org, p. 10). While various factors contribute to the gender gap, such as cultural norms and cost-benefits, girls' lack of self-confidence has been found to be directly correlated to "girls' enrollment, retention, attendance, and learning" (King & Winthrop, 2015, p. 27). Further, a lack of academic self-efficacy is strongly linked to academic success (King & Winthrop, 2015). Therefore, quality education helps affect positive change in the agency of girls with low self-confidence and low self-efficacy (King & Winthrop, 2015).

- The *Do You Know?* series is premised on evidence that show gender bias in textbooks, specifically underrepresentation of females and stereotyped female roles and traits (King & Winthrop, 2015). Moreover, research found increased female participation in sports, as a result of Title IX legislation in which provided "equal athletic opportunities for males and females" (p. 37), linked to increased attendance at university; and female role models have a "positive influence on girls' education and career aspirations" (King & Winthrop, 2015, p. 48). Thus, anchoring the series on two women in history, Katherine G. Johnson and Billy Jean King, aims to show that women have made and can make positive contributions to society. Further, these lessons aim to sustain the legacy left behind by the women highlighted by encouraging student development of self-confidence, self-efficacy, empathy, and self-empowerment to affect positive change in twenty-first century global issues.

Lessons
- **Lesson 1** – *Do You Know* WHO? Female Role Models in History
- **Lesson 2** – *Do You Know* WHAT? Gender Inequality in Society
- **Lesson 3** – *Do You Know* WHY? Gender Equality Leads to Peace and Prosperity
- **Lesson 4** – *Do You Know* HOW? Ways I Can Make a Difference

Lesson One: *Do You Know* WHO? Female Role Models in History
Grade: 2nd   Time Frame: 50 minutes

Summary and Rationale

Lesson one aims to highlight the important role women play in society by showcasing women who have made positive impacts in science and sports and the lesson aims to serve as a catalyst for self-confidence and self-efficacy in girls and encourage empathy and respect for others. Lesson one explores the lives of two successful women in science and sports in order to highlight that women are valuable and can accomplish great achievements.

Subjects

Social Studies, Language Arts

Instructional Goals

Students will:

- Learn about the contributions women have given to society
- Recognize women succeed in a variety of employment sectors
- Develop self-empowerment and self-efficacy
- Recognize the value of all human life
- Develop empathy and respect for others

Standards

Quality Education (SDG 4), Gender Equality (SDG 5)

The *Do You Know* WHO? lesson aligns with the SDGs related to quality education and gender equality. The lesson is designed to achieve competency in 1) intrapersonal skills, specifically appreciating oneself and others, 2) ethical orientation, particularly equality of all people, and 3) knowledge and skills, particularly in appreciating the past and learning from the past.

Understanding Goals

Grade 2 students will understand that people regardless of gender or race can be valuable citizens in society through their capacity, determination, and self-efficacy.

Essential Questions

- How does studying history help students to appreciate women?

259

- What obstacles did the women overcome in order to achieve their potential?
- What qualities do the women in history share with each other?
- What factors help foster these qualities in the women studied in class?
- What qualities do students feel are needed to succeed?
- What factors help and don't help support the development of these qualities in students?

Student Learning Objectives

Students will be able to (with 80% accuracy):
- Name one women they learned about in history and explain why she is important
- In small groups of two, apply the concept of a role model by naming one person each who they admire and why they chose this particular individual
- In groups, analyze two similarities between the women in history and their role model
- Compare similarities with class and narrow list reflecting qualities of a role model
- Summarize the main points of discussion and why it was important to learn about the women showcased

Assessment

Teacher will assess student participation and teamwork skills through informal checks during group activity. Teacher will assess mastery of learning objectives by 1) grading activity sheets with a scoring rubric and 2) reviewing *Do You Know* journals. Points for each question on the activity sheet should be on a graduated scale, specifically low value questions assess recall and basic understanding versus high value questions assess critical thinking. Journal entries will be reviewed to assess student progression in the particular area of study.

Sequence of Activities

Step 1: (10 minutes) Opening Activity:

Teacher introduces each lesson in the *Do You Know?* series. Teacher charges two students with distributing the Lesson One Activity Sheet to each student (see Appendix A). Teacher instructs students to write their names at the top of the sheet and to fill out the chart during the lesson when prompted. Teacher proceeds to give a brief outline of lesson one. To engage students in the lesson, the teacher writes on the board, *Do You Know* WHO? Famous women in history.

Step 2: (35 minutes) Main Activity:

Teacher highlights the contributions mathematician and former NASA "computer" Katherine G. Johnson and tennis champion Billy Jean King gave to history. Teacher instructs students to complete the first two questions on the activity sheet. Following the brief biographies, the teacher puts students in groups of two. Teacher prompts the group discussions with this question, "Which female do you admire (look up to) in your life and why is she important to you?" Students will briefly discuss this prompt with their partners, then write their own answers on the activity sheet. Teacher will call upon students to share their thoughts with the class. Groups re-confer and think about two similarities their role models share. Students discuss these similarities with the class and the class agrees on three qualities shared by their role models. Teacher instructs students to note these common traits on the activity sheet. Teacher prompts deeper thinking in students by asking a *So What?* question, "Why are role models important to people and society in general?" Students engage this prompt with their partner and share their thoughts with the class. Teacher instructs students to complete the final question on the activity sheet. Teacher guides the discussion enabling students to reflect on themselves by asking a final question, "What qualities do each of you have or need to obtain in order to be a role model to someone else?"

Step 3: (5 minutes) Closing Activity:

Teacher tasks students to write their reflections on this final question and on what they thought about the women studied in class; i.e. were they

261

inspiring and were they good role models, in their *Do You Know?* journals in the hope students develop self-empowerment and self-efficacy. Teacher encourages students to engage in conversation with their families about important women in history furthering students' curiosity, knowledge, and deeper thinking. Students may ask their families who their female role models are and why they chose that person.

Resources

For teachers:
- *Katherine Johnson: The Girl Who Loved to Count,* Nov. 24, 2015, https://www.nasa.gov/feature/katherine-johnson-the-girl-who-loved-to-count
- *Billie Jean won for all women, By Larry Schwartz,* Special to ESPN.com, https://www.espn.com/sportscentury/features/00016060.html

Lesson Two: *Do You Know* WHAT? Gender Inequality in Society

Grade: 2nd   Time Frame: 50 minutes

Summary and Rationale

This lesson aims to build upon the knowledge gained in lesson one by contextualizing the plight of females regarding inequality in schools and society.

Subjects

Social Studies, Language Arts

Instructional Goals

Students will:
- Develop awareness of inequality of people
- Recognize that inequality serves as an obstacle to many people reaching their potential
- Develop empathy and respect towards all people

Standards

Quality Education (SDG 4), Gender Equality (SDG 5)

The *Do You Know* WHAT? lesson aligns with the SDGs related to quality education and gender equality. The lesson is designed to achieve competency in 1) intercultural skills, specifically interpersonal skills of empathy towards women and intrapersonal skills of recognizing gender prejudice, 2) ethical orientation, specifically appreciation for other cultures and both genders, and 3) knowledge and skills, particularly in studying the past.

Understanding Goals

Grade 2 students will understand that gender disparities that keep girls away from primary education hampers their efforts to become successful and productive women in society like the women studied in lesson one.

Essential Questions

- What does inequality look like?
- Why do you think girls are treated differently than boys?
- What factors may foster inequalities at school, in society, and in different countries?
- How do you think girls feel when they are treated equally?
- How should boys and girls treat each other? What does respect look like?

Student Learning Objectives

Students will be able to (with 80% accuracy):
- Describe the meaning of inequality and give two examples of inequality
- In groups of two, produce one example each of a time they felt unfairly treated
- Analyze factors that help perpetuate unfair treatment of people
- Generate a class list of behaviors that show respect towards people
- Evaluate the importance of respect and empathy towards others

Assessment

Teacher will assess students' participation and collaborative skills using informal checks during group discussions. Teacher will use a scoring rubric to grade activity sheets in order to formally assess student's mastery of learning objectives. Points for each question on the activity sheet should be on a graduated scale, specifically low value questions assess recall and basic understanding versus high value questions assess critical thinking. Teacher will informally review student journals in order to track student growth from lesson to lesson.

Sequence of Activities

Step 1: (10 minutes) Opening Activity:

Teacher briefly recaps lesson one and answers any questions students may have regarding the prior lesson. Teacher gives an overview of lesson two. Teacher selects two students to distribute the Lesson Two Activity Sheet to each student (see Appendix B). Teacher instructs students to write their names at the top of the sheet and fill out the chart when the teacher prompts. Teacher proceeds by writing on the board, *Do You Know* WHAT? Gender inequality exists in primary schools.

Step 2: (30 minutes) Main Activity:

Teacher groups students in sets of three. Teacher begins discussion by asking groups, "What is inequality and gender inequality?" Teacher gives a brief example of unfairness, i.e. the cafeteria serves pizza to six grade students only (inequality) or recess is given to girl students only (gender inequality). Each group develops their own definition of gender inequality. Teacher selects one group member in each group to share their group ideas. Teacher compiles a list on the board and the class narrows inequality down to a simple definition. Teacher instructs groups to come up with two examples of gender inequality. Each group shares their examples. Teacher shares real-world examples of gender disparities in primary schools in low-income countries (see links in Teacher Resources). Teacher then asks students, "How would you feel if there were only boys' bathrooms or only girls' bathrooms in school? Would you still want to go to school? What if it was more expensive for girls to attend school than boys? Is that fair to girls?"

Students contemplate these questions and complete the first to prompts on the activity sheet. Teacher asks students, "What words or behaviors helps encourage unfair treatment of either boys or girls?" Groups discuss and share their thoughts with the class. Teacher lists on the board factors that may lead to more gender inequality. Teacher then guides students as they try to answer the following questions, "How do you act towards someone to show that you respect and value them as a person, and how do you think a person feels when they are being mistreated?" Groups re-confer to discuss the questions and then share their ideas with the class. Teacher lists the behaviors on the board and the class narrows the behaviors list. Teacher asks a final *So What?* question, "Why is it important to learn about gender inequality?" Groups discuss this question and complete the last question on the activity sheet. Groups share their thoughts with the class. Teacher asks follow-up questions to spark deeper thinking on inequality and the behaviors and actions that perpetuate this particular gender issue.

Step 3: (10 minutes) Closing Activity:

Teacher asks students to share their final thoughts on inequality and gender inequality. Teachers task students to take note of gender inequality in their communities and write down any observations and reflections in their *Do You Know?* journals, i.e. how does inequality make you feel and what do you think when someone is treated unfairly because of their gender.

Resources

For teachers:
- Sub-Saharan Africa: Lack of basic services in primary education http://uis.unesco.org/sites/default/files/school-resources-and-learning-environment-in-africa-2016-en/school-resources-and-learning-environment-in-africa-2016-en.pdf
- King, E. and R. Winthrop. 2015. Today's Challenges for Girls Education. Brookings Institution. [pps. x-xi] https://www.brookings.edu/wp-content/uploads/2016/07/Todays-Challenges-Girls-Educationv6.pdf
- Printout of an acrostic poem with the word EMPATHY. Teachers may distribute to each student to take home and display in class as a visual reminder of the importance of good behavior.

https://i.pinimg.com/originals/56/df/f4/56dff4fe5a06410c644a30c
29c27a1c7.jpg

Lesson Three: *Do You Know* WHY? Gender Equality Leads to Peace and
Prosperity

Grade: 2nd   Time Frame: 50 minutes

Summary and Rationale

Lesson three builds upon previous lessons and aims to show a need
to achieve gender equality by highlighting the link to negative social outcomes
in societies.

Subjects

Social Studies, Language Arts

Instructional Goals

Students will:
- Develop awareness of the interconnectivity and interdependence of
  people and societies
- Strengthen empathy towards all people
- Foster an environment that encourages people to discover their
  talents

Standards

Quality Education (SDG 4), Gender Equality (SDG 5)

The *Do You Know* WHY? lesson aligns with the SDGs related to
quality education and gender equality. The competencies that the SDGs help
students gain through this lesson series is 1) intercultural skills, specifically
interpersonal skills (empathy) and intrapersonal skills (identifying gender
prejudices), and an interest in cultures and global issues, 2) ethical orientation,
particularly appreciation for other cultures and genders, and a responsibility
to basic human rights of equality, and 3) knowledge and skills, in particular in
studying the past and the impact of an uneducated population on society.

Understanding Goal

Grade 2 students will understand the interconnectedness of the world, such that inequality in one region has the potential to negatively impact global stability.

Essential Questions

- What value do societies gain by educating girls?
- How can one region with low rates of educated girls affect other regions with high rates of educated girls?

Student Learning Objectives

Students will be able to (with 80% accuracy):
- Describe two ways educating girls helps their communities
- Compare economic and health outcomes in countries with low educated female populations and highly educated female populations
- Analyze how educating girls in one country helps the world stay safe
- Evaluate the importance of interdependence and interconnectivity

Assessment

Teacher will assess students with informal checks during group discussions to assess teamwork skills and participation during group sessions. Teacher will use a rubric on the activity sheets to formally assess a students' mastery of the learning objectives described above. Points for each question on the activity sheet should be on a graduated scale, specifically low value questions assess recall and basic understanding versus high value questions assess critical thinking. Teacher will informally review student journals in order to track student growth from lesson to lesson.

Sequence of Activities

Step 1: (10 minutes) Opening Activity:

Teacher groups students in sets of three. Teacher briefly reviews the takeaway from the previous two lessons and answers any questions students may have regarding the prior lessons. Teacher gives an overview of lesson three. Teacher selects two students to distribute the Lesson Three Activity

Sheet to each student (see Appendix C). Teacher instruct students to write their names at the top of the sheet and fill out the chart when the teacher prompts. The teacher proceeds by writing on the board, *Do You Know* WHY? Gender equality leads to peace and prosperity.

Step 2: (30 minutes) Main Activity:

Teacher begins discussion by asking groups, "What are two ways educating girls helps your community?" Student groups discuss the prompt and share their thoughts with the class. Teacher calls on one member from each group to list on the board their groups two examples. The class discusses the examples and narrow the list down to three examples. Teacher instructs students to write their examples on the activity sheet. Teacher shares real world data to show the impact education has on developing and developed countries' economy and health outcomes (see link in Teacher Resources). Teacher prompts groups to discuss and give two reasons of why education is connected to a society's wealth and health outlooks. Groups share their thoughts with the class. Teacher instructs students to fill out the sheet with their answers. Teacher follows-up this line of thinking with the following *So What?* question, "Why does it matter to the rest of the world if some countries do not educate girls?" Teacher guides group discussion by telling students to keep in mind the concept of interconnectedness. Student groups ponder this question and share their ideas with the class. Teacher instructs students to fill out the appropriate question on the activity sheet.

Step 3: (10 minutes) Closing Activity:

Students share their final thoughts on the importance of gender equality. Teacher tasks students to reflect on the question, "If gender equality and quality education is important to world peace, then how can you help this cause?" Teacher instructs students to write their reflections in their *Do You Know?* journals.

Resources

For teachers:
- Social Outcomes in Sub-Saharan Africa. Majgaard, K. & Mingat, A. (2012). *Education in Sub-Saharan Africa: A comparative analysis.* Washington, D.C.: The World Bank [Appendix H].

Lesson Four: *Do You Know* HOW? Ways I Can Make a Difference

Grade: 2nd   Time Frame: 50 minutes

Summary and Rationale

Building upon the competencies developed in the previous lessons, lesson four aims to encourage personal and civic responsibility and deep collaboration in the pursuit of a shared goal and highlight the various mechanisms by which students can affect positive change in their communities.

Subjects

Social Studies, Language Arts

Instructional Goals

Students will:
- Develop personal responsibility and civic duty
- Strengthen interpersonal and intrapersonal skills
- Develop ways to promote quality education and gender equality in their communities

Standards

Quality Education (SDG 4), Gender Equality (SDG 5)

The lesson of *Do You Know* HOW? aligns with the SDGs related to quality education and gender equality. The competencies that the SDGs helps students gain through lesson four in particular is work and mind habits, specifically in finding creative ways to mitigate gender inequality.

Understanding Goal

Grade 2 students will understand that development of knowledge and skills strengthens individual agency enabling them to fully contribute to improving global issues.

Essential Questions

- What are the skills needed to affect change?
- What are the steps needed to bring about change?
- How can I make a lasting difference?

Student Learning Objectives

Students will be able to (with 80% accuracy):
- Identify three competencies needed to impact twenty-first century issues
- In groups, design a process of change in order to demonstrate their creativity
- In groups, evaluate the process in order to promote effective and sustainable change

Assessment

Teacher conducts informal checks during group sessions to assess teamwork skills and uses a rubric on activity sheets to formally assess individual mastery of the learning objectives. Points for each question on the activity sheet should be on a graduated scale, specifically low value questions assess recall and basic understanding versus high value questions assess critical thinking. Teacher will informally review student journals in order to track student growth from lesson to lesson.

Sequence of Activities

Step 1: (15 minutes) Opening Activity:

Teacher groups students in sets of four. Teacher briefly reviews lessons one to three and answers questions from students regarding previous lessons. Teacher gives a brief outline of lesson four. Teacher selects three students to pass out the Lesson Four Activity Sheet to each student (see Appendix D). Teacher instructs students to write their names at the top of the sheet and fill out the sheet when the teacher prompts. Teacher proceeds by writing a question prompt on the board, *Do You Know* HOW? Ways I can make a difference.

Step 2: (30 minutes) Main Activity:

Teacher instructs groups to ponder the question prompt and come up with three ways their group can take action in order to promote gender equality. Teacher may offer an example to guide student thinking, i.e. create a poster campaign in school that promotes respect for all people. Teacher calls on one group member from each group to share their group ideas. Teacher adds each idea to a list on the board. Teacher instructs students to confer in groups and narrow down the class ideas to three ways the class can impact global change with regards to gender inequality. Each group shares their final three examples. Teacher lists final ideas on the board. Teacher instructs students to fill out the appropriate prompt on the activity sheet. Teacher instructs groups to think of two ways that will help make sure their collective actions are effective and sustainable, i.e. are the gender responses to the action they take positive and are the actions taken realistic enough to be repeated? Groups share their ideas with the class and teacher lists measures on the board. Class narrows the list down to two measures. Teacher instructs students to complete the appropriate prompt on the activity sheet. Teacher asks, "What skills are needed to affect positive change?" Students discuss this prompt in groups and share their thoughts with the class. Class narrows competencies down to three. Students fill-out the activity sheet with their answers. Teacher asks students two *So What?* questions in order to spark self-reflection, "What skills do you have that can help contribute to making a difference? How can you develop the needed skills to make a positive impact in society?" Teacher instructs students to fill out their answers on the last prompt of the activity sheet. Teacher encourages students to share their final thoughts on the importance of gender equality.

Step 3: (5 minutes) Closing Activity:
Teacher instructs students to record in their Do You Know? journals their reflections on what competencies they think they will need, how they can develop these skills, and what actions they would like to take in order to make a difference in promoting gender equality in their home, school, and community. Teacher encourages students to continue reflecting in their Do You Know? journals at home regarding the global issue of gender equality and record the progress they make in creating an environment of sustained gender equality.

Resources

For teachers:

- UNICEF   Heroes   for   Change   magazine
  https://www.yumpu.com/en/document/view/53587356/heroes-for-change

Appendix A: Lesson 1 Handout
Name:

LESSON ONE
Do You Know **WHO?**

What is the name of the women I learned about in class?	
Why is she famous?	1. 2.
Who is my role model?	
Why do I admire (look up to) this person?	1.
List the qualities your class agreed upon that represent the qualities of a role model?	
Summarize the main points of the lesson (2 sentences) and why it was important to learn about the women in history (1 sentence).	1. 2. 3.

Appendix B: Lesson 2 Handout

Name:

LESSON TWO

Do You Know WHAT?

Define inequality and give two examples of inequality?	1. 2.
Give one example of a time you felt unfairly treated.	1.
Give two examples that may cause people to be unfairly treated.	1. 2.
List two behaviors that show respect towards people.	1. 2.
Give two reasons why it is important to respect and show empathy towards others	

Appendix C: Lesson 3 Handout
Name:

LESSON THREE
Do You Know **WHY?**

Name two ways educating girls helps society.	1. 2.
List two ways, discussed in class, education is related to a country's economic growth and health outlook.	1. 2.
List two reasons one country that has a less educated female population may affect a country that has more educated females.	1. 2.

Appendix D: Lesson 4 Handout
Name:

LESSON FOUR
Do You Know HOW?

List three ways your class can promote gender equality in school and community.	1. 2. 3.
List two things you can do to make sure your actions to lessen gender inequality are adequate and maintainable, i.e. are the responses to your actions positive and can you repeat your actions?	1. 2.
Identify three competencies (skills) needed to impact gender inequality in the twenty-first century.	1. 2. 3.
What skills to do you have that can help you make a positive impact on gender inequality?	1. 2. 3.

References

Global citizenship a growing sentiment among citizens of emerging economies: Global poll.

(2016). *Globescan.com*. Retrieved from https://globescan.com/wp-content/uploads/2016 /04/BBC_GlobeScan_Identity_Season_Press_Release_April%2026.pdf

Grimley, N. (2016, April 28). Identity 2016: "Global citizenship" rising, poll suggests. *BBC.com*. Retrieved from http://www.bbc.com/news/world-36139904

King, E. M. & Winthrop, R. (2015). *Today's challenges for girls education*. Retrieved from https://www.brookings.edu/wp-content/uploads/2016/07/Todays-Challenges-Girls-Educationv6.pdf

Unpacking sustainable development goal 4 education 2030. *Unesco.org*. Retrieved from http://unesdoc.unesco.org/images/0024/002463/246300E.pdf

Food on the Global Table: From Food Waste to Responsible Consumption

By June Chung, Rachel Hunkler, Idia Irele, Gillian Foster Wilkinson, Cicy Zhang

Unit Overview:

This four-lesson unit addresses the issue of food waste around the world while empowering students to think globally and act locally to improve responsible food consumption. By learning about food waste and its local and global implications, students will work together to develop creative solutions to tackle the issue of food waste in their local communities.

Unit Scaffold:

Lesson 1	What is food waste and why is it a problem?
Lesson 2	Think globally: Food waste around the world
Lesson 3	Global Food Waste Poster Exposition
Lesson 4	Act locally: How can the local community tackle food waste?

Main SDG Target:

- SDG 12.3 By 2030, halve per capita the global food waste at the retail and consumer levels and reduce food losses along production and supply chains, including post-harvest losses.

SDG Sub-Target:

- SDG 2.1 By 2030, end hunger and ensure access by all people, in particular the poor and people in vulnerable situations, including infants, to safe, nutritious and sufficient food all year round.

Target Audience

This unit plan is designed for lower or upper secondary education students ages 15 and older. It can be integrated into a social studies, citizenship, geography, or history classroom or could serve as part of a specific global citizenship course. We have attempted to create lessons that are adaptable and flexible for schools in any type of cultural or institutional setting; however, we recognize that these lessons are most-readily implementable for schools which have access to technology and Internet connection. In addition, this unit is most readily used in schools located in communities where food waste is a relevant issue; however, these lessons could be adapted to settings where food waste is less of an issue. As such, we encourage teachers to add more resources or content materials as they see fit to adapt to their local setting and further enrich the global citizenship experience in their classrooms.

Special Considerations

Teachers working with low-income students who may be suffering from hunger will likely need to take extra care to frame these lessons in a way which empowers students to improve their situations rather than leaves them feeling disenfranchised. By shedding light on the disparity of sustainable food practices around the world, our intention is not to create an "us versus them" attitude between wealthy and impoverished students, communities, or countries; rather, it is to challenge students to think of the role they can play in solving these challenges, regardless of their own socioeconomic status.

Learning Goals

Students will become more responsible global and local citizens and recognize their personal agency to creatively address food waste challenges. They will gain knowledge of the state of food waste and/or responsible consumption in other countries as well as their own local community. They will strengthen their interpersonal skills, particularly teamwork, negotiation, diplomacy, and conflict resolution. Students will increase their sense of personal responsibility and their understanding of the individual role they can play in addressing important global issues within their own local context.

Unit Learning Objectives:

• Students will gain knowledge about food waste in individual communities and countries.

• Students will compare differing realities and perspectives of food waste and responsible food consumption across geographic locations and apply learnings to their local context.

• Students will demonstrate innovation and creativity by contributing to formulating solutions to challenges of food waste.

• Students will tackle a real-world problem through collaboration and negotiation to identify viable steps towards reducing food waste in their local communities.

Rationale

We designed this unit to immerse students in a project-based learning experience centered around specific targets of the Sustainable Development Goals (SDGs) and anchored by a global citizenship framework that fosters twenty-first century competencies.

The topic of food waste directly relates to SDG target SDG 12.3 pertaining to sustainable food production and consumption. It also indirectly relates to the SDG Goal 2 of "Zero Hunger," as eliminating food waste can lead to less hunger in communities. We chose the topic of food waste because it is an issue that is easily transferable across many different levels of discussion - global, national, local, and individual. By designing our unit around a global issue that students can work to address in their own local communities, we intend for students to both think globally and act locally.

The unit begins with an introductory lesson on the topic of food waste and its importance, asking them to observe how food is wasted in their communities throughout the duration of the unit. The second lesson then moves to the global scale, where students learn about food waste around the world and are broken into small groups to research food waste in specific countries. The third lesson allows students to present their research at a poster exposition, at which students compare and contrast policies regarding food waste in various countries in order to search for best practices. The fourth culminating lesson brings the focus once again back to the local context by asking students to apply the knowledge they have gained about best practices from other countries to collaboratively design an innovative solution to any issues with food waste in their own local community.

Twenty-first century skills and global citizenship competencies are woven throughout this unit. The overall aim of this unit is that by applying a comparative global perspective to students' local context, they will be empowered to be both citizens of their communities and of the world with a personal responsibility to pursue the goal of reducing food waste set forth in the SDGs. These specific competencies include the ability to:

- understand differing ideas and global perspectives by asking students to research and represent the current situation of food waste in various countries around the world

- find, present, analyze, and synthesize information about the countries researched and presented within the class

- form and defend an opinion

- communicate and collaborate effectively in teams as the unit's final problem-solving exercise, which encourages interpersonal skills by learning to work together with those with differing viewpoints and intrapersonal skills by formulating and expressing their own opinions in respect to those of their peers

- diagnose problems in their local communities

- utilize design thinking to identify innovative solutions to complex problems

- enhances analytical and critical thinking skills by asking students to formulate a concrete plan through weighing and evaluating existing and new options against alternatives

A Final Note

This unit was initially inspired by the "Food Security" unit developed by the United Nations Association of Greater Boston for Model UN classrooms in middle schools across the Greater Boston area. While we did not use any specific lessons from their curriculum, we did use many of their research sources as a springboard for our own research and ideas.

Lesson 1 - What is food waste and why is it a problem?

Time Frame: 1 class period (60 minutes)

Summary and Rationale:

In the first lesson of the unit, students look at the issue of food waste as not simply as a global issue far removed from their lives but as a day-to-day problem that exists in many communities. Students develop an understanding of what is food waste and why it is a problem, thereby also increasing their understanding of the urgency of global hunger.

*Note that this lesson assumes that most students in the class typically waste food at home. If students in the class do not have consistent access to food at home, teachers should reframe the discussion questions to address this context and ask students to consider how eliminating food waste could benefit their own access to food.

Instructional Goal: From this lesson, students will learn about the challenge of food waste on a global level, with specific examples of how food is wasted around the world and the impact of food waste.

Understanding: Although there is enough food in the world to feed everyone, food waste is a serious problem. Food waste contributes to the problem of hunger, and responsible food consumption is relevant for everyone to practice.

Essential questions: *What is food waste? How severe is the problem? Why does it matter?*

Student Learning Objectives:

• Students will develop an understanding of food waste around the world and its repercussions.

• Students will learn to analyze, interpret and present information.

• Students will gain awareness of the local resources available to support responsible food use.

• Students will develop their own brief definition of food waste and share it with the class

Assessment: By the end of this lesson, students will articulate their own definition of food waste and why it is an important issue. They can demonstrate this understanding in a variety of ways, such as on social media, in a written reflection, in short oral presentations, or through art work.

Sequence of Activities ("4As" approach used with permission from Global Learning Partners, Inc):

Anchor (10 minutes) - Students will take a true-or-false quiz about the situation of food supply and food waste across the world to understand that there is enough food in the world to feed everybody, but still a lot of people suffer from hunger (see first resource at the end of this lesson for an example).

Add (20 minutes) - The teacher will divide the students into four groups and assign one of the four videos in the resources list to each of the groups. The videos are meant to give students an overview about the reality and consequences of food waste. (Note: teachers could also provide substitute written material for students to read as a group if that better fits the class context). Once students have watched their group's assigned video, each group will use the information from the video to create a short representation that they present to the class, using visualizations or role-play. The teacher is encouraged to give an example, using the case of video 4 about fruit waste, where students could design a story like "An Apple's Life Story" to demonstrate how fruits are wasted in our kitchens and supermarkets.

Apply (20 minutes) - In these same groups, students will discuss the following questions, based on the learnings from the videos and the observations from their own life:

- Who wastes food around the world?

- What are the causes of food waste, from the perspective of both household and industry?

- What consequences does food waste cause to the environment and people's' lives?

- How would the world be different if food waste stopped today?

The teacher will ask each group to choose one representative to talk about their discussion results in front of the class and post unanswered questions and generate more discussions on these questions between the groups. In recognition that some students may be currently facing food scarcity or be unaware that these issues face their community, the teacher will inform the students of local organizations that are helping address the issue of hunger and food waste.

Away (10 minutes) - In the same groups, students will discuss and summarize the learnings of this lesson in 2 to 3 sentences with a 140-character limit, mimicking the average length of a 'Tweet" or social media post. Students will then share these with the whole class. After the class, students are encouraged to share their 140-word learning outcomes on social media if possible. As the class concludes, the teacher will introduce the ongoing assignment for the remaining classes of the unit.

Homework:

Throughout this unit, students should gather visual evidence of the problem of food waste in their own community for the teacher to display in the classroom. Additionally, they should be encouraged to highlight contrasts in food waste and responsible food consumption within the community if any exist. Ideally students will send in photos that the teacher can print and display in the room but understanding that not all students will have access to a camera and not all teachers will have access to printing, teachers can encourage students to bring any visual evidence that can be displayed in the classroom. Examples evidence may include photos of excess waste in a garbage can, a drawing of an empty plate, or a poem about what it is like to be hungry.

"Community" could mean classroom, grade, school, town, state, etc. but the teacher should decide what community the whole class will focus on before introducing the artistic evidence activity and this lesson to ensure that recommendations can actually be implemented and held accountable for throughout the year.

Resources:

- Quiz source: https://goo.gl/UiB3yh

286

- Video 1: Food Waste - The story of our garbage bins: https://goo.gl/62Hcm9

- Video 2: Help Us End Food Waste: https://goo.gl/uWH6iy

- Video 3: Food Waste is the World's Dumbest Problem: https://goo.gl/B8T0s3

- Video 4:Food Waste: Why It Matters: https://goo.gl/id2Fgx

- More activities to refer to: Change Food Lesson Plan: https://goo.gl/Cs5mNU[7]

Lesson 2 - Think globally: Food waste around the world

Time Frame: 2 class periods (Ideally 90-120 minutes)

*To provide ample scaffolding throughout the research process, we suggest that the instruction on food waste in different countries encompass one class period and that the student group work encompass another.

Summary and Rationale: In this lesson, students are introduced to the realities of food waste in different countries. Students will learn about 2-3 countries through the lens of (1) how much food is wasted in the country, (2) challenges the country faces in reducing food waste, and (3) current practices in the country to improve sustainable and responsible food use and/or ideas for future action. Students will then be divided into teams to begin preparing to present on a specific country at the "Global Food Waste Poster Exposition" in the next lesson.

Instructional Goal: From this lesson, students will build on their knowledge of food waste to understand it on a global scale, including learning about international organizations addressing the issue. They will strengthen their analytical skills by focusing on the state of food waste and/or responsible food practices in one specific country and preparing a presentation of their findings to classmates. They will develop interpersonal skills, particularly teamwork, as they work in groups to prepare for the poster exposition.

Understanding: Food waste and responsible food usage have distinctions and similarities across countries around the world. Different countries have different challenges and opportunities to improve the sustainability of their food usage and reduce waste, and there is a global movement to help address the issue.

Essential questions: *What does food waste look like on an international level? What are specific countries doing to improve responsible food practices and food sustainability, and how might we learn from them?*

Student Learning Objectives:

- Students will identify how food waste and sustainable food practices are similar and distinct across contexts.

- Students will practice critical thinking, teamwork, and creative problem-solving skills by working in teams to synthesize information about improving responsible food usage in their assigned countries and develop ideas on how challenges could be addressed.

Assessment: Student teams will create a poster with key information about their assigned country organized into three sections: (1) the state of responsible food usage in the country, including how much food is wasted, (2) challenges the country faces in reducing food waste, and (3) what the country is currently doing to improve responsible food usage and/or ideas for future action.

Sequence of Activities:

Anchor - The teacher will ask questions to review the previous lesson, then introduce the idea that food waste and responsible food usage vary across countries around the world and within individual countries. Students are introduced to the names of organizations addressing the challenges of food waste on an international level.

Add - The teacher will share 2-3 examples of food waste and/or responsible food usage from countries around the world. Students will start becoming familiar with using the following framework to analyze countries:

(1) status of food production and consumption in the country, including but not limited to population, per capita GDP, examples of popular food and foods produced there, amount of food eaten per year, etc.

(2) challenges the country faces in food waste, amount of wasted food, measures of hunger, food security issues, etc. paying attention to how these may differ among areas *within* the country

(3) what the country is currently doing to improve responsible food usage - are there good examples of initiatives or policies that reduce food waste? If so, what are they? If not, what could be an idea the country could consider?

Apply - Students will be divided into teams of 2-4 people and be assigned a country to analyze through the three-step framework presented by the teacher. Students will receive guidance on how to present their findings in a poster and how to access information on their assigned country.

(At this point, it is recommended to give students time to work on their posters in their groups with the teacher available to help as needed. This could be in the same session or an additional working session at a later time).

Away - In their teams, students discuss which learning surprised them most and what they think the key food usage challenges are in their assigned country.

Resources:

A note on country selection:

According the World Economic Forum, the world's top producers of food waste can be found in North America and Europe, the world's wealthiest regions. Thus, to examine some of the greatest challenges of food waste, we suggest using countries from the World Bank or OECD's list of wealthiest countries per capitas. These countries include: Luxemburg, Ireland, Switzerland, Norway, the United States, Saudi Arabia, the Netherlands, Austria, Iceland, and Denmark. Of course, many of these countries are also making efforts to improve food sustainability. In addition, many lower-income countries are also leading the way in responsible consumption. It may be interesting to choose the country of origin to compare to other similar-income countries to see how food waste and responsible consumption compare. Ultimately, country selection should be up to the teacher's discretion of what comparisons will be most helpful and appropriate.

For student teams to research assigned countries

● World Bank database on food and beverage consumption
https://goo.gl/LFVFJY

● FAO food wastage facts and figures, including a 2013 report
https://goo.gl/Sth7i1

● If internet and computer access are limited for students, teachers should direct students to relevant books in a local or school library or share printed summary information with student teams on their assigned country.

290

About the general topic

- Food Tank "10 Facts You Might Not Know About Food Waste" https://goo.gl/vYSZXW

- New York Times Article "One Country's Table Scraps, Another Country's Meal" https://goo.gl/1rTZsK

- FAO Video "Food Wastage Footprint" https://goo.gl/f6dd58

- Blog "13 Resources for Teaching About Food Waste" https://goo.gl/tVy57f

About presenting information on a poster

- Perfecting the Project Display Board https://goo.gl/Yv4VGQ

- Sample poster layout:

Country Name

1. Status of food consumption and production

```
_____
_____
_____
```

2. Challenges the country faces in food waste

```
_____
_____
_____
```

3. Current or potential future actions to reduce food waste and improve responsible food use

```
_____
_____
_____
```

Examples of organizations addressing the issue

- UN Food and Agriculture Organization http://www.fao.org/save-food/en/

- World Resources Institute https://goo.gl/8mfWBc

- World Food Programme http://www1.wfp.org/

- FoodTank https://goo.gl/PochUq

- List of 101 additional examples with global and regional activities https://goo.gl/PochUq

Lesson 3 - Global Food Waste Poster Exposition

Time Frame: 1 class period (60 minutes)

Summary and Rationale: In this lesson, students present the research they have done on food waste and responsible food usage in their assigned countries. Students will learn about the situations in various countries by perusing their displays and taking notes on food waste in each of those countries and current actions each country is taking to reduce or eliminate food waste. At the end of the expo, students must submit their reflection on which countries they think are best addressing the issue of food waste and what specific practices or policies exist in these countries. By comparing different country contexts and policies to improve responsible food usage, students are expanding their worldview while also preparing to apply these best practices to their local context in the final lesson of the unit.

Instructional Goal: From this lesson, students will gain knowledge of food waste in other countries. They will think critically to compare and contrast the situations in various countries and analyze best practices in eliminating food waste and promoting sustainable food use.

Understanding: Food waste has distinctions and similarities across countries around the world. By comparing different situations and strategies for reducing and eliminating food waste, countries can discover best practices that can be adapted to their local context and work collaboratively to solve the issue.

Essential questions: *How is food used or wasted in countries around the world? What successful policies have countries implemented to help eliminate food waste?*

Student Learning Objectives:

293

- Students will present information on countries' situations and perspectives on food waste.

- Students will analyze information about various countries to compare best practices when it comes to food waste and responsible food usage policies.

Assessment: At the end of the expo, each student group will submit a one-paragraph written response in which they choose which countries they think currently best address food waste and what specific policies or practices they think are most effective in those countries.

Sequence of Activities:

Anchor - The teacher, acting as the moderator of the Global Food Waste Poster Exposition, will give some brief opening remarks. These remarks should remind the students of the importance of the issue of food waste and the end goal of the expo, which is to decide which countries are most effectively addressing the issue of food waste, given their current contexts.

(Note: Remind students that they should base their decisions on country best practices based on the content of the posters in term of current actions, not on the actual poster design nor on the student representatives for the countries).

Add - Students travel around with the other member(s) of their assigned country to peruse each country's poster displays. They can use the provided graphic organizer for jotting down notes comparing a set of two countries or develop their own note-taking strategy.

Apply - Students reconvene with their country groups to discuss their individual findings. Allow for some Q&A time if students need to ask any clarifying questions to specific country representatives. Then the country groups will compare and contrast their findings to pick which three countries they think are doing the best job in addressing food waste and why. They must write this down in a one-paragraph reflection, which will be submitted at the end of class.

Away - Ask for student volunteers to share their reflections with the class. After students have shared and the teacher has collected the reflections, the teacher should challenge students to begin thinking about the ways in which

294

these best practices could be adapted to their own local community in order to begin the brainstorming process for next class.

Resources:

- Worksheet to compare and contrast two different countries: https://goo.gl/vS5brX

Lesson 4 - Act locally: How can the local community tackle food waste?

Time Frame: 1 class period (60 minutes)

Summary and Rationale:

In this lesson, students reflect on what they have learned throughout this unit and apply it to a local context. They will examine the visual evidence that each student has brought in throughout the lesson, make sense of key issues in their community, and work together to think about interventions.

Through talking about local issues in groups with students who presented on different countries, students will sharpen their reasoning skills, practice clearly presenting an idea, and work with a team to generate a concise action proposal. Students will also learn how theory can translate to action and recognize their agency in addressing a global problem by first starting with their immediate surroundings.

This culminating lesson is meant to be adapted to the needs of the community in which it is implemented. The ultimate goal for this lesson is to help students develop responsible practices and attitudes towards food, no matter the local community's challenges regarding food waste or food scarcity. Classrooms with students experiencing food scarcity may develop concrete steps to ensure that their community is fed. Conversely, students in communities with food waste can use these same skills to find solutions to food waste in their community, thinking creatively to incorporate some learnings that they gained from the poster exposition.

Understanding:

Food waste is an issue that affects each community differently, however, one country's actions can inform solutions in other contexts. In order to deal with the issue, all communities must be able to place themselves within this global context and strategize how they can mitigate local problems that contribute to global issues.

Essential questions: *How is our community affected by this issue? In what ways do our actions tie into the global issue and vice versa? What strategies can we learn from other countries to tackle this problem at home?*

Student Learning Objectives:

• Students will observe evidence and make conclusions from that observation.

• Students will share findings with a group and interpret them.

• Students will transfer information from one context to another.

• Students will work in groups to negotiate and produce one clear, concise response.

Assessment: Each group will present their recommendations to the entire class. The class will then vote on the recommendations they think are the most thoughtfully designed and most feasible given their local context.

Sequence of Activities:

Anchor – Students will do a gallery walk and observe the photos/visual evidence that they each brought in throughout the unit. They will note their observations on notebooks or a worksheet using the See, Think, Wonder format: (1) What do you **see**? (2) What do you **think** about that? (3) What does it make you **wonder**?

Add – Concentric Circles: Students will form two circles, one inside and one outside, so that each student is facing another. They will have one minute to discuss with their partner what they observed from the gallery walk. They will rotate three times so that in the end they will have discussed the problem with three people.

The teacher will ask the prompting question: *Based on what you have observed, what is the problem that our community faces concerning food consumption and waste? Where could we improve in responsible food use?*

Apply – Students are split into medium-sized groups, so that each group is comprised of members who represented a different country at the exposition. They will then be asked to share their findings and within their group generate one essential recommendation for their own community that deals with the issue of food waste. In order to determine their group recommendation, groups may use a visual organizer like the example in the resources to write multiple ideas and evaluate their impact and feasibility.

Away – **1)** Each group will have two minutes maximum to present their recommendations to the class and the teacher will record the recommendations publicly. The teacher's discretion and creativity will guide the recording method: the teacher can record the recommendations on a chalkboard or chart paper, each group could write or draw their recommendation on a paper to be hung up in the classroom, they could create some sort of blog or written guidebook, or groups could prepare a formal written resolution. Finally, the teacher will ask students to vote on which group's recommendations are the most well-designed and the most feasible to implement, given the context of their local community. See "Resources" for an example for a layout for a worksheet for students or a chalkboard to record recommendations and note the feasibility and impact.

2) After voting, students will have three minutes to reflect individually and write a brief journal entry on what they have learned in this lesson. The teacher should ask students prompting questions: *What do you know about global food waste that you did not know before? What did you learn about this issue in our community? What will you do personally to help solve this problem, either globally or at home?*

Resources:

- Visual organizer for recommendations (see next page for worksheet).Use this worksheet to compare your recommendation ideas. Think about how easy it would be to implement in the community (viability), and how many people it would reach (impact). Circle the recommendation that you believe would be the most appropriate for this community.

- Should the United States follow France's lead in eliminating food waste? https://goo.gl/VZdptd

- Impact/Effort Matrix example for evaluating the students' creative solutions:
    - https://goo.gl/BozLph
    - https://goo.gl/ubh9ee
- World Resources Institute "10 Ways To Cut Global Food Loss and Waste" https://goo.gl/RHhcDZ

- New York Times Lesson "Clean Your Plate" https://goo.gl/nZ5cjd

Recommendation Visual Organizer

Recommendation	How easy would it be to implement in our community?	How many people in the community would it reach?
# 1		
# 2		
# 3		
# 4		

References

Global Learning Partners. (2012). *Four Steps for Learning that Lasts.* Retrieved from http://www.globallearningpartners.com/blog/4-steps-for-learning-that-lasts

OECD. Country GDP Data. Retrieved December 29, 2017 https://data.oecd.org/gdp/gross-domestic-product-gdp.htm

Project Zero. (2015). See / Think / Wonder. Retrieved from http://pz.harvard.edu/resources/see-think-wonder

Reimers, F., Chopra, V., Chung, C., Higdon, J. and O'Donnell, E.B. (2016). *Empowering Global Citizens.*

Reimers, F. et al. (2017). *Empowering Students to Improve the World in Sixty Lessons.*

United Nations. (2015). *Transforming Our World: The 2030 Agenda for Sustainable Development.* Retrieved from https://sustainabledevelopment.un.org/post2015/transformingourworld/publication

United Nations Association of Greater Boston - Model UN. (n.d.). Retrieved September 24, 2017 from the UNAGB-MUN Wiki: http://unagb-mun.wikispaces.com/Food+Security+for+Teachers

World Economic Forum. (2015). *Which Countries Waste the Most Food?* https://www.weforum.org/agenda/2015/08/which-countries-waste-the-most-food/

Constructive Participation in Dialogue

Shannon O'Brien

This series of four lessons (and a final project) is designed to be taught, one lesson per week, in order for teachers to give students some time outside of class to research if they want and for students to properly digest the material and prepare for the final presentation and essay. The time frame, however, is flexible. Ideally, this project would be contextualized and used in each grade level throughout elementary, middle and high school, in any school.

It is meant to follow a lesson on how to distinguish between objectivity and subjectivity, as well as how to find reputable news sources and avoid depending on others. It is also meant to come after a lesson on listening to others. Therefore, as the full implementation of this lesson, as described below, assumes many academic and social-emotional skills, it is meant for high schoolers (or anyone who already has command of the pre-required competencies). Teachers for lower grades would need to adjust the objectives to their students' abilities and needs. Please see more details on objectives for different grade levels in Appendix A and ideas for lesson topics in Appendix B.

Teachers can choose any topic that is recent, relevant and controversial for their students. In order to use this lesson, teachers would need to choose topics, material and resources that are age and language-appropriate and relevant to their students. Teachers can also adjust the time-frame and team sizes, depending on their specific students' needs and the topics chosen. If a teacher chooses to use this series of lessons for younger children, less rigorous activities than presentations and essay-writing could be used. This lesson plan's extremely flexible structure should make it easy for any teacher to use.

The role of the teacher in the lessons will vary, depending on the context. Some classes or students may need more support than others. For example, Barry Overeem's Three Levels of Listening could be specifically taught to the children. However, if the class has already worked on

301

something similar or if students are already more developed in these areas, this will not be necessary. The worksheets they fill out about how they think the other students feel will suffice.

The skills learned and practiced throughout this series of lessons are prerequisites to achieving SDG #15, Peace, Justice and Strong Institutions. Currently, many institutions do a thorough job of teaching students how to debate, back up their arguments and how to make their opinions heard. However, in order for constructive dialogue to take place, students also need to learn to *listen* to others in order to understand the reasons behind different opinions and to innovate together despite those differences. This lesson will remind students to use legitimate resources and fact-check their material and it will give them a chance for teamwork and dispassionate dialogue as they problem-solve together. Such skills are necessary for the goal of Peace, Justice and Strong Institutions to be achieved by our society.

This activity is meant to reflect reality in that we are presented with many problems, globally, and we must be able to weed out unhelpful information and base decisions on facts, as well as listening to others in order to realize teamwork, dialogue and inclusivity.

This lesson has been tested once.

Please see the results in Appendix C.

Grade 9

Learning Goal

Throughout this series of lessons, students will deepen their knowledge of previously-learned skills, learn new ones and practice all of them throughout the various stages of a collaborative project. The skills to be learned and/or practiced throughout this series are: distinguishing between objective and subjective evidence, creative problem solving, understanding both the difficulties and possibilities associated with working in teams and with people who have different opinions, listening to others, looking for similarities and differences in their own beliefs and others', compromising, active and productive participation in discussions, collaboration, presentation skills, essay-writing and reflection.

Lessons

- Lesson 1: Intro to Lesson: Collaboration, Fact-Checking and Finding a Solution

- Lesson 2: Finding Opportunity in Different Opinions

- Lesson 3: Presentation Preparation

- Lesson 4: The Final Compromise

- Lesson 5: Final Individual Essays

Learning Objectives

- Students will practice collaboration, creative problem solving and distinguishing facts from fiction while they explore different aspects of a particular controversial topic with classmates.

- Students will learn listen to others, look for similarities in distinct viewpoints, participate constructively in dialogue, compromise and peacefully come to a consensus through a team activity.

- Students will put together a coherent and reflective explanation of their experience throughout this project.

- Students will participate in activities that review constructive dialogue, listening and collaboration skills and using fact-based evidence to make decisions. They will also practice communication, writing and presentation skills.

Lesson 1: "Collaboration, Fact-Checking and Finding a Solution

Time Frame: 60 minutes | Subjects: English, Social Sciences, Civics | Standards: SDG 4 (Quality Education) and 16 (Peace, Justice and Strong Institutions)

Summary and Rationale

To give students an opportunity to practice their recently-learned skill of critically evaluating resources; To give students an opportunity for

303

creative thinking; To give students an opportunity to work as a part of a team; To give students a starting point for the new skills to be gained throughout this series of lessons.

Instructional Goals

- Students will practice critically evaluating resources.

- Students will engage in creative thinking and provide a solution to a problem.

Understanding Goals

- To recognize the benefits of diverse teams.

- To listen to others openly and dispassionately.

- To understand the benefits of compromise.

Essential Questions

- How do I check that my ideas to solutions are based on legitimate evidence and, therefore, more reliable?

- How do I work with others?

Student Learning Objectives

- Students will be able to successfully work as a part of a team.

- Students will engage in productive dialogue.

- Students will be able to fact-check resources.

- Students, as a part of a team, will be able to come up with a solution to a problem.

Assessment

Participation in team discussion; Filled-out team worksheet.

Sequence of Activities

Step 1: (5 minutes) Introduction

The teacher presents the class with a currently relevant, controversial, age-appropriate problem, that is difficult to solve, in paragraph form. The class should then be divided into six teams of three (to be adjusted, depending on class-size). If students already have opinions on the matter, they can be grouped with those that they agree with in order to articulate and solidify their arguments together. However, if it is a problem that the students are unfamiliar with, they should be given information packs to utilize in order to come up with their opinions. The teacher will decide which of these options is necessary (if not a mixture of the two).

If information packs are used, Teams A, C and E are given Information Pack 1, while Teams B, D and F receive Information Pack 2. An important note is that Information Packs 1 and 2 should be designed to lead the groups to very different conclusions. (For example, Pack 1 might lead them strongly towards a "yes," while Pack 2 leads them strongly towards a "no" on a yes or no question posed). There is not meant to be a "right" or "wrong" answer but the resources are meant to bring the different groups to different conclusions. Teachers can also choose what sorts of resources they provide but it is highly encouraged to include some erroneous sources so that students have the chance to practice their recently-learned skill of eliminating illegitimate information. (This skill will also be necessary if the students are working without Information Packs and, instead, using their own knowledge and resources that they find on their own.)

Step 2: (20 minutes) Reading Time

Each team takes time to read through the problem and the information from the different articles in their Information Pack (or the internet or any other resources the teachers allows/asks them to use instead of or in addition to the Information Packs).

Step 3: (15 minutes) Fact-Checking & Discussion

Each group is encouraged to check (most likely online) if the sources of their information are reputable and if their information is factually correct or subjective/biased. They then discuss what they think the best solution to the problem would be.

<u>Step 4: (10 minutes) Report</u>

Each team designates a leader for the day who writes the group's answer.

Lesson 2: "Finding Opportunity in Different Opinions"

Time Frame: 60 minutes | Subjects: English, Social Sciences, Civics | Standards: SDG 4 (Quality Education) and 16 (Peace, Justice and Strong Institutions)

Summary and Rationale

The student teams of three will be combined into teams of six; groups that have come to opposite conclusions will be put together and students will be encouraged, once again, to fact check and, now, to work together with students who have different opinions on the same problem but based on different evidence. They will work as a team to come up with a new solution to the problem.

Instructional Goals

- Students will learn to truly listen to others and look for similarities in distinct viewpoints.

- Students will participate constructively in dialogue.

- Students will practice compromising.

- Students will come to a peaceful consensus.

Understanding Goals

- Students will come to understand the importance of fact-checking.

- Students will be able to recognize the reasons for other people's opinions.

- Students will understand that looking for similarities between their viewpoints and others' is a good way to find possibilities to work together and build something new and innovative together.

- Students will understand some of the benefits as working as a part of a team, rather than individually or with people who have only seen the same resources as they have.

Essential Questions

- What are the benefits of engaging with people with different viewpoints from my own?

- Is it better to work as a team or individually?

- What is the importance of fact-checking and knowing what organizations my sources

  come from?

- How do I know that I'm truly and fully listening to another person?

- How do I compromise with someone who has a very different opinion than mine?

Student Learning Objectives

- Students will be able to have productive dialogue with students who have different beliefs.

- Students will learn to recognize (and assess) their own listening abilities.

- Students will be able to come to compromises and agreements with other students.

- Students will be able to find solutions to problems based on legitimate evidence.

Assessment

Individual answer sheets filled out; Participation in group discussion; Ending discussions with an agreement/compromise between the six people in the group; Final answer written as a group on worksheet.

Sequence of Activities

Step 1: (5 minutes) Introduction

Teams learn that, in the previous lesson, their counterpart teams (A & B, C & D and E & F), who were given different Information Packets or had different opinions on the matter, came up with a very different solution to the same problem. The teacher gives every student in the class a worksheet and explains that they have to listen carefully to their counterpart team's explanation and write down the similarities, differences and the reasons for the differences. They also have to pay close attention to the other team members' emotions when they speak on the controversial topic and try to identify why they might feel the way they do. This will encourage students to listen empathetically, rather than listening only to respond or argue. Teachers must gauge their students' necessities in this area, as well, giving more or less direction and explanation as necessary.

Step 2: (25 minutes) Joint-Team Explanation of Solutions

Each individual fills out a worksheet as their counterpart team presents:

Similarities in our interpretations of and solutions to the problem:	Differences in our interpretations of and solutions to the problem:	Reasons for differences: (Are they based on accurate and reliable evidence?)	What emotions do you think each of the other team members felt as they told you about their solution? Why do you think they felt that way?

Once both teams have presented their solutions, the teacher explains that Teams A and B (as well as C-D and E-F, etc.) will now join together to form their official team for the project and that they will be graded as one group (AB). They now have the *opportunity* to improve their solutions (and, therefore, grade) by having access to each other's evidence and creative ideas and working as one big team. They are allowed to completely change their current ideas if they decide that's best. The teacher should remind students to listen carefully as they discuss and to not be offended by or scared of other opinions, but rather to look for similarities and opportunities to build a creative solution together. They should be reminded that they are one team now, looking for the best possible solution to the problem that takes all of the evidence into account.

Students from the original Teams A and B (and so on) take turns showing each other the evidence behind their decisions and listening intently to one another (while filling out their worksheets).

Step 3: (10 minutes) Joint-Team Fact-Checking & Discussion

The teacher reminds the students to make sure that they are only to use reputable sources and objective information when coming up with their solution. The students engage in fact-checking and discussion before they come up with their final answer to the problem.

Step 4: (10 minutes) Joint-Team Decision

Each team designates a leader for the day who writes the summary of the new joint-team solution to the problem.

Lesson 3: "Presentation Preparation"

Time Frame: 60 minutes | Subjects: English, Social Sciences, Civics | Standards: SDG 4 (Quality Education) and 16 (Peace, Justice and Strong Institutions)

Summary and Rationale

Students will work together, once again, to create a reflective and coherent summary of their work in the previous class and then present it to their teacher and classmates.

Instructional Goals

- Students will engage in self-reflection.

- Students will continue to practice working peacefully in groups.

- Students will practice presentation skills.

Understanding Goals

The reflection involved in this activity will solidify students' appreciation for the importance of working with others and using fact-based information to create ideas and solutions.

Essential Questions

- How did the solution my team came up with differ from the one my original team of three came up with? How did it differ from what I first thought on my own?

- What benefits came out of working as a team?

- What was difficult about working as a team?

- Is it possible to compromise with those who think differently than me? If so, how?

Student Learning Objectives

- Students will be able to successfully work as a team.

- In teams, students will be able to put together a coherent and reflective explanation of their experience in this project.

Assessment

Participation in the creation and practicing of the group presentation

Sequence of Activities

Step 1: (5 minutes) Introduction

The teacher explains that each joint team will now work together to create a presentation to give to the rest of the class, explaining the following:

- The problem, as their joint team (Team AB, etc.) sees it

- Group [A's] original solution

- Group [B's] original solution

- The new and final combined team's (i.e. AB) solution

- How they came to that solution

- Whether it was easy or difficult to combine the two teams, and why, as well as how it changed the outcome of their solution to the problem presented

Step 2: (40 minutes) Presentation Preparation Time

In the same joint groups, students come up with their answer to the questions above and prepare their presentations.

Step 3: (15 minutes) Presentation Practice Time

Students practice presenting their presentations.

Lesson 4: "The Final Compromise"

Time Frame: 60 minutes | Subjects: English, Social Sciences, Civics | Standards: SDG 4 (Quality Education) and 16 (Peace, Justice and Strong Institutions)

Summary and Rationale

Students will present their work to the class. Students will then become one large team (the entire class) and will continue working together peacefully in an expanded form. The importance of source legitimacy and fact-checking will be reviewed, and students will listen to one another in order to compromise with each, as a larger group, other one last time.

Instructional Goals

- Students will be able to explain their work in a presentation.

- Students will be able to state the benefits of working with people of diverse opinions.

- Students will be able to listen carefully to other, different opinions.

- Students will participate in collective reflection.

- Each student will be able to write an essay, demonstrating the new skills learned throughout this series of lessons.

Understanding Goals

- Students will solidify the understandings (on teamwork and fact-checking) gained in the previous lessons.

Essential Questions

- What possibilities can come out of having a calm and productive discussion with someone who disagrees with me?

- Why is checking facts and resources so important?

- How are we able to compromise with others?

Student Learning Objectives

Review of skills learned in previous lessons: fact-checking, listening, teamwork, engagement in productive dialogue, compromise and putting together coherent and reflective explanations.

Assessment

Participation in group discussion; Final individual essays

Sequence of Activities

Step 1: (30 minutes) Group Presentations

Each joint group gives their presentation (10 minutes each)

Step 2: (25 minutes) Whole-Class Discussion

The teacher facilitates a whole-class discussion, eliciting a summary from the students of the three joint-group solutions presented. The students and teacher, together, have one final discussion about the legitimacy of the evidence presented by each group and then decide which of the three solutions is best. If there is not exact agreement, they can do a vote (majority rules) and the teacher can discuss compromise and agreeing to disagree with students.

Step 3: (5 minutes) Assigning of Project Capstone: Reflective Essay

The teacher explains that each student will be responsible for writing an individual essay answering the following questions:

- What are some possible benefits of people having different opinions on the same topic?

- Why is it so important to check facts and the legitimacy of our sources of information?

- How were you able to compromise with people who had different opinions than you?

- How can you tell if something is a fact or an opinion?

Appendix A: Objectives for different grade levels

Students will need to exemplify each of the competencies from one level before they move on to the next. The grade levels below are a rough idea but this will vary greatly, depending on students' contexts. Teacher discretion will be necessary in deciding which level of the lesson to implement.

Rough outline of objectives for each grade:

- Elementary grades 1-3

    o Creative problem solving

    o Teamwork

    o Listen dispassionately to others

    o Small presentation to explain to the class what they've decided

- Elementary grades 4-6

    o Creative problem solving

    o Teamwork

    o Listen dispassionately to others

    o Reflective paragraph and presentation

- Middle School

    o Creative problem solving

    o Teamwork

    o Listen dispassionately to others

    o Distinguish between fact and bias/opinion

    o Reflective essay and presentation

- High school
  - Creative problem solving
  - Teamwork
  - Listen dispassionately to others
  - Weed out erroneous sources of information
  - Distinguish between fact and bias/opinion
  - Reflective essay and presentation

Appendix B: Topic Ideas

Lower grades:

1. Which person should be chosen for [the job]? (Perhaps they have to choose who they think would make a better teacher or choose a coach for a sports team.)

2. School lunches (This, and other ideas, would be even better if they had real-life application.)

3. Zoos (Are they okay or not okay? - Some argue that they are good for families, schools and children to learn about animals; They take care of the animals, etc. - Others argue that the animals are depressed, they've been taken from their homes, they don't have enough space, etc.

4. Something about sports or games

5. Recess time (Teachers don't have time to teach everything they need to and their job is on the line vs. Research backing importance of recess for learning) — This could be for older grades, too.

Older grades:

1. Political problems (for example: bills that are currently under consideration or which candidate should be chosen in an election)

2. Current topics in the news (what do they think should be done about a given problem? Etc.) (What should be done about police brutality? How much control should the government have over news organizations? Should the current tax reform proposed be passed? Should neo-Nazis be allowed to speak on public campuses? Etc.)

Appendix C: Pilot Results

Rúbia Marzochi, a Portuguese teacher for foreigners in Rio de Janeiro, Brazil, implemented a trial run of this lesson in a class of five adult students. They used a topic that is currently controversial in Brazil: agro-business. The students found the topic interesting and some already had very informed opinions before the discussion began. One, in fact, had been working in the industry for years and was, therefore, fully in-favor, while two of them were very against Agro-business.

The class was implemented over a two-day period (an hour and a half in each of the classes, plus related homework between the two days). On the first day, Rúbia divided the students into two groups (those who were already in-favor of and those who were already against, based on their existing opinions. They discussed the topic as a class and Rubia provided them with additional information (videos and articles). She then gave them the homework of looking up additional information and preparing arguments for their positions for class the next day.

On the second day, the students presented their findings to their counterpart teams and Rubia then announced that they needed to all work together in order to come up with a solution. The students used the majority of the class to listen to one and another, find similarities and come up with a solution. In the end, they decided that Agro-business was necessary in order to sustain everyone, but that it needed to be implemented more responsibly and they came up with rules that would allow this.

The results were that the students deepened their knowledge on an important, current and polemic topic in Brazil, improved their Portuguese and successfully came to an agreement, even though they'd had very different opinions at the beginning. One student still didn't fully agree that Agro-business was necessary, but he was able to agree to disagree and also thought that implementing the new rules they'd come up with would be better than the current Agro-business situation in Brazil. Rubia evaluated the students, both in their Portuguese and in their productive and peaceful participation in the collaboration process. She also jumped in to guide the conversation a bit, at times, to make sure that all students were able to speak for an equal amount of time.

This trial was done with a group of adults from different countries and backgrounds, who already have formed many important academic capacities. This is obviously a different situation than implementing the lesson in public elementary, middle and high schools around the world. Less guidance and information were necessary from the teacher and many of the students were already quite informed. Not all were, however, and this mix is a good reflection of what the situation in classrooms will likely be; since teachers will be choosing relevant topics to their students, many of them will already have opinions and some will be more informed than others. The successful results of the implementation demonstrated the importance of the activity. Adults with partially-formed opinions looked to further-inform themselves, came up with solutions as a group, listened to another group's different opinions and reasoning, then worked together to combine their ideas and come up with a newer and more productive solution that included everyone's ideas. The implementation was more less guided than public school classroom implementations will be but, step by step, the hope is that all students will gain and utilize such peacefully collaborative strategies.

A Journey of Empathy

A curriculum to encourage individuals to develop empathy, whilst gaining 21st century skills required for global citizenship.

Aarushi Singhania, Dahlia Maarouf, Hui Helen Liu

Introduction

We live in an ever-changing globalised world, that brings with it an increase in technological innovation, development and economic growth. However, at the same time there have been emerging challenges and obstacles, as seen in recent years by the increase in wars, conflicts and extreme ideologies across the globe (Delors, 1996). It is becoming ever more critical to equip our children and youth with the skills, knowledge and experiences needed to become positive and effective global citizens in the 21st century. Further, it is crucial to provide them with the ability to effectively deal with arising new challenges and obstacles that we face as a global population. As Professor Reimers clearly states; "Global citizenship education is essential for creating a world with sustainable peace." (Reimers, 2016: xix). Moreover, global citizenship is essential to working towards achieving the Sustainable Development Goals presented by the United Nations.

In the curriculum presented in this chapter, we will target Sustainable Development Goal 4, 'Quality Education', specifically focusing on target 7, which blueprints that "By 2030, ensure that all learners acquire the knowledge and skills needed to promote sustainable development, including, among others, through education for sustainable development and sustainable lifestyles, human rights, gender equality, promotion of a culture of peace and non-violence, global citizenship and appreciation of cultural diversity and of culture's contribution to sustainable development" (United Nations, SDG). Our emphasis is particularly on global citizenship for all

319

learners. To that end, we present a curriculum of empathy that not only provides students with an ability to develop their empathetic skills but is also coupled with life skills needed to become effective global citizens. These skills are essentially transferable, and can be used for the betterment of themselves, their families and communities. The skills students will develop are the seven survival skills, proposed by Dr Tony Wagner (2014) in order to bridge the Global Achievement Gap.

The Global Achievement Gap is the "gap between what even the best schools and universities are teaching and testing versus the skills that *all* students will need for careers, college and citizenship in the 21st century" (Wagner, 2014). The seven skills required are; critical thinking and problem solving, collaboration across networks and leading by influence, agility and adaptability, initiative and entrepreneurship, effective oral and written communication; accessing and analysing information, and curiosity and imagination (Wagner, 2014).

Why a Journey of Empathy?

Empathy is the "ability to step into the shoes of another person, aiming to understand their feelings and perspectives, and to use that understanding to guide our actions" (Krznaric, 2012). Often empathy can be confused with sympathy. However, students must not only develop the ability to empathise with those less fortunate than themselves but also those more fortunate. Empathy is not necessarily something that can be explicitly taught but rather something that can be experienced at a personal level, moreover it can be solicited and encouraged to be continuously developed at all stages in life. How then can we teach empathy? The idea behind this curriculum is to allow students to experience different scenarios of how other individuals may live their lives, the obstacles and struggles they face as well as their opportunities. Through various interactive activities such as simulation, role play, and reflective exercises, students are taken on a journey of empathy. If we allow students to observe and listen to others, take on their perspectives in a non-judgmental manner, and recognize their emotions we can encourage them to continuously think of the scenario 'What if that was me? How would I feel and act? What opinions or perspectives would I have?' Empathy is the foundation needed to effectively build the skills required to become dynamic global citizens. By teaching students the skills through both theory and experiential learning and guiding them through a journey of empathy, we can provide them with an opportunity to learn to develop these skills at a deeper and more sincere level. For example, if they begin to practice empathy they can then communicate with others more effectively or work in teams in a more collaborative manner. The essence is having the ability to always try to put themselves in the shoes of others. To be able to understand others' perspectives and where they are coming from, even if they don't agree or hold the same opinions and views, it will help them to develop their critical thinking and essentially become more effective communicators and collaborators. All these skills are needed to become effective global citizens and work towards common goals for their betterment of not just themselves but their communities.

A Breakdown of Empathy

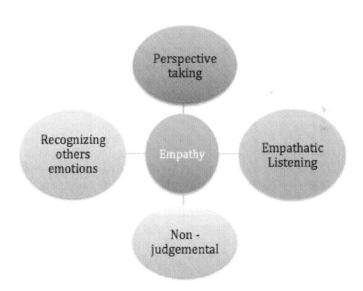

By breaking down the meaning of empathy into four subgroups, as presented in the diagram above, we can ensure that lessons are designed to incorporate activities that elicit students' feelings, thoughts and opinions. Students will take part in activities that allow them to actively listen in a non-judgmental manner, take on the perspectives of others and recognize others' emotions while reflecting on their own journey and process of development.

Vision of the curriculum

To develop students' empathy skills in order for them to become productive and inspirational global citizens in the 21st century.

Description of the curriculum

The scope and purpose of the curriculum is to ensure that students begin to empathise at a deeper and more sincere level. As well as encourage students to continuously empathise with others around them, despite their differences. To learn to use the empathy they have gained, to guide their actions for the improvement not only of their individual situations but for others around them. In end, encouraging them to become more productive members in their local communities and as a result becoming more positive global citizens.

Audience

The curriculum is initially designed for students in public schools in London, the UK, for 9-11-year-olds, in grades 3-5. The curriculum will be made up of individual one-hour sessions, totaling 21 hours to be delivered over 21 days. It will be built into the UK's current citizenship curriculum. The 21 lessons will be spread out over five weeks. Students will be guided through different activities and themes, designed around a 'journey of empathy', where they will have an opportunity to develop the seven survival skills, through bloom's taxonomy. The curriculum can also be adapted to students below 3rd and above 5th grades as well, even adults. For the lower graders, one-hour daily session can be shortened to 40 minutes from Monday to Thursday given younger pupils' attention span and a review session added on Friday to reinforce the module lesson. For older students above 5th to 12th grade, the activities can be more sophisticated to intertwine multiple survival skills. For adults, especially in a corporate setting, the theme could be modified to reflect the real needs of the target audience. For example, to replace "What if I was a billionaire" with "What if I was the CEO" to walk employees through a journey of empathy during professional development and training seminars.

Pedagogy

To ensure that lessons are designed to incorporate various methods of teaching such as role play, simulation, visuals, aesthetics, field trips, socratic method of dialogue and presentations mapped to bloom's taxonomy.

Overview of units

The themes were specifically chosen to try and ensure that students will have an opportunity to put themselves in the shoes of others, especially those from different socioeconomic backgrounds, age groups and of different abilities. Hence, allowing students to think and reflect on opportunities, challenges, daily lives, opinions and thoughts about those that they may not have previously interacted with.

Bloom's taxonomy will be incorporated throughout the individual lessons at various stages. For example, in any give lesson students could be analysing, evaluating and creating. To further ensure a systematic approach of teaching and to maximise the potential of developing empathy and building their skills to a more rigorous level, we have aligned the overview of the curriculum with the six stages of Bloom's taxonomy. Below is a summary of the five lessons, the first lesson plan is provided in more detail as an example template with a brief description of the rest four units presented for reference.

Title/Theme	Hours/ Week	Description	Survival skill (Taught through activities of the lessons)	Bloom's Taxonomy
What if I had nothing?	4 hours (Week 1, Monday to Thursday)	The lesson is designed on reflecting the daily lives of street children	• Effective oral and written communica tion • Accessing and analysing information	Remember Understand
What if I couldn't see/hear?	4 hours (Week 2, Monday to Thursday)	The lesson is designed on reflecting the daily lives of the blind or deaf	• Collaborati on across networks and leading by influence	Apply
What if I was different age?	4 hours (Week 3, Monday to Thursday)	What if I was much older or younger- lesson is designed	• Curiosity and imagination	Analyze

		on reflecting the daily lives of the elderly or baby		
What if I was a billionaire?	4 hours (Week 4, Monday to Thursday)	Lesson is designed on what if I got a billion dollar	• Agility and adaptability	Evaluate
Community initiative (A walk in my shoes)	5 hours (Week 5, Monday to Friday)	Students will identify a problem in their local community and design a solution or contribution to help ease the problem	• Critical thinking and problem solving • Initiative and entrepreneurship	Remember Understand Apply Analyze Evaluate Create

Unit 1 Detailed Lesson Plan Example: 'What if I had nothing?'[1]

Summary and Rationale:

Below is an example of one lesson from the curriculum, which is the first lesson of the first module 'What if I had nothing?'

1. Dream Exercise (15 mins) - In teams, pupils will be asked to create a piece of work among themselves to depict their future dreams.

Students will be divided into teams of five and provided with one flip chart, crayons and colouring pens. They will be asked to draw their dreams on one sheet. The idea is that all members of the team contribute to one joint drawing or collage, in any way they choose. For example, if students in one group dreamt of being a footballer, or ballerina or astronaut, there could be a large drawing of a young man or lady, wearing a football boot on one leg, ballerina shoe on the other and an astronauts helmet. Children will have an opportunity to develop their team building skills and creativity. They will be asked to choose one person to stand up and present all their dreams to the rest of the group. They will need to think of ways to choose the person presenting, e.g. by voting, picking out of a hat, tossing a coin etc.

2. Survival exercise (20 mins) - The pupils will be given challenges to demonstrate the daily struggles that street children their age have to face in order to survive.

In this activity students are split into two large groups, and using a team building activity they will be competing to win the opportunity to rummage through a large bin liner of rubbish for an activity hidden in a plastic bottle. Students will volunteer to complete each activity. The activities are designed around using the children's senses. One example is they are presented with a prepared meal and asked if they are willing to taste it, students are presented with old and mouldy food on a plate and discuss if they would ever eat it? Perhaps if they were extremely hungry and hadn't eaten in a few days?

[1] This lesson plan was built on a project by Layla Shirreh for 'Walou', a British registered charity supporting street children in Morocco.

3. Hot seat exercise (15 mins) - Images of street children in difficult circumstances will be shown to pupils. Pupils will then be asked to internalise the thoughts and emotions, and experience life in the shoes of a street child.

Students are split into smaller groups of five and asked to sit in a circle. One person is chosen from each group and provided with a photograph of a child covering his/her face with their hands. That person is in the 'hot seat' and has to imagine being that child. Numerous images of street children, sleeping on the streets, rummaging through rubbish, walking alone in alleyways are placed on the floor in front of the other students. Students are requested to ask any questions they want to the pupil in the 'hot seat' who answers as if he or she were that child. This activity allows for students to develop their imagination and critical thinking skills. (Walou, 2010)

Subjects: Citizenship

Instructional Goal: Students will learn to develop two main skills from the seven survival skills, through the activities designed for the lesson;

1. Effective oral and written communication

2. Accessing and analysing information

They will also develop team working skills.

Standards: SDG 4 (Quality Education), target 7 (Global citizenship)

Target seven specifies that all learners will acquire knowledge and skills to promote sustainable development, including global citizenship.

Essential questions: What if you were in his/her shoes? What would be the most valuable thing to you? What do you think would be some of your daily challenges? How would you feel? What would your dreams be?

Student Learning Objectives:

1. To raises awareness about children less fortunate than themselves, living in different countries.

2. Encourage pupils to question their own perceptions of the challenges faced by children in developing countries.

3. To encourage students to recognize and appreciate the opportunities they have and face new challenges positively.

4. For students to identify their future goals and aspirations.

Resources for students: List print or online resources that can support students in carrying out the activities.

Resources for teachers: flip charts; mark pens; video clip on street children; sticky notes

Unit 2 Detailed Lesson Plan Example: 'What if I was couldn't see or hear?'

Summary and Rationale:

Students will be asked to think about three things they value most in their lives and to write them down on a piece of paper. They will then be split into pairs, one and two. Group one will be asked to speak to their partner about 'what they value and why?'. Group two will be taken outside and told to act as if they cannot hear anything their partner is saying, for example, look away with a bored or confused face. Group one will then be asked how they felt, if they felt their partner was paying attention or what they think was happening.

Another activity is the blind simulation over lunch. Students will be provided with lunch but will have to eat their lunch with blindfolds on. They will then be brought back to discuss what they felt. The purpose of the activity was to ponder on the questions below:
- How did students use their other senses during the exercise?

- Could they imagine walking to school with a blindfold on?
- What daily obstacles would they face if they were asked to wear a blindfold for a day?

They would go back to reflect on the first activity where they may have felt their partner was not listening or paying attention and asked to think about how they could try to communicate with someone who had lack of hearing? In smaller groups they would discuss both the advantages and disadvantages of individuals who are either visually impaired or have lack of hearing, including the daily obstacles and challenges they may face and how they may overcome them.

Unit 3 Detailed Lesson Plan Example: 'What if I was different age?'

Summary & Rationale:

Students will be given the opportunity to live the daily lives of people above 60 years old who have Parkinson's disease. By imagining the moveabouts and emotions of such elders, pupils are encouraged to analyze and eventually empathize with the different and difficult lives of people ~50 years older than themselves.

Sample scenarios:

- If you couldn't hold a glass of water due to uncontrollable shaky hands, what would you do and how would you feel?
- If you couldn't sleep well constantly and act out dreams injuring your bed partner, what would you do and how would you feel?
- If you lost your way home on a busy street and just couldn't remember your address and the phone number of your family members, what would you do and how would you feel?

Parkinson's disease affects millions of people over 60 years old globally. The above-mentioned scenarios reflect some common symptoms of the disease in elderly people: shaking, memory dysfunctioning and sleep disorder. For pupils 9-11 of age, who are at one of the prime time of their physical life, such symptoms may be hard to empathize unless they proactively think about it. The design of this unit offers a unique opportunity to feel for themselves the difficult lives of people ~50 years older than themselves, so that eventually they would be able to empathize rather than tease those elders who are affected by Parkinson's disease and co-live a harmonious life together for the sustainable development of society.

Unit 4 Detailed Lesson Plan Example: 'What if I was a billionaire?'

Summary & Rationale:

Students will be made to go through situation analysis and write their opinion piece. Two situations would be given at the same time to spark a child's empathy IQ.

For example:
- If you get ticket to world tour or an opportunity to win 100 kgs of gold, what would you choose and why?
- Now if you chose world tour and later you realized that one of your closest family member is in hospital living his last breath, what would you choose and why ?
- If you chose a bag full of gold to buy all the luxurious items and later realized you need this gold to give away debts that your parents owned, otherwise they would be sued. What would you choose and why?

Giving such contrasting situations to a child will trigger an element of empathy unconsciously and getting children to debate and discuss their reasons after such an exercise will enable them to see the same situation from their friends' perspective. These situations can be changed as per the rigor of the classroom and the need of different children.

Unit 5 Detailed Lesson Plan Example: 'A Walk in my shoes?'

Summary & Rationale:

Students will be asked to walk in their communities/ localities and do a need finding study of a problem that needs to be resolved.

This will be the final capstone project, where groups will be allocated and there would not be a lot of structure, just that students will have to conduct a research on what is one problem that their respective community faces. Students will go through technical and design thinking lessons in school to design a solution for a community problem.

This unit will push children beyond their initial awareness of the problem. The problem-solving attitude will encourage children in groups of 4-5 members to actually solve a problem and test solution in their communities and beyond.

In this exercise, children will receive technical support and guidance from teachers but not direct answers to the problem. The idea is for children to actually walk in to other people's problem and do something about it rather than just discussing it with friends and teachers. It is a way to actually contribute to society as 21st century students.

Teachers can assess this in multiple ways, depending on what are other elements along with Empathy that teachers want to measure. In terms of soft skills, teachers can measure the following:

Criteria	Member A	B	C	D
Did all members have equal voice in the group?				
Did all members collaborate at all points?				
Did all members follow the team rules?				
Was the work equally divided among the members?				

With regards to academics, teachers can measure what evidence have children collected to say, that this problem needs to be solved? what statistic measures did children use to come to the conclusion of which problem needs the most attention? And so on...

Assessment:

The assessment for 'A Journey of Empathy' would be in the form of Capstone project. In this project, students will be asked to identify a problem in the community and design a solution to the problem. In developing and presenting the capstone problem, students will be assessed on the seven survival skills and also level of empathy they have used in tinkering with problem and solution. It is somewhat difficult to measure such skills, and even more so level of empathy, as it is largely abstract and based on one's individual interpretation. Evaluators will be trained on the measurement tool and how to remain as objective as possible, by giving clear examples of when they have seen students demonstrate a skill or level of empathy during the exercise. Note empathy will also be measured in terms of their behaviour to others in their group. We will use the Likert scale (the most commonly used rating scale regarding attitude), which is used to allow evaluators to assess how much they agree or disagree with a particular statement, defining a student's potential to showcase their ability of a skill or level of empathy (McLeod, 2008)

Feedback from Government Schools

We tested the first unit in two government school classrooms in Bangalore, India. The context of the classroom included 70% students from Muslim communities and 30% from Hindu Communities. The community had numerous incidents of noticeable religious conflicts every now and then, which affected student mindset towards other fellow students.

The average income of parents in communities where these schools were located was INR 7000, approx. $100 to support family of five members. We felt that teaching empathy to these students, who were surrounded by constant violence and conflict, was the right thing to do and we chose these sites to examine how would this curriculum perform if taught to the group that needed it the most but was subject to uncertain reaction from children.

It turned out that, students in the class showed phenomenal improvement with just 1 exercise. Sagar, a Teach for India fellow from Bangalore, India mentioned that throughout his first year of the fellowship he struggled with kids raising hands to ask questions but in second year he saw challenges of overconfidence and he felt that "Journey to Empathy" curriculum was exactly what his class and context needed the most. He also said in order to see sustainable change in student behavior, he needs his student to go through all the module of empathy curriculum.

Conclusion

In order for students to have the opportunity to become positive and inspirational global citizens, students need to be provided with a strong global citizenship curriculum that works towards achieving the Sustainable Development Goals. If we can provide students with specific skills, such as the 7 survival skills, these skills can be transferred to all aspects of their lives, from personal, to their future careers, to their families and communities. Further by providing them a chance to interact with a curriculum like 'Journey of Empathy' we can help students not only develop empathy skills, but further allow students to maximise the potential that these transferable skills have to offer and essentially achieve a higher level of self-actualization.

However, the most difficult aspect to designing and delivering a curriculum founded on empathy is 'assessment'. As mentioned above how individuals display empathy is largely subjective and down to individual interpretation. Although we have suggested an assessment based on evaluators observing students during the capstone project, it needs a rigorous training programme to try and ensure that all evaluators are remaining as objective as possible. More research needs to prove effective ways of measuring empathy.

Despite the limitations, if successful the 'Journey of Empathy' has the possibility of mitigating the risks of children and young adults from potentially developing individualistic behaviour and/or extreme views and ideologies, against others, that could lead to oppression within their communities as well as at the global level. Through this curriculum, we hope to encourage students to leverage the survival skills they have gained and to guide their behaviours and actions for the benefit of their communities and beyond.

References

Delors, J., & UNESCO. (1996). *Learning, the treasure within: Report to UNESCO of the International Commission on Education for the Twenty-first Century.* Paris: Unesco Pub.

Krznaric, R. (2012, November 27). Six habits of highly empathic people. *Greater Good Magazine.* Retrieved from https://greatergood.berkeley.edu/article/item/six_habits_of_highly_empathic_people1

McLeod, S. A. (2008). Likert Scale. Retrieved from www.simplypsychology.org/likert-scale.html

Reimers, F., Chopra, V., Chung, C., Higdon, J & O'Donnell, E. B. (2016). Empowering global citizens: a world course. North Carleston, South Carolina: Create Space.

United Nations Sustainable Development Goals. Retrieved from http://www.un.org/sustainabledevelopment/education/

Wagner. T. (2014). Seven survival skills. Retrieved from http://www.tonywagner.com/7-survival-skills/

Walou. (2010). 'Streetz' workshop delivered by Walou

Empowering Student Leadership for Change: Using Design Thinking Tools

Ameya Kamath & Sharon Zacharia

Overview

The overall objective of this curriculum is to enable students of Grades 5-8, to contribute to the attainment of the Sustainable Development Goals at a community level and to develop global citizenship skills in the process. By working on projects that address the SDGs, they will i) learn about the SDGs, ii) develop competencies necessary to achieving the SDGs and iii) directly contribute to the attainment of the SDGs. The idea is to make students passionate about addressing these global challenges, create a ripple effect and spark a grassroots movement in local communities, empowering them in the process.

The proposed curriculum is hence designed in a manner that is highly modular and easily adaptable to different levels of resources and settings. In addition, few curricula manage to use one structure of lessons to address all SDGs; only the first lesson changes, since each topic needs a slightly different introduction. Furthermore, we incentivise school leaders to add this curriculum to their school program via a global competition and grant system in partnership with UNDP (see below). We believe this gives schools and communities a platform to display and share their efforts on a global level. Lastly, school leaders are able to select the SDGs most relevant to their school's context, rather than being limited to a curriculum that is limited to a narrow range of SDGs. The key criterion is for this curriculum to be customisable; ie. it should be easy to integrate in resource-constrained, low-income settings, yet equally relevant to use for high-income schools; not country-specific or location-specific. Learning will occur through student centered techniques such as design thinking and project-based learning.

Overview

One SDG is addressed through a sequence of 5 lessons:

Lesson 1 is SDG specific whereas Lessons 2 - 5 are the same for all SDGs. In our curriculum, we have presented sample lesson 1 for SDG 4 and 11. A similar structure can be followed for an SDG of your choice.

Schools, through school leaders and teachers, can pick and choose the SDGs that are most relevant to their school environment and community. To incentivise schools to participate and to implement the curriculum well, schools enter a competition and a ranking system when they sign up. To be eligible to participate in the competition, schools have to go through all five lessons for at least one SDG within one school year and document their progress. The evidence is to be sent to an evaluation committee.

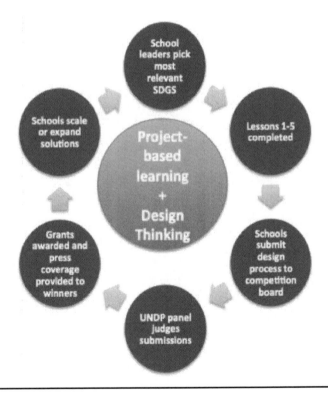

Learning Goal
This unit of 5 lessons helps students build awareness, understand and empathise with a specific and relevant Sustainable Development Goal. It then builds in the students the tools of root cause analysis in order to deeply understand where this social issue is stemming from. It then builds the skill of designing ways forward to work through the problem innovatively, resourcefully yet mindfully. Students prototype their ideas for change, learn to love to fail, engage with stakeholders, receive feedback. They use this to redesign their ideas and redevelop it. They finally test their improved ideas for change but learn that this is an iterative process. This is done through 5 consecutive lessons using the tools of Design Thinking and Project Based Learning.
Lesson Scaffold
Lesson 1: LOOK, LISTEN, LEARN - Building Awareness & Empathy
Lesson 2: QUESTION - Identify the Causes & Understand the Problem
Lesson 3: IDEATE - Understand own Agency & Brainstorm Solutions
Lesson: PROTOTYPE - Prototype, Redesign, Reiterate, Redo
Lesson 5: TEST - Test, Reflect, Redesign
Learning Objectives
• Lesson 1 - Students will build awareness and empathise with a specific relevant social issue on which an SDG is based.   • Lesson 2 - Students will identify the underlying root causes of the specific SDG in order to deeply understand the problem that is leading to the

social issue

- Lesson 3 - Students will understand the power of their own agency and use it to brainstorm ideas that in order to begin to create change towards achievement of the specific SDG

- Lesson 4 - Students will prototype their ideas with stakeholders in order to receive feedback in order to redesign their ideas

- Lesson 5 - Students will test their improved ideas and continue the process of reflection and reiteration of the solution

LESSON PLAN #1: LOOK, LISTEN, LEARN (Build Awareness & Empathy)

Time Frame: 90 minutes | **Standard:** SDG 5 - Gender Equality |
Subjects: Social Science

Summary and Rationale: This is the first lesson plan in the set of five lessons. In this lesson, students dip their toes into understanding the SDG 5: Gender Equality. Students learn to empathize with the problem by analyzing their own community. They draw connections between the problem at their local level and the larger global goal. They question the goal and understand its specific targets and the relevance of the goal to their community.

Instructional Goal: Empathy skills, analysis skills, ethical orientation, intercultural competency, work and mind habits, understanding of the concept behind the SDG (gender inequality)

Understanding: Students understand that their community is failing to achieve this SDG and that it is important that they achieve the SDG at a local level.

Essential questions:

- What does gender equality mean?
- Do we have gender equality in our community? If not, how are boys and girls treated differently?
- How will our community - your family, your friends, all of us - benefit from achieving this goal?

Student Learning Objective: Students will prototype their ideas with stakeholders in order to receive feedback in order to redesign their ideas.

Sequence of Activities

From Where I Stand? *[Pre-work]*
- Students conduct a survey of their vicinity and report it using the table in *Appendix A1.*

(http://cdn.worldslargestlesson.globalgoals.org/2016/07/Project-Pack-11.pdf)
• Additional task: Students can create multiple tables, each looking at numbers of males and females in their local leadership over different time periods. For example, they can create one table for my generation, one for parents' generation and one for grandparents' generation, and compare them. They can use the internet/ ask their parents or other seniors to help tabulate this.

Debrief / Reflection: *[20 minutes]*
o Teachers can also use techniques of visible thinking to help students reflect on their observations:
■ What do you see? *I see...*
■ What do you think about that? *I think...*
■ What does it make you wonder? *I wonder...*
o Sample response: *I see that some professions are dominated by males, especially in the past. I think why is it so? I wonder how we might change this.*
o Introduce the phrase "gender equality".
■ Ask students to outline their understanding about this.
• Sample Response: Students come up with their own definition for gender equality
■ UN's definition is as follows:
http://www.un.org/sustainabledevelopment/gender-equality/
■ Do you agree with this definition?
■ What would you add to this? Why?
• Sample Response: Definition doesn't involve roles of men. Teacher can point at the big questions that students can draw from this.

Understanding and Empathising with Gender Equality in their community: *[20 minutes]*
• Split students up into groups to discuss the following questions. Ask groups to share their ideas out loud with the rest of the class once they have discussed their ideas.
o How do you see / experience Gender Inequality in your community? Share personal experiences.
o What advantages and disadvantages do boys and girls have in your community?

o   Is this fair?

o   How does it impact you / people in your community?

o   If gender roles became more equal, what would be better in your community? What could be worse? Who may benefit? Who may lose?

Questions beyond the UN's goal. *[15 minutes]*
- Split students up into groups to discuss the following questions. Make them think out loud and share within their groups. Ask groups to share their ideas out loud with the rest of the class once they have discussed their ideas.

o   Are boys allowed to cry? Are men?

o   Why is the chef industry dominated by men, whereas in households across the world, women are the main providers of food?

■   Sample response: *People might think it is a woman's duty to provide food, whereas when men cook, it might be considered a profession. This ideology has loopholes.*

Summarize: *[15 minutes]*
- with video on Gender Equality: https://vimeo.com/174213067
- https://www.youtube.com/watch?v=J5ic-oOE4fw

Closing: *[10 minutes]*
- Students independently fill out their End of Activity Reflection sheet (*Appendix A2*).
- Students pair up (with someone different they haven't interacted with yet) and share. Ask students to share out loud to the whole class.

Assessment / Homework: *[Out of class]*

- Rewrite an existing short story using any format (story / comic strip / video / script for a play / song / spoken word poetry / etc). Switch gender roles played by different actors.
- Write a short essay on your reflections from the experience. OR Discuss your experience with your classmates in the next class.

Resources:

-      Pre-study materials for teachers:
  - http://www.un.org/sustainabledevelopment/gender-equality
  - http://www.globalgoals.org/global-goals/gender-equality/
  - http://worldslargestlesson.globalgoals.org/global-goals/gender-equality/
-      Appendix A1 and A2
-      Device for video playback

LESSON PLAN #2: QUESTION

(Identify the Causes, Understand the problem)

Time Frame: 90 minutes | **Standard:** Any SDG | **Subjects:** Social Sciences

Summary and Rationale: This is the second lesson plan in a cycle of five plans. It builds student skills to analyse the root cause of a problem, in this case the reasons why their community is still behind in attaining the SDG. They reflect on why it is important to identify the correct root cause in designing solutions to problems. They use the '5 Why' model towards root cause analysis.

Instructional Goal: analysis, critical thinking, ethical orientation, work and mind habits

Understanding: There are clear, identifiable causes that create the current situation and these causes can be manipulated to improve the situation.

Essential questions:

-      What are the causes of this blockage to attaining the SDG?

-      Which do you think is the most important cause?

Student Learning Objectives: Students will be able to carry out a thorough self-directed root-cause analysis

Sequence of Events	

Titanic: *[30 minutes]*
- You are the designer of Titanic 2.0. You must look at the pros & cons of Titanic and redesign the Titanic 2.0. What is the first thing you want to do? Maybe think about why the titanic sank and ensure that that is taken care of in Titanic 2.0. Ok, so let's think. Why did the Titanic sink? What is the first thing that comes to mind?
- Ok, now let's do an investigation. Teachers use the graphic organizer *[Appendix C]* to guide the investigation. Teachers help students realize that there were more nuanced reasons that contributed to the disaster.
  - https://www.thinkreliability.com/case_studies/the-sinking-of-the-titanic-cause-map/

- Debrief:
  - What was different from the first response that came to mind and the graphic organiser we used to discuss the causes to why the titanic sank? With this activity, let's go through the See-Think-Wonder routine.
    - What do you see? *I see...*
    - What do you think about that? *I think...*
    - What does it make you wonder? *I wonder...*
- Sample Response: *Iceberg wasn't the root cause of why the Titanic sank. We need to ask ourselves why several times to get to the real reason or the root cause of why a problem is occuring. It is important to understand the exact problem.*

Wait, but why?! *[20 minutes]*
- Students use a graphic organiser *[Appendix B.2]* to break down the specific SDG to understand the root cause of where this problem stems from in their community. Teacher uses the graphic organiser to model by making their thinking visible.
  - Sample Response: *Gender Inequality. Why? Lower pay for women. Why? Women may be considered less productive. Why? Traditional mindsets and so on..*

Root Cause Tree: *[20 minutes]*
- Small Group Activity: Students use the graphic organiser *[Appendix D]* in teams to break down their problem into roots and its causes. Teacher uses the

graphic organiser to model by making her / his thinking visible.
o   Sample Response: *See Appendix D*

Strength Test: *[5 minutes]*
● Students pair up with one group and present their root cause analysis and their rationale. The other groups must ask questions to push the groups to think. Teacher models this process.

Closing: *[15 minutes]*
● Students independently fill out their End of Activity Reflection sheet *[Appendix A2]*
● Students pair up (with someone different they haven't interacted with yet) and share. Ask students to share out loud to the whole class.

LESSON PLAN #3: IDEATE

(Understand own Agency & Brainstorm Solutions)

Time Frame: 150 minutes | **Standard:** Any SDG | **Subjects:** Writing

Summary & Rationale: Students begin to understand the power of their own agency. They use this to frame their root cause analysis into a question statement. This will allow them to ideate specific ideas as solutions to answer their problem statement question. By ideating without any restraints allows them to truly think creatively which allows for innovative solutions. They then add restraints to check the strength and feasibility of their solutions. On narrowing in on a specific idea, they present this in order to elicit feedback and improve their idea.

Instructional Goal: Students will understand the power of their own agency. They will use this to ideate solutions to the root problem they identified. They will check how feasible and strong their proposed solutions are in achieving the SDG they are working towards.

Understanding: Agency is not limited by age. Agency is a function of determination and the willingness and drive to create change. As students, we have great agency and are important change makers. We can harness this super power into coming up with innovative and creative solutions to social issues. We must translate our root cause analysis into a problem statement question. This will help us identify specific ideas.

Essential Questions:

- Do we as students have agency? Can we truly have an impact in society?
- What is our 'How Might We' question that we need to address in order to brainstorm ideas?
- Can we ideate creative and innovative ideas without any restrictions limiting our idea flow?
- How strong are our ideas in creating the change we intend to have?

Student Learning Objectives: Students will be able to understand the power of their own agency and use it to brainstorm ideas that in order to begin to create change towards achievement of the specific SDG

Sequence of Events

Students as Change Makers: *[15 minutes]*

○ Choose one of the stories (or show video) about students who used their own agency to create change: *(See Appendix E)*

■ Muzoon Almellehan, Syria

■ Malala Yousefzai, Pakistan

○ **Debrief the activity:** Pair up student who read a different story. Discuss: Is age important for having agency and creating change? If not, what are the key factors to create change? What does this mean for us? (Get the students excited about their own agency and being change makers.)

■ *Sample Response: These girls were able to create change at a really young age and hence age is not a key factor. Key Factors could be different values like - Determination to want to create change, Passion to want to change things, Grit, Resilience, etc. Even if we are students, we can create change. In fact, we can create more change as students!*

School on Fire: *[30 minutes]*

o   Partner students up. Give each partner a disability. One student acts blind and the other acts mute as well as physically paralysed. Call the mute partners aside. Tell them that the school is on fire and that they need to seek support of their blind partners to help get them out of the school.

o   **Debrief the activity:** Pair up students who had success & who didn't. Discuss: Did the handicaps make it impossible to achieve the goal? If yes, why? If not, what made you successful?

■   *Sample Response: Even if some things are not perfect, we are able to find a way out. In fact, some form of lack of resources and capabilities can make us more creative and resourceful. Hence, if we think creatively, there is always a way forward!*

o   What does this reflection make you think about in regards to the Root Cause Analysis activity?

■   *Sample Response: There are lots of real problems that could hinder us from achieving our goal of gender equality (or insert name of SDG that students are working towards) in our community. However, if push ourselves to think creatively, with determination and grit, we will be able to make an impact and be successful in creating change!*

'How Might We' Question: *[20 minutes]*

o   Support students to formulate their Root Cause into a "How Might We" question .

■   *Sample Response: (See Appendix F)*

o   Get students to work in small groups. Ask them to share out loud with the class. The facilitator's role is to help fine tune the first 1 - 2 group responses by by modelling how they gave feedback. The facilitator then gradually releases responsibility to students to give each other feedback.

Idea Machine: *[20 minutes]*

o   Students are divided into equal groups of 4. They must come up with a list of 50 solutions to solve this problem. Explain to them that they can be the silliest, craziest, most impossible and unfeasible ideas - but they need to have 50 ideas! Be sure to not limit the way different students express. Allow them to list out their ideas or express them in any other form of their choosing.

o   Remind them that their ideas can be - digital work or a tangible product, a work of art or something they engineer. It might even be an action or an event or a system.

o   Ask students to share a few of their crazy ideas out loud to the everyone.

■   *Sample Responses: (See Appendix G)*

Strength Test: *[20 minutes]*

●   Students use the Strength Test graphic organiser to evaluate the strength of an idea. Keep or remove ideas to come up with 1 idea that they want to prototype. Teacher models this using the graphic organiser.

o   *Sample Responses: (See Appendix H)*

Presentation & Feedback: *[30 minutes]*

●   Groups share their ideas & their rationale with one other group. The other group poses questions in terms of feedback on how well their prototype addresses the root cause of the problem.

Closing: *[15 minutes]*

●   Students independently fill out their End of Activity reflection sheet. *(See Appendix A2)*

●   Students pair up (with someone different they haven't interacted with yet) and share. Ask students to share out loud to the whole class.

LESSON PLAN #4: PROTOTYPE

(Prototype, Redesign, Reiterate, Redo)

Time Frame: 210 minutes | **Standard:** Any SDG | **Subjects:** Writing

Summary & Rationale: This lesson is designed to support students to build a prototype of their proposed solution idea. They first start with a prototype on paper that details out their logic model for their solution. On breaking this down into a logic model, students will be able to self-identify the gaps in their idea and hence this acts as a self-improvement tool. This will also help them identify details of everything they need to build a physical prototype. On building the physical prototype of their idea, they present that to other students, soliciting feedback and using this to improve their models. The purpose of giving them limited time to prototype is to build an action bias towards solutions as a reminder that solutions to social issues are an iterative process and can only improve by testing them in different ways.

Instructional Goal: Students will detail out their prototype onto paper using a simple logic model. This will help them make clear connections between their proposed idea and how this intends to make a positive impact and advance the specific identified SDG. Once their logical flow of thoughts are strong, they build their prototype. They showcase this to elicit feedback and improve their prototype.

Understanding: It is essential to break down the process of designing a solution into mini- steps. We must start by ideating our solution on paper and breaking this down into a paper prototype and detailing out our logic model to make our thinking visible in terms of how we see this idea hope to create change towards the identified SDG. Once that is clear, we will build a prototype in a short time span and elicit feedback. We will remember that an action bias is key in developing effective solutions.

Essential Questions:

- How does your proposed idea help advance the SDG you identified?
- How strong is your prototype?
- How can your prototype be improved?

Student Learning Objectives: Students will be able to prototype their ideas with stakeholders in order to receive feedback in order to redesign their ideas.

Sequence of Events

Level 1 of Prototyping: Paper Prototype *[40 minutes]*

- **Build a Paper Prototype:** *[20 minutes]*
- o Students will design a paper prototype (logic model) for their chosen idea. Facilitator models using the simple logic model. *(See Appendix H2)*
- o Facilitator models how students must build their prototype around

these questions:
- What variables do you want to better understand?
- What questions to we have about our idea?
- How can we make our idea tangible and in a way that gives us the feedback we need?

- **Present, Feedback & Combine:** *[20 minutes]*
o   Student present a 2 minute elevator pitch of their their paper prototype to another group. The other group poses their feedback in the form of questions aligned to how well their prototype addresses the root cause of the problem. Facilitator models this process.

Level 2 of Prototyping: Physical Prototype *[60 minutes]*

- **Build a Physical Prototype:**
o   Encourage students to be resourceful with available resources to build their prototype. (It might be a digital work or a tangible product, a work of art or something they engineer. It might even be an action or an event or a system.)
o   Facilitator reminds students that their prototype must be built around these questions:
- What variables do you want to better understand?
- What questions to we have about our idea?
- How can we make our idea tangible and in a way that gives us the feedback we need?

Gallery Walk & Feedback: *[60 minutes]*
- Split the Gallery Walk into 2 sections. In each section have half the number of groups. Each group presents their prototype. The other students walk around (individually, not in groups) and experience different prototypes. Each student must provide feedback in the form of questions to each group.

Reflect: *[15 minutes]*
- Students reflect on their ideas using the "Gibbs Reflective Cycle" graphic organiser. Teacher models. *(See Appendix K)*

Redesign: *[20 minutes]*
- Groups use the feedback to improve their prototypes.

Closing: *[15 minutes]*
- Students independently fill out their End of Activity reflection sheet. *(See Appendix A2)*
- Students pair up (with someone different they haven't interacted with yet) and share. Ask students to share out loud to the whole class.

LESSON PLAN #5: TEST

(Test, Reflect, Redesign)

Time Frame: 210 minutes | **Standards**: Any SDG | **Subjects**: Writing,

Summary & Rationale: In this lesson, students begin by understanding that the best way to build a solution is by keeping the end user in mind. They thus test their improved prototypes on real stakeholders, to the extent possible. The purpose is to solicit real time feedback that helps them reflect and improve their prototypes.

Instructional Goal: Students develop an action bias in designing ideas and solutions to social problems. They understand that the best solutions are built with the end user in mind and by constantly engaging with these stakeholders. One important way to do this it to test the prototype on the end user and elicit real time feedback to improve their prototype.

Understanding: It is important to understand, involve and engage with the end user closely every step of the way in order to build a solution that will be effective and sustainable in creating change.

Essential Questions:

- How must you test the robustness of your solution?
- What are your reflections and learnings from this journey of building

this prototype towards achieving this SDG?

Student Learning Objectives: Students will be able to test their improved ideas and continue the process of reflection and reiteration of the solution

Sequence of Events

Blind Room: *[30 minutes]*

o Students must redesign the room (or whatever space is available) as blind friendly, by physically changing things around. Once they are done, get them to write down one change they would make to their model. Now, blind half the team and allow them to use the design of another group, while the other group observes their design being used. Again, ask student to write down one change they would make.

o **Debrief the activity:**

■ How useful was your first change after you watched the blind person use your room? How useful was the second change? What is your reflection from this activity about testing on your end user?

• *Sample Response: It is important to understand the end user and engage with them during designing and building a solution for it to be useful to the end user. Lots of iteration processes are good and make the solution better. A bias for action is important to test the idea and not wait for perfection. The best feedback comes from the end user.*

TEST! *[75 minutes]*

• Students go into the community and test their ideas.

• Students note down feedback using the graphic organiser provided. *(See Appendix I)*

Reflect: *[15 minutes]*

• Students reflect on their solution using the 'Gibbs Reflective Cycle' graphic organiser. Teacher models. *(See Appendix K)*

Redesign: *[30 minutes]*

• Groups use the feedback to improve their prototypes.

Showcase: *[75 minutes]*

• Each group needs to present their journey of learnings from beginning to end in any form and present the whole journey as part of the final showcase including the final redesigned prototype.

Appendices

A1 : From Where I Stand

"From Where I Stand"

A Survey of Your Local Community Influencers and Decision Makers.

Fill in your survey by putting a cross in the relevant box.

	Female	Male
POLITICAL LEADERSHIP		
Your Prime Minister / President		
The person that represents you in your national parliament		
LOCAL LEADERSHIP		
The local leader of your district or town council / tribal chief / head of county / mayor etc.		
LOCAL COMMUNITY INFLUENCERS AND DECISION MAKERS		
Your head teacher		
Your doctor		
The boss of one of your parents		
The head of your local police		
Your local bank manager		
Newsreader on the TV news channel you watch or the editor of the newspaper you read		
The lead singer of your favourite song		
The coach of your sports team (optional)		
Your religious/spiritual or pastoral leader (optional)		
TOTAL:		

Source: worldslargestlesson.org
http://cdn.worldslargestlesson.globalgoals.org/2016/07/Project-Pack-11.pdf

Appendix A2: Reflection Sheet

End of Activity Reflection Sheet	
I used to think...	
Now I think...	
Something new I learnt today was...	
Something I learnt about myself today was...	
1 question I have...	
On a scale of 1-5, today I pushed myself....	
2 things I did well today were...	
1 thing I want to work on is...	

B.1 : "5 Why" model

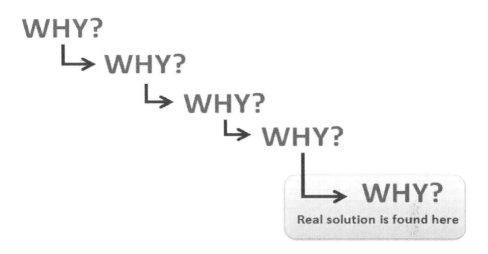

B.2: Graphic Organizer

Problem	Gender Inequality / Lack of Quality Education
Wait, but why?	
Wait, but why?	
Wait, but why?	
Wait, but why?	
Wait, but why?	

C: Titanic Infographic

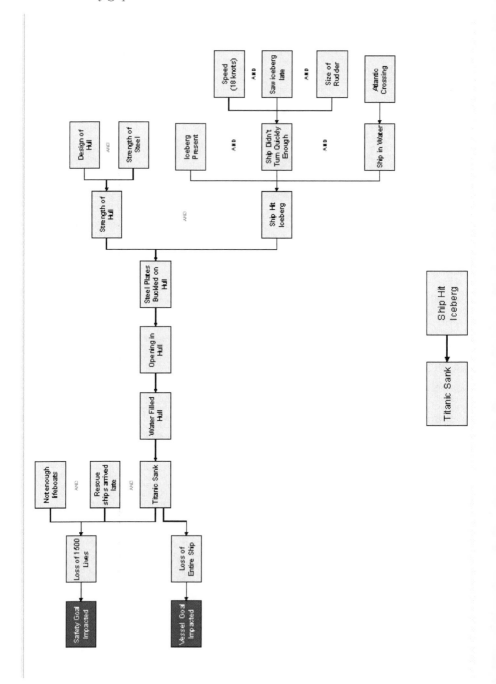

D: Root Cause Tree (Example)

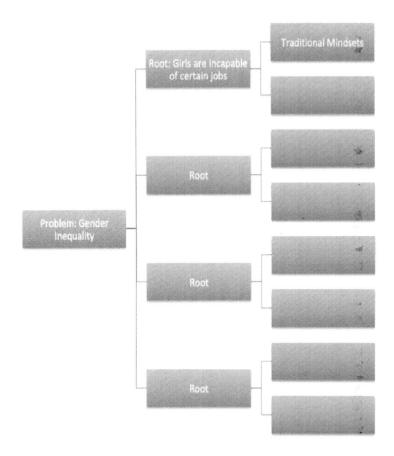

E: Story of Mala Yousefzai and Muzoon Almellehan

- Story of Malala Yousefzai, Pakistan
- Story of Muzoon Almellehan, Syria

F: "How Might We" Activity

Root Cause Problem (from Root Cause Analysis worksheet)	Sample "How Might We" Question
Community is dirty because there are not enough garbage cans.	"How might we have keep our community clean given that there are no dustbins / garbage disposal cans?"
Samples	"How might we induce use positive narration to encourage women to be given equal opportunities?" "How might we increase awareness of the problem of girls not having equal rights in our community?" "How might we make the change easy for people in our community who support equal opportunities for girls and boys?"

G: Activity: Idea Machine!

Sample Ideas:

- Start a campaign in your community to get signatories to a letter asking your local leader to mandate paternity leave.
- Start a podcast documenting positive and negative stories of change in your community
- Get the most popular radio station that the community listens to start a segment about Gender
- Get local newspapers to print stories your / your journalism team about gender equality
- Street Plays in the community

- Create posters / flyers & stick it / distribute it around the community
- Create comics & give it to students in the community, etc.

H: Activity: Strength Test

Is our idea....	
Bold in nature?	
Easily to replicate?	
Impacting maximum possible people?	
Have long lasting impact?	
Be hard to convince people to do?	
Been tried before?	
Compare to other solutions?	

H2: Paper Prototype

Resources (Who, What)	Activities	Result	Short Term Outcome	Goal

Sample filled out Paper Prototype:

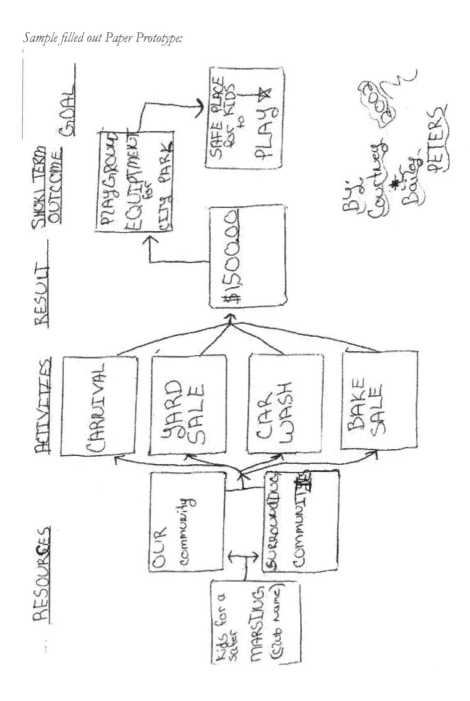

I: Feedback from Stakeholders

Idea	What works about this?	What does the community have questions about? What are they skeptical about?	What would they want to change?
Idea 1 -			
Idea 2 -			
Idea 3 -			

K: Gibbs Reflective Cycle

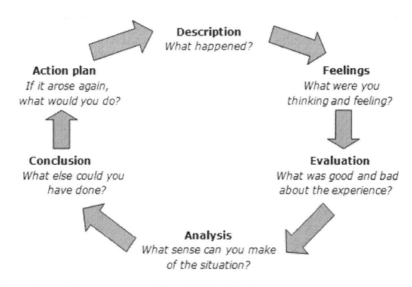

Source: https://www.emaze.com/@ACQOWQFZ/Gibbs-Reflective-Cyc

Bridge: A Teacher's Tool for Experiential Learning based on the Sustainable Development Goals

Minahil Adeel, Lior Avrahami, Sayeda Unsa Shah Bukhari, Renée
Contreras, Benjamin Gulla, Gabriela Anzo Gutiérrez, Leonardo
Parraga

Summary

Recently, learning has been reframed as a lifelong process,
entrenched in both formal and informal educational experiences, and aimed
to promote students' 21st century skills. *Bridge* is an adaptable out of class
activity list, designed to supplement teachers' curriculum with experiential
learning opportunities. *Bridge* aims to address the United Nations' Sustainable
Development Goals by promoting critical thinking, collaboration and
mindfulness. This prototype includes an example of a set of activities, meant
to be implemented at middle- high schools' settings and is designed to
facilitate an interaction between students' and their environment.

Philosophical Underpinnings

Globalization has generated the conditions required to fundamentally
change what it means to be a citizen of the world. Globalization, a process
that has been intensifying during the last century, has created a new, global,
society; developed a humanist, collective epistemology; and cultivated de-
facto interdependence between all people (Reimers, 2016). Throughout the
20th century however, postmodernism exposed science, art and language (i.e.
literature) as based on ethics and politics, indicating that these do not hold
meaning outside of their context and particularity (Aylesworth, 2015). The
dynamics between globalization's humanist, all-encompassing perspective and
post-modernism's narrative-based, contextual approach - have put forward
individuals entrenched in particularity and cosmopolitanism, simultaneously.

Significant Frameworks

Multiple educational frameworks have aimed to recharge education
with a new vision of agency and citizenship of the globalized-postmodern
age. In line with globalization, Delors (1997) claims learning happens

365

throughout life, and places "lifelong education" at the heart of future societies. This shift includes, among other things, four educational "pillars": Learning to know, do, be and live together. Delors asserts that there should be *bridges* between formal education and educational manifestations of learning to live together, do and be. Therefore, educational opportunities to experience vocational training, collaboration and teamwork, differences in ethics, cultures and contexts (locally, nationally and internationally) - should be tangent to traditional educational efforts.

Aligned with Delors' notion of education are 21st century skills. Little (2013) claims 21st century skills are based on the ideas of progressive education and include skills that are necessary in order to address advancements in technology and globalization. These skills include: critical thinking, collaboration, creativity and innovation, self-direction and independence, global connections, and using technology as a learning tool.

From the postmodern point of view, Kahane (1997) argues that the non-traditional and chaotic "new world" order requires new educational institutions and experiences, aimed at helping youth cope with the multiple complexities presented by global living. These establishments and experiences, he claims, are characterized by freedom, choice, rebellious and innovative spaces, spontaneity and "order-less leisure". Keeping Kahane and Delors in mind, an important concept relevant to our discussion is experiential learning. Experiential learning theory defines learning as "the process whereby knowledge is created through the transformation of experience" (Kolb, 1984, p.41). In other words, the mere experience elicits meaningful learning.

Pedagogy

Our curriculum is positioned at the intersection of globalization and postmodernism: incorporating 21st century skills, Delors' (1997) concept of lifelong education, Kahane's (1997) postmodern approach to the design of educational experiences, and tenets of experiential learning. In pedagogic terms, this requires designing non-formal, experiential learning opportunities, in order to develop students' 21st century skills, as supporting elements to traditional curriculum. Importantly, the content we have chosen to apply this framework to is the United Nations Sustainable Development Goals ("SDGs"). The SDGs elaborate a plan to stimulate action towards solving the world's most exigent problems by 2030: eradicating poverty, supporting the planet's sustainability, and ensuring prosperity for all (United Nations, 2015; Reimers, 2016).

Bridge

The overarching goal of *Bridge* is to resolve the world's most pressing problems by providing teachers the resources to extend a student's learning beyond the boundaries of the classroom. We believe that personal development is advanced by building relationships among individuals, communities and nations (Delors, 1997). To truly develop 21st century skills, students must be given the tools to understand and grapple with complex issues present in their everyday lives. Therefore, learning should not be contained to classrooms and to school hours. Thus, we have designed activities that promote interaction and provide a *Bridge* for students to cross over into diverse and varied contexts within their own communities, but also connecting them with the larger world. By linking in and out of school learning, we reveal to students how engaging with the world around them can create rich, meaningful educational experiences.

Our second goal is to make clear connections between the UN SDGs and the everyday life of students. Community involvement invests students in the wellbeing and improvement of their environments (O'Donoghue et al, 2003). Therefore, even though students may not have had an active role in the creation of the SDGs, the design underlying the activities encourages students to grasp how the SDGs are relevant to their lives and the well-being of their communities. Moreover, it reveals to students the agency they have to accomplish the SDGs targets and how their actions matter.

Design

We have designed *Bridge* to provide a ready-made list of activities that connects directly the SDGs, especially designed to be simple, context-adaptable, ready to be implemented without the use of extensive resources. *Bridge* provides an activity connected to each major SDG and comes with an instruction manual for teachers. We attempted to create a list that would be easily implemented in classrooms and could be accessible to students in a variety of environments. We appreciate that teachers around the world feel immense pressure to help their students find success and we wanted to

367

provide a means to do that without asking them to spend more of their own time and energy teaching. Moreover, we were intentional in making the activities low-cost and low-resource as we wanted multiple learning communities around the world to be able to use this tool.

Bridge is designed for teachers and will enhance the work that teachers are doing. The strength of the curriculum lies in its ease of integration. Because activities are carried out by students outside of school, implementation requires minimal effort in the form of time and external support, from teachers. The activities do not encroach on teaching time, which may already be overly constrained by academic demands. Importantly, our curriculum extends learning opportunities for students to engage with ideas and develop critical competencies, such as critical thinking, collaboration and teamwork, and mindfulness. By creating more constructive, purposeful spaces for students in the informal realm, *Bridge* effectively magnifies a teacher's capabilities, provides opportunities to deepen conceptual understanding, and makes visible the value of experiential learning. One important aspect about *Bridge,* is that it generates spaces for dialogue within the classrooms, where students are able to exchange their experiences and learn through the experiences of their peers, by engaging in a discussion led by the teacher.

We foresee *Bridge* having the most impact at the beginning of secondary school. This age range is capable of responsibly carrying out independent activities while also benefiting from more active and experiential learning methodologies (Conrad & Hedin, 1982). The activity set is a way of allowing students to see how their time and effort inside school has a direct relevance to addressing the problems and injustices they observe outside of school. In this sense, *Bridge* has the potential to be a method for increasing student investment and interest in academic content, and possibly help to reduce school absenteeism or drop-out in areas that face these particular challenges.

Competencies and Desired Outcomes

In order to promote the SDGs by 2030, there are key competencies *Bridge* must work to develop in students. These are competencies that can be broadly applied to move us towards attainment all 17 SDGs. A joint report prepared by UNICEF and the Education in Crisis and Conflict Network

(ECCN) emphasized that peace education requires the internalization of knowledge, skills, and attitudes (Reily, 2013). Literature supports the idea that experiential learning is a key method to facilitate that internalization (Salomon & Nevo, 2005). Thus, the competencies we believe would help resolve global challenges are mindfulness, critical thinking, cooperation and teamwork. These competencies would create mindsets that can tackle global challenges and create a larger sense of interconnectedness and agency. Here we define the competencies that *Bridge* builds.

Mindfulness

The concept of mindfulness has roots in Buddhist and other contemplative traditions. It is commonly defined as the state of being attentive to and aware of what is taking place in the present (Braman, 1998). Mindfulness plays a key role in fostering informed and self-endorsed behavioral regulation, which has long been associated with well-being (Ryan & Deci, 2000), and improving social relations (Liu et al., 2013). Mindfulness is also connected with emotional intelligence and openness to experience (Brown & Ryan, 2013), thus helping to increase empathy, reduce discrimination and engage in prosocial behaviors. Mindfulness creates a sense of responsibility and system-thinking in people, that could shape global trends and the entanglement between the local and global spheres.

Critical thinking

Encouraging students to think critically is the first step towards helping them reflect critically. Jack Mezirow (1991) defines the term "critical reflection" as "a critique of the presuppositions on which our beliefs have been built." He contends that it is through critical reflection that one ultimately achieves "perspective transformation."

Additionally, there are two components essential to the critical thinking process: identifying and challenging assumptions; imagining and exploring alternatives (Brokefield, 1987). This can help develop "contextual awareness" and identify how certain assumptions are based on social or cultural characteristics. Thus, critical thinking can be crucial to enhance intercultural understanding, increase empathy and solve problems in non-violent ways.

Cooperation and Teamwork

Trust is seen as an expression of confidence between individuals - confidence that they will not be harmed or put at risk by the actions of the other (Jones & George, 1998). Trust can lead to cooperative behavior among individuals, groups and communities (Jones & George, 1998). To create a sustainable peace, it's necessary to create the conditions for groups with diverse individuals to come together, trusting one another and being willing to collaborate.

Teamwork enables trust building. When there is collaboration between different individuals there must also be the capacity to work through disagreement and difference with respect and mutual cooperation. The process of improving the value of the ideas and thinking critically about a plan can lead to enhanced trust among group members (Davey, Su, Celia de Anca, Salvador Aragón, & Kniffin, 2017).

Adaptability

Bridge aims to empower teachers with an adaptable framework to facilitate meaningful learning experiences for students outside of the classroom. We define 'adaptable' as non-dependent on resources, relevant to culture and social context, and supplemental by adding concrete value to current curricula. *Bridge* strategically sits at the intersection of these three points to achieve optimal adaptability. As well, it generates a space to actively reflect on the learning generated during the experiential learning, key to internalize the lessons and make them transferable to the long-term memory (Canziani & Weng, 2013).

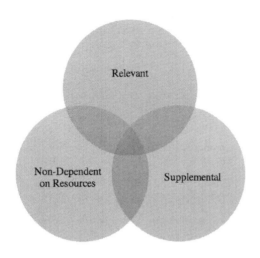

Rather than taking a technocratic or 'one size fits all' approach, *Bridge* intentionally does not depend on materials so that it may be adapted to a wide variety of student populations and contexts. While teachers are provided with a protocol of ready-made list of activities related to the SDGs, they have complete freedom to change an activity depending on the learning needs of the students and the resources available to them. For example, in some developing contexts where there is a lack of access to drinking water teachers may choose to adapt the activity associated with *SDG 6: Ensure access to water and sanitation for all* (The United Nations, n.d.). Rather than measuring and reflecting on consumption, the activity could be adapted to encourage students to map their route to collect water or create an advocacy campaign to raise awareness of the right to clean drinking water.

In addition to a lack of dependency on materials, *Bridge* is designed to complement already existing curricula. For example, a science teacher may choose to supplement a unit on climate change with an adapted list of activities for students to complete outside of the classroom related to *SDG 7: Ensure access to affordable, reliable, sustainable and modern energy for all* (The United Nations, n.d.). Similarly, a vocational training program in construction could draw from *SDG 9: Make cities and human settlements inclusive, safe, resilient and sustainable* by developing a series of activities for students to practice their trade by building affordable housing in their community. The curriculum protocol could also be used during a study abroad or exchange program orientation to facilitate team-building and inspire inquiry about the challenges specific to a particular country.

Conclusion

The Sustainable Development Goals (SDGs) serve as a call to action for people all over the world to work together towards solving issues of poverty, inequality, and climate change. Our curriculum prototype does not offer solutions to these complex problems, but rather seeks to facilitate students' understanding of how the SDGs are relevant to their everyday experiences and local context. Utilizing a framework of experiential learning activities, students develop critical competencies in critical thinking, collaboration, and mindfulness of self, others, and their community. Through *Bridge* and with the support of teachers, students drive their own learning experiences outside of the formal classroom and develop a sense of personal responsibility to contribute to the achievement of the SDG goals within their own community.

Bridge Protocol

Summary and Rationale:

Bridge aims to connect students with their communities and the outside world. SDGs will be the framework by which students will learn from themselves, their communities, and the world. At the beginning of the school period, teachers will provide students a description of the SDGs, so that students could become familiar with them. Teachers will provide students a list of activities related to the SDGs that they will have to fulfill during the school period. These activities will help students comprehend, apply, and analyze the SDGs to make this knowledge relevant to their lives and to strengthen their agency through experiential learning. The activities will be developed outside of school and the students will be responsible for their compliance. The flexibility of these activities will help teachers select those that could be more nuanced to their context. Teachers will only guide students to fulfill these activities but are not meant to develop them during class.

Grade: Middle and High School.

This protocol targets middle and high school students because adolescence is an important developmental period in which individuals refine their social skills. Moreover, during this period students can have experiential learning by their own with a lower supervision from adults. Hence, this protocol aims to develop competencies that will help students become active agents of their communities. Furthermore, in many countries, the highest risk of dropout school rates is during adolescence, in middle school in some places and in high school in others.

Time Frame: One semester/One academic year

Subjects:

Bridge could be incorporated to the full school curriculum because the activities are not developed during class time. These activities will be developed outside of school and entirely carried out by the students. The teacher of any subject can use them to develop competencies that the students will use inside and outside of the classroom. To generate this bridge, class discussions about the activities carried out outside the classroom will be held.

Competencies: Critical thinking. mindfulness, and collaboration and teamwork.

Standards: This protocol aims to work with the seventeen Sustainable Development Goals (SDGs).

Understanding Goals: The teacher will provide an introduction about:
1. The importance of the relation between the individual, the local community, and the global community.
2. The definition of the SDGs.

Essential questions: These questions will guide the introduction and reflection lesson to stimulate the discussion and exalt inquiry and critical thinking:

Introduction:
1. Think about something that you would like to change about yourself?
2. Think about something that you would like to change about your community (e.g. school, neighborhood, club)?
3. Do you think you have the power to change it?
4. How can you do it?

Reflection lesson:

1. What do you think about this SDG? Why do you think it is important/not important?
2. Have you ever learned, listened, or read something about this issue?
3. How did you feel when you read the instructions for the activity?
4. How did you feel while doing it?
5. Did the activity change your perspective?
6. Did you talk to someone about your endeavor? Why yes/no? How did they react?

Student Learning Objectives:

- Students will develop their agency as individuals immersed in their community.
- Students will learn the importance of collaboration and teamwork to improve outcomes.
- Students will understand that they can be agents of their own learning process.
- Students will learn to find critical solutions to individual and collective problems.
- Students will understand that education can be through formal and informal processes.

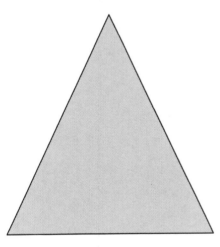

Sequence of Activities:

The activities are developed to follow the Blooms Taxonomy (Figure 1)

Evaluation (6)

Synthesis (5)

Analysis (4)

Application (3)

Comprehension (2)

Knowledge (1)

Figure 1: Bloom's Taxonomy

(1) Knowledge:

The teacher will introduce the SDGs and the instructions of the activities. The instructions will clearly state each activity, the period of time they have to fulfill them all, the questions they will have to respond for the reflection process, and the final product that the teacher will choose. The teacher can use the essential questions mentioned above as a guide for the final product he/she asks to the students.

(2) Comprehension:

- The teacher will make sure that the students understand the SDGs as well as the objectives, the sequence, and the outcomes of the activities.
- Students will be responsible of carrying out more research to thoroughly understand each SDG.
- Students will write a paper with their expectations about the activities.

(3) Application:

- Students will be responsible to fulfill each activity during the school period.
- Students will have to plan the allocation of time and resources they need for each activity.
- Students could develop some of the activities individually or in teams. Collaboration among students is highly encouraged for some activities.

(4) Analysis:

This objective will be fulfilled initially by the students using guiding questions provided by the teacher. Teachers can use the essential questions mentioned above or nuance them to their context.

(5) Synthesis:

At the end of the semester:

- teachers will receive the final portfolio of the activities; and
- teachers will have a session to discuss the reflections of the activities.

(6) Evaluation:

Students will provide a portfolio documenting the activities with pictorial evidence, reflection statements, and written products. They will have to include a general reflection about their progress to better

Bridge: A Teacher's Tool for Experiential Learning based on the Sustainable
Development Goals

know themselves, understand their communities, and engage with their communities.

Resources for students and teachers:

Sustainable Development Knowledge Platform:

https://sustainabledevelopment.un.org/

References

Aylesworth, Gary, "Postmodernism", *The Stanford Encyclopedia of Philosophy* (Spring 2015 Edition), Edward N. Zalta (ed.),URL: https://plato.stanford.edu/archives/spr2015/entries/postmodernism/

Braman, O. R. (1998). Teaching Peace to Adults: Using Critical Thinking to Improve Conflict Resolution. Adult Learning, 10(2), 30.

Brokefield, S. D. (1987). *Developing Critical Thinkers.* San Francisco, CA: Jossey Bass.

Brown, K. W., & Ryan, R. M. (2003). The benefits of being present: Mindfulness and its role psychological well-being. *Journal of Personality and Social Psychology, 84*(4), 822-848. doi:10.1037/0022-3514.84.4.822

Canziani B., Hsieh (Jerrie) Y,, Hsieh WC, Weng L.C. (2013) *Guided Student Reflection: A Critical Imperative for Experiential Learning.* J Tourism Res Hospitality S1. doi:10.4172/2324-8807.S1-003

Conrad, Daniel and Hedin, Diane, "The Impact of Experiential Education on Adolescent Development" (1982). School K-12. Paper 20. http://digitalcommons.unomaha.edu/slcek12/20

Davey, L., Su, A. J., Celia de Anca and Salvador Aragón, & Kniffin, K. (2017, May 03). If Your Team Agrees on Everything, Working Together Is Pointless. Retrieved September 27, 2017, from https://hbr.org/2017/01/if-your-team-agrees-on-everything-working-together-is-pointless

Delors, J. (1998). *Learning: The treasure within.* Unesco.
376

Gordon, G. M., & Young, L. E. (2017). Cooperation, information, and keeping the peace. *Journal of Peace Research, 54*(1), 64-79. doi:10.1177/0022343316682063

Itin, C. M. (1999). Reasserting the philosophy of experiential education as a vehicle for change in the 21st century. *Journal of experiential Education, 22*(2), 91-98.

Jones, G. R., & George, J. M. (1998). The Experience and Evolution of Trust: Implications for Cooperation and Teamwork. *The Academy of Management Review, 23*(3), 531. doi:10.2307/259293

Kahane, R. (1997). *The origins of postmodern youth: Informal youth movements in a comparative perspective* (Vol. 4). Walter de Gruyter.

Kolb, D. A., Boyatzis, R. E., & Mainemelis, C. (2001). Experiential learning theory: Previous research and new directions. *Perspectives on thinking, learning, and cognitive styles, 1*(8), 227-247.

Liu, X., Xu, W., Wang, Y., Williams, J. M., Geng, Y., Zhang, Q., & Liu, X. (2013). Can Inner Peace be Improved by Mindfulness Training: A Randomized Controlled Trial. *Stress and Health, 31*(3), 245-254. doi:10.1002/smi.2551

Little, T. (2013). 21 st Century Learning and Progressive Education: An Intersection. International Journal of Progressive Education, 9(1).

Mezirow, J. (1991). *Fostering critical reflection in adulthood: a guide to transformative and emancipatory learning.* San Francisco: Jossey-Bass.

O'Donoghue, J., Kirshner, B., & McLaughlin, M. (2003). *Introduction: Moving youth participation forward. New Directions for Youth Development, 2002* (96), 15-26.

Reily, E. (2013). Peacebuilding, Education and Advocacy Program. Retrieved September 26, 2017, from https://eccnetwork.net/wp-content/uploads/PBEA-Adolescents_PB-KAP-desk-review-and-recommendations.pdf

Reimers, F. Education Policy Analysis and Research in Comparative
Perspective. uBloom's Taxonomy. [Powerpoint slides]. Retrieved September
29th, 2017. https://canvas.harvard.edu/courses/33493/pages/learning-and-
policy-2?module_item_id=301832

Reimers, F., Chopra, V., Chung, C. K., Higdon, J., & O'Donnell, E. B.
(2016). *Empowering*
    global citizens: a world course. CreateSpace Independent Publishing
Platform.
Ryan, R. M., & Deci, E. L. (2000). Self-determination theory and the
facilitation of intrinsic motivation, social development, and well-being.
American Psychologist, 55, 68–78.

Salomon, G., & Nevo, B. (2005). *Peace Education The Concept, Principles, and
Practices Around the World.* Mahwah: Taylor and Francis.

The Global Risks Report 2017. (2017). Retrieved September 26, 2017, from
https://www.weforum.org/reports/the-global-risks-report-2017
The United Nations. (n.d.). *Sustainable Development Goals.* Retrieved 09 29,
2017, from https://sustainabledevelopment.un.org

The United Nations. (n.d.). Sustainable Development Knowledge Platform.
Retrieved 09 27, 2017, from Sustainable Development Goal 7:
https://sustainabledevelopment.un.org/ sdg7

The United Nations. (n.d.). Sustainable Development Knowledge Platform.
Retrieved 09 27, 2017, from Sustainable Development Goal 6:
https://sustainabledevelopment.un.org/sdg6

UNESCO. (1945). The Constitution. Retrieved September 26, 2017, from
http://www.unesco.org/new/en/unesco/about-us/who-we-
are/history/constitution/

Zucker, L. G. 1987. Institutional theories of organization. Annual Review of
Sociology, 13: 443-464.

Appendix: **Full activity list**

1. No Poverty
   a. Pie chart spending - For a week, record how much you/your family spend every day. Put your spending into categories i.e. food, travel, school, see what category you have spent the most money on.
   b. Most of the world lives on less than $2.00 a day. Try to only spend $2.00 in one day. At the end of the day, write about what it was like. What you would have bought if you could spend more? How it felt to be so limited in what you could buy? What did you spend your $2.00 on? Why?
   c. There are many programs governments around the world design in order to help people living below the poverty line. For this activity you can research a program that you think is particularly effective and write a short explanation about what it does and why it is successful. You can also design your own program aimed at assisting those living in poverty. Your program can focus on shelter, nutrition, health care, or any issue that directly affects the poor.
2. Zero Hunger
   a. What's on your Plate - Choose a meal of your liking. Ponder and write about it using the following questions as guidelines:
      i. Who grew or helped produce my food?
      ii. How far did my food travel to get to me?
      iii. Am I making healthy choices?
      iv. What was my food packaged in?
      v. How much food am I wasting?
   b. Many communities have organizations that help feed those who can't afford daily meals. If such an organization exists in your community, ask if you can volunteer a day to help wherever help is needed. Take pictures of your experience or write a journal entry reflecting on what you learned.
   c. A famine is a widespread scarcity of food, caused by a range of different factors. Research one historical famine. Write a one-page paper about the famine explaining the background,

how it occurred and what the effects of the famine were on the local or national population.

d. In this activity you will go to your local grocery store or market. In a notebook record the prices of foods you would eat over the course of a given week. Try to be as realistic as you can in your choices and only pick those foods you would eat for breakfast, lunch and dinner. After you are done, add up the prices of each item and see what you would spend if you were an adult.

3. Good Health and Well-Being

a. Up and About - Exercise daily for 30 minutes for a week. Record what activity you do and how you feel before and after each session. You could do this as a group activity or individually.

b. Visit a doctor, nurse or health-care provider in your community. Check if you can ask them some questions about staying healthy. See what you can find out about what young people should do to stay healthy. Make a list of at list five things you can do, based on the responses you are given. Have the interviewee sign your sheet at the end of the interview.

c. Identify one problem in your community that you think leads to poor health outcomes for people. Design an advertisement that can be used to try to prevent people from making these kinds of choices in the future.

4. Quality Education

a. Volunteer to Educate - It's your turn to be a teacher. Choose a topic you are interested in and plan how you will teach others about the topic. Choose some friends, family members of community members who can be your students. After you teach about your topic, write a journal entry with your reflections on how it went.

b. Interview a Teacher - Interview a teacher at your school. Ask them why they chose to become a teacher, what they think about the role of a teacher, and any other questions you might find interesting. After you are done, create a reflection on how your opinions of teaching have changed or stayed the same after the interview.

    c.   School Suggestions - Create a survey for students at your school around what they like about school or what they would hope would change or improve. The survey should be short and simple to fill out. After you have a good number of responses, organize the main themes and ideas and present it to a leader at your school.

5.   Gender Equality

    a.   Girl Power - Find and interview a woman in your community who you consider a role model. Why did you choose her as a role model? Ask her about her life, the obstacles she faced in life, any prejudices that she faced at work, in her community or in her family. After your conversation, write a reflection about what you learned from the conversation. How did what what was said make your think differently about being a woman in the world?

    b.   Mothers and Fathers, sons and daughters - Think about the roles of mothers, fathers, sons and daughters in your community. Write down a list of responsibilities and roles that each family members takes on in your community. Afterwards, write a reflection about how these roles could be different how you feel about your own responsibilities as one of these members.

    c.   Gender Stereotypes - Write down a list of common stereotypes or assumptions you have about the opposite gender. These stereotypes should be ones you have commonly heard or seen expressed in conversation or in the media. Afterwards, find a friend of the opposite gender and ask them about your list. Write down their thoughts and ideas next to each stereotype.

6.   Clean Water and Sanitation

    a.   Water Works- Write down every action you take in a day that requires you to use water. Estimate how much water you might use in the course of a day. Try to measure as accurately as you can. Next, write a reflection about how life would be different if you didn't have easy access to water.

      b. Water Route - Draw the route that water travels to get to your home. Try to draw each stage of the process from where it begins to where it ends. What steps does it travel along the way? Does the water get cleaned before it gets to your home?

      c. Inventor - Try to think of one way your community or your family could save water. What could you do different or even invent that would help reduce the amount of water you used. After you have thought of something, either create a poster advertising your idea.

7. Affordable and Clean Energy

      a. Dark Age - Don't use electricity or any electronics for a day (sunrise to sunset). Three times during the day, write down how you feel without electronics and what you are doing instead. Record what you were able to achieve, and how difficult you found to adjust to this routine.

      b. What is energy? - Use your science teacher, science books, or anyone else to try to find an answer to the question, what is energy? Try to find out where energy comes from, how it is produced, how it travels or what it is used for. After you have collected as much information as possible, create a poster that shows others what you have learned.

      c. Alternatives - Where else can we get energy from? Choose an alternative energy source such as wind, solar, hydroelectric and create a poster describing how it works. Explain in your poster whether or not this kind of energy alternative might be feasible for your community.

8. Decent Work and Economic Growth

      a. Dream Team - Pick someone in your community who has a job you admire, ask to shadow them for a day to learn more about their career path. After the day is over, pick out two things you enjoyed about the job that you didn't know before and two things you didn't like.

      b. Start a business - Come up with an idea for a business that you might like to start in your community. Create a 'prototype' for the product or service that you would like to sell to customers. Write a business plan where you talk about what you will sell, who will buy your product and why you think it could be a successful business.

c. Market or Mall - Go to a market or mall in your community. Walk around and record your observations about what you see and hear. How are the people behaving? What are they saying? What are the smells and sounds? Afterwards, write down your full description of the experience.

9. Industry, Innovation, Infrastructure

a. Homeland - Using materials available to you, design an ideal home. You can use lego or any other available materials like clay. If you don't have access to materials, you can draw your ideal home. After you do this, write a reflection talking about why you made the choices you did. For an extra challenge, try to make your design as sustainable as possible.

b. Exports & Imports - Research what your country exports to other countries. Write a page report detailing what your country's biggest exports are, how much is produced and shipped, and how much money is earned from it. Next, do the same for the country's imports.

c. I Innovate - Make a "Top 3" list of the inventions or innovations that you believe have helped human society progress or improve the most. For each invention, write a brief explanation why you picked it. As the end, have some fun and try to predict that you think will be the next big innovation that will propel humans into the future.

10. Reduce Inequality

a. Borrowed Lens - Draw, paint or take a picture of an example of injustice or unfairness in your community and explain what you think causes this injustice, and how you could help address it.

b. Spokesperson - Think about your community and how inequality might be present within it. Pretend that you are now the leader in the fight to reduce this inequality. Write a short speech where you try to persuade people in your community to join in the fight with you.

c. Uncovering Discrimination - Carry out an interview with a friend in your community or at school. In this interview try to find out if the friend has ever been bullied or discriminated against in any way. If they have had this kind of experience, find out how they responded to it and how they dealt with it afterwards.

11. Sustainable Cities and Communities

    a. Space for All - Experience a day in the shoes of a disabled person. For example, spend a day blindfolded, using crutches, or one hand in a sling. After the day, write about the difficulties you faced in getting from one place to another. Think and write on how you can help to make your village or city more tolerant or accessible for all.

    b. Home Improvement - Find a friend that is willing to help you. You and a friend are going to go to each other's houses and make a list comparing how they are similar and how they are different. Next, you and the friend will make recommendations to community leaders about how all houses in your community could be improved or made more sustainable.

    c. City Connections - Write about the closest city you live in, or if you live in a city write about the city you live in. In your description write about what you see in the city. What is a typical street like? What are the sounds, smells and sights? What are some things you like about the city and what are some things you don't like? Present your description in a poster or small essay.

12. Responsible Consumption and Production

    a. Craft Master - Use recycled goods around your home or community to make an arts or crafts project. Record all the materials that you used. Write a description of your art and then write of the impact of each of these materials on the environment.

    b. Compost Bin - You are going to start a compost bin or hole. Compost is made up of perishable food and can be used a fertilizer for other plants. You can put food items such as fruit skins, eggshells of leftover vegetables. Document the experience by writing what you see or taking pictures.

c. Nature Walk - Take a walk outside your community somewhere that is out in nature. Observe what you see around you carefully. Either create a journal entry about what you experienced or make a drawing about one of the scenes you encountered on your walk.

13. Climate Action
   a. Green Bean - Plant something in your community and document its growth. Each day write what you do to the plant and sketch one drawing of the plant each week.
   b. Natural Disasters - Has your community ever experienced natural disasters like floods, fires, droughts or earthquakes? If so, describe what this experience was like and how it affected your community. If you haven't, interview a parent or grandparent to see if they have ever experienced living through a natural disaster and record their responses.
   c. Vegetarian - A lot of the energy human beings use comes from raising livestock for food. If you or your family eats meat, it took a lot of energy to get that food to you. Try to eat vegetarian for one full week. Each day describe what you eat instead and and how you feel. If you are already a vegetarian, you can discuss why you make that choice and how you have found the vegetarian lifestyle.

14. Life below water
   a. Get to know a fisherman - If you live near body of water, find a local fisherman and discuss how fishing may have varied over the years. Ask them about how their knowledge of fishing has changed over time, and any other questions you might be curious about. Record their responses and be able to share them with the class.
   b. Marine Life - What is one ocean species that you know of? Or what is one living ocean species that interests you? Do research into this species, and collect basic information. Where does it live? What does it eat? What are its greatest threats? Put the information into a poster, a paper, or a drawing.
   c. Coral Reefs - What are coral reefs? On a map of the world, indicate where some of the largest coral ocean reefs can be

found. Research any information you can around what is happening to coral reefs around the world? Why is it happening? What will these reefs be like in 20 years?

15. Life on land

a. Animal Visit - Go to a zoo, nursery or a park. Make a list of all the animals you see and sketch a drawing of at least one. Afterwards, think about where the animals come from, what they eat and if they are important to you.

b. Plant Sketch - What plant life exists in your community. Walk around your community and pick a plant to make a drawing of. You can either draw the full plant or just a part, make sure to include the name of the plant and write down any interesting parts you noticed while you did the drawing.

c. Endangered Species - What does it mean for an animal to be endangered? Collect information on the internet, from books or from your science teacher about species of animals that are endangered. Find out why they are endangered. Make a poster that helps spread awareness about what people can do to protect the species.

16. Peace, Justice and Strong Institutions

a. Conflict Journal - Maintain a conflict journal where you write about the conflicts or disagreements you encounter in a day. Write a reflection and think about why these conflicts occurred, the different perspectives of the people who are part of the conflict and the actions you can take to deal with future conflict.

b. Honest Confession - Have you ever done something that you knew was wrong, but you did it anyway? In a journal, write down what happened and how you feel about it now. Explain why you did it and what effect it may have had on other people.

c. Identity Documents - What documents do you have that prove your identity? Do you have a birth certificate? A ID document? Find out what documents exist that prove who you are and recreate a sketch of them to show the class. You can also make up your own identity document and include what information you would like.

17. Partnerships for the Goals
    a. Talk to someone in your community or your school. From your conversation with them discover how similar and different they are from you. What things do you have in common? What do you see differently? What else did you learn from your conversations with them?
    b. Fundraising - Is there a cause you really care about? Think about an issue that you want to help to address then think about a way you can raise money for this issue. Maybe you can make food and sell it, or make art and sell it? Think about what you can create that other people might like to buy. Afterwards you can donate the money you make to that cause.
    c. Reflection - Is there a leader in your community that you can talk to? Or maybe write a letter to? In this letter write about what you have learned by conducting these activities around the SDGs. Do you think they are more important than you used to? In your conversation or letter, you can suggest ways that your community should work to make these goals more central to their activity.

Gender Equality

Josué Lavandeira & Edwin Coleman

This exercise is meant to initiate the conversation on gender disparities in society, raising awareness on how gender roles have been socially constructed and the consequences of these in the lives of individuals.

Learning Goal

Learners will learn the importance that gender, and gender roles play into the choices people make in modern day societies, as well as the relevance of gender equality for development.

Lesson 1: What is gender? What are gender roles? What is gender equality?

Grade level: 3rd-8th   Time frame: 60 minutes

Learning Objectives

- Students will learn about how genders are defined.
- Students will identify gender roles present in everyday life and the way they play out in modern societies.
- Students will explore gender roles in different cultures and geographical settings, as well as in different times in history in order to understand how gender roles have shaped the way we interact with each other.
- Students will learn about the implications of gender roles in the pursuit of gender equality, and the importance of gender equality for development.

Subjects

Civic Education, Social Studies.

Standards

Quality Education (SDG 4), Gender Equality (SDG 5)

Gender Equality

Summary and Rationale

This lesson aims to make students aware of the similarities and differences of people of different genders and how genders are defined in modern society. This will allow them to move forward in their studies with a gender perspective that gives them a broad scope to analyze the settings in which civic and social matters take place in different cultures, geographical locations and times in history. It will also teach them to reflect on the underlying problems of conforming to traditional gender roles and the implications this has for sustainable development.

Instructional Goals

Students will:

- Understand what defines a gender, and what gender roles are
- Learn about the differences and similarities of people of different genders and develop an understanding of what are gender biases
- Compare the gender roles of men and women in their households and families
- Discuss how gender roles might have limited their choices in the past.
- Reflect on how one may overcome obstacles that gender roles might represent for future goals.
- Share their understanding of gender roles in cultures different than their own.
- Understand how gender roles have shifted over time.

Understanding

Students will understand the differences that make up genders as a social construct and the inequalities that these create and have created in different geographical, cultural and historic contexts.

Essential Questions

- What are genders and how are they created?
- What are gender roles and how do they affect a person's behavior?
- How are gender roles different around the world and how were gender roles played in the past?

- What is gender equality and why is it important for future development?

Student Learning Objectives

Students will be able to:
- Discuss and compare from their own experiences
- Effectively communicate to the class their perspectives on gender and gender roles
- Share their critical views of the impact of gender roles
- Work in pairs to discuss and actively listen to each other's perspectives
- Present their work to the class as a team
- Effectively express in writing their reflections on this lesson

Assessments

Students will be assessed on how much they engage in participating in the activities, as well as short reflections.

Rubric for discussions:

5 Very Active participation	4. Active Participation	3 Moderate Participation	2. Low Participation	1 Passive Participation
Student participates and communicates reflections with the teacher and others, contributes to discussion and listens to other's opinions	Student participates and communicates reflections with the teacher and others, contributes to discussion but does not consider other's opinions	Student participates and communicates reflections with the teacher and others	Student participates in activities communicating only when prompted	Student participates passively and vaguely participates when prompted

Rubric for written reflections:

5 Understood all concepts	3 Understood most concepts	1 Understood some concepts
Student communicates effectively what gender is and provides a clear example of a gender bias	Student communicates what gender is and has some concept of what is a gender bias	Student struggles to communicate what gender is and doesn't know what a gender bias is

Necessary Resources

- Sticky notes or paper with adhesive
- Pens & Pencils
- Board, flipchart, or wall

Piloting

This lesson will be piloted in different settings, including conservative and progressive, and mixed and gender specific schools both in developing and developed countries, in order to get relevant data from different perspectives that allows for more successful scaling.

Sequence of Activities

Step 1: (5 minutes) Gender Descriptions:

The teacher has already prepared a stack of small pieces of paper with various adjectives written on them. Examples of adjectives include: strong, loving, ambitious, brave, gentle, etc. The teacher passes out one or two adjectives to each student and then writes the words "men" and "women" on opposite ends of the board. The students are given 60 seconds to think about their adjectives and decide whether to place them on either the "men" or "women" side of the board. Once all the students have placed their adjectives, the teacher should give the class 2 minutes to look at the board and think about where their classmates placed their adjectives and why. In most cases, students will assign adjectives according to the prevailing societal conceptions of masculinity, femininity, and gender roles, which is likely to reveal underlying gender biases among the students and within the society.

Below are questions the teacher can use to guide the students' thinking:

- Where did you place your adjective(s) and why?
- Do you notice any similarities or patterns in the types of adjectives selected for men and women?

Important Considerations

1. *The teacher should avoid over-explaining this activity at the start.* The students should not be able to anticipate the "right" answer or have the time to think about the purpose of the activity. The activity works best when students respond intuitively and individually to the choice they are given.

2. *Keeping time is important for the success of the activity.* The best way to have students to respond intuitively to the question is by forcing them to make a quick decision. This is achieved by limiting the amount of time students allotted to place their adjectives. The resulting atmosphere of urgency and chaos limits opportunity for collaboration and encourages intuitive responses from the students.

3. *The adjectives should be age appropriate and culturally relevant.* Adjectives that are beyond the vocabulary level of the average student in the classroom are likely to cause confusion and disrupt the flow of the activity if the teacher is forced to define words that students do not understand. Similarly, the activity is most effective and runs most efficiently when the adjectives relate to the cultural contexts of the students.

4. *In contexts where gender topics are a sensitive social issue,* the teacher should try to use tools to measure the applicability of this lesson, here are some of these available tools:

   a. Pilot the lesson with parents and/or teachers to receive feedback on the applicability within the classroom.

   b. Use a case study perspective explaining it as an experiment that occurred in a different setting and get feedback on without bringing it into the student's actual context.

   c. The teacher may adapt the language to talk about "gender roles", or "gender studies" instead of "gender equality" to avoid a politically charged language.

5. *The teacher could bring in data into the classroom* in the form of charts to present data on the current state of affairs for women in the national or regional context compared to either the state of affairs for men in that same context or compared to the state of affairs of people of the same sex in a different regional or national context.

Step 2: (5 minutes) Reflections with a partner:

Students are asked to find a partner for a brief discussion about where they placed their adjectives on the board. This is a chance for the students to share their reflections on the activity with a classmate and consider a different perspective. The teacher should encourage honesty when sharing reflections and active listening skills when listening to their partner's reflections. The teacher should tell the students that they will be asked to report what their partner said during the discussion to the class. This accountability mechanism will further encourage to activate their listening skills during the discussion.

Below is an example prompt for introducing this discussion:

The Teacher: *Now I would like for you to find a partner from across the room. Take turns sharing the adjective(s) you had, where you placed them on the board, and your reasons for the decision you made. Be honest. Be open to your partner's perspective. And listen carefully when it's your partner's turn to share because you will have to share with the class what your partner shared with you. You have 5 minutes to discuss.*

Important Considerations

1. *Make sure both partners get time to share their reflections.* It is easy to get carried away with sharing reflections and forget to save time for the partner's turn to share. One way to avoid this scenario is to alert the students when half of the allotted time has expired.

2. *Older students may desire more time to discuss in pairs.* Students' reflections are likely to be more complex and require more time to discuss at higher age and education levels. Teachers can accommodate for this complexity by doubling the activity time.

Step 3: (15 minutes) Class Discussion:

The teacher asks the students to bring their attention back to the whole class for a group discussion about the activity. By asking for pairs of volunteers to share the reflections of their partner with the class, the teacher can both jump start the conversation and check whether the students practiced good listening skills. As pairs of students report the details of their discussions, the teacher should encourage the class to think critically about the perspectives of their classmates by asking whether they agree with the decision their peers made and the rationales that motivated them.

At an appropriate time, the teacher should transition into a discussion that challenges the students' intuitive responses, assumptions, and biases. Below are questions the teacher can use to facilitate the discussion:

The teacher switches an adjective from one gender to the other and asks, for example: Can a man also be loving? Can a woman also be strong? If so, then why didn't we assign the adjective differently?

- What does it mean to be a man or a woman?
- Who teaches us what being a man means?
- How do we learn what it means to be a woman?
- Are there differences between men and women? If so, what are those differences.

Step 4: (30 minutes) Gender vs. Sex, Gender Equality, and the Global Context:

The teacher writes the words gender and sex on the board and asks for volunteers to explain the difference between the two. After a few volunteers have shared their thoughts, the teacher presents both definitions to the students and opens a discussion about their differences. Teachers should first check that all students understand both definitions and offer additional explanations when necessary. After a 10-minute discussion, the teacher repeats the same steps with the phrase "gender equality" by asking volunteers to define the phrase, giving the official definition of the phrase, and opening a discussion about gender equality relates to the definitions of gender and sex. Lastly, the teacher leads the class in a conversation about gender roles in other parts of the world and in other time periods.

Below are the official UN definitions for gender, sex, and gender equality[1]:
- Gender: Gender refers to the roles, behaviors, activities, and attributes that a given society at a given time considers appropriate for men and women.

395

- Sex: the physical and biological characteristics that distinguish males and females.
- Gender Equality: refers to the equal rights, responsibilities and opportunities of women and men and girls and boys.

Questions to guide the 1st discussion:
- Do you agree with these definitions? Why or why not?
- How are the two definitions different?
- What conclusions can you draw from comparing the two definitions?

Questions to guide the 2nd discussion:
- How is gender equality related to the definitions of gender and sex?
- How equal is our society for both genders?
- Why is gender equality important?

Questions to guide the 3rd discussion:
The teacher should prepare examples of gender roles in other countries and ask the students to reflect on the similarities and differences.
- Have gender roles changed over time?
- What were the gender roles for your parents and grandparents?
- How may gender roles in our society change in the future?
- How do our gender roles compare to those of other societies from around the world?
- Do you know of any behavior from a specific gender in a different culture that seems odd to you?

Resources
- World Bank Group Gender Action Plan, Four-Year Progress Report (January 2007-December 2010)
- http://siteresources.worldbank.org/INTGENDER/Resources/4year_progress_report_May5.pdf
- https://www.mckinsey.com/global-themes/employment-and-growth/how-advancing-womens-equality-can-add-12-trillion-to-global-growth

Step 5: (20 minutes) Assessment Activity:

Students are given sheets of paper and spend 10 minutes writing down their responses to the following questions:

1. What is one new thing you learned from today's lesson?
2. How has your perspective on gender equality changed?
3. What actions can you take to achieve gender equality in our society?

The teacher spends the last 10 minutes asking volunteers to share their responses to the questions with the class. The teacher should end the lesson by encouraging the students to reflect more and act on gender equality is a great way to end the lesson.

Resources

- http://www.hbs.edu/faculty/Publication%20Files/10-097.pdf
- http://www.oecd.org/social/gender-development/1896320.pdf
- http://www.pbs.org/independentlens/content/two-spirits_map-html/
- https://www.oldbaileyonline.org/static/Gender.jsp
- http://apworldhistory2012-2013.weebly.com/gender-roles.html
- https://www.ncbi.nlm.nih.gov/pmc/articles/PMC3131694/
- https://www.youtube.com/watch?v=N433aXwj59E

---

[1] United Nations' Gender Equality Glossary:
https://trainingcentre.unwomen.org/mod/glossary/view.php?id=36&mode=letter&hook=G&sortkey=&sortorder

Building 21st Century Competencies for Girls

By Aakriti Kalra and Aarati Rao

Introduction

There has been a significant focus on defining and building 21st century competencies among today's children. A key aspect of this discourse is exploring the different ways in which 21st century competencies can be built through formal and informal learning spaces. These are identified as a set of knowledge, skills and dispositions that are essential to the development of individuals and collectives in the present day. Here we present a 21st Century Competencies-centric curriculum especially contextualized for adolescent girls from developing countries. The underlying belief is that young girls have much to gain from developing competencies identified as 21st century - collaboration, critical thinking, problem solving, creativity, perseverance, leadership, economic and financial literacy, curiosity, global awareness (Kober, 2016).

It is rooted in the Sustainable Development Goal (SDG) 5 – "Achieve gender equality and empower all women and girls". While a lot has been done to develop legal frameworks to further basic rights and opportunities for women, they continue to be one of the most marginalized sections of the population accruing to social discrimination, exclusion from education and career opportunities, violence and underrepresentation (United Nations Economic and Social Council, 2017). Thus, education for young girls needs to be designed specially in a manner that promotes their capacity building.

The framework of 21st Century Competencies (Reimers & Chung, 2016) and the context of progress on SDG 5 (United Nations Economic and Social Council, 2017) has been the defining themes for this curriculum. The curriculum is developed across 5 content areas which assist progress towards SDG 5. These include Identity and Leadership, Menstrual Health and Hygiene, Financial Literacy, STEM for Girls and Fighting Violence Finding Voice. Each of these is further developed into 6 sessions of 1-1.5-hour duration each. The 6 sessions are scaffolded across the levels of Blooms

Taxonomy. The Blooms progression will help educators organise their instructional goals and build rigor gradually among learners.

Audience and Context:

This curriculum is designed to be implemented in both formal and informal learning spaces such as schools, NGO run community programs, learning centers etc. Instructors for this curriculum thus be trained teachers in schools or social workers or individuals running community learning NGOs and informal centres. However, it is dependent on basic technological support such as mobile phones, tablets, computers or projectors which can be used as alternates, and internet connection. These can be provided by government run ICT programs or sponsored by private organizations regionally. The program also assumes a basic level of literacy among girls which can be further bolstered through the various activities of the program.

Assessment:

Each activity in the curriculum is mapped on a framework of learning goals, Blooms', learning experiences and pedagogy, resources, connect to SDGs and 21st century competencies that it helps to build. The modules include different learning experiences of students based on global case studies, project-based learning, group discussions and debate, community interviews, designing projects and implementing them, etc. Aligned assessment can test for specific skills and competencies on the corresponding Blooms level. Since this curriculum aims to expand overall opportunities and basic rights for women, already existing regional assessments such a ASER in India and PASEC in Africa can be useful for evaluating overarching impact of the curriculum for specific groups that receive instruction of this curriculum. Additionally, the results can be measured by looking at indicators such a school-attendance, dropout numbers among girls and school level test scores.

LESSON 1: Identity and Leadership

Summary and Rationale:

This module seeks to build self-awareness among young girls through learning experiences such as reflection, identifying strengths and weaknesses, self-discovery, peer-reviews and team-leading. A key part of this module on the remember and understand [1] level includes historical narratives of gender-based discrimination, violence and present day legal frameworks for women's rights. It introduces girls to the idea of gendered identities and pushes them to connect it to their daily experiences of being a girl in their community. By looking at case-studies of Rosa Parks and women's rights movements [2] around the world, blog posts from women college students, the curriculum expands exposure of girls to the contemporary discourses on gender. The latter sessions focus on developing leadership and collaboration skills of girls through public speaking opportunities, simulations and developing an election campaign in groups by the girls. It is based on the model of transformational leadership opportunities which combine both training and opportunities for acts of leadership.

Time Frame: 6 sessions of 1-1.5 hours each

Subjects: Social Science

Competencies: Collaboration, Communication, Scientific Literacy, Creativity, Curiosity, Communication, Social and Cultural Awareness, Communication, Global Awareness, Leadership, Critical Thinking, Higher Order Skills, Leadership

Instructional Goals: Participants will be able to build the foundation of 21st century skills by developing self-awareness, access opportunities of leadership, collaboration.

Sequence of Activities and Resources:

Session 1: REMEMBER

A-Z Women Leaders:

Introduce participants to the stories of women leaders - local, national, international in the A-Z activity format.

Participants will create a scrapbook of women leaders from A to Z. They will reflect in small groups what stands out to them about their qualities and strengths.

Resources: https://www.biographyonline.net/people/women-who-changed-world.html

Instructors can choose to build their own library of A-Z women leaders based on the context of participants.

Session 2: UNDERSTAND

Trust Fall: In the Trust Fall activity, one person has to fall on purpose while the other has to catch him. Let your kid stand with another partner in an opposite direction. One of the partners has to stand in front of the other and make his body go stiff. They have to give a signal that they are about to fall backwards. As the kid falls, the partner has to catch him gently and prevent him from hitting the ground. Sometimes it helps to have two people catch one person falling. The activity begins with less distance between the partners. As the levels increase and the partners start trusting each other, the distance increases with each level.

Reflect on what each participant felt after the activity - what I thought before, how I acted differently, did I get to know something new about myself?

Resource: http://www.creativeyouthideas.com/resources/game-ideas/trust-fall/

Know thyself! True leadership comes with a high level of self-awareness. Use the Empowerment star Self-assessment tool to assess your own competencies (Appendix 1). Mark the level that you are at on each skill. Share with the group why you are at that level and support it with a rationale, story or anecdote. Take turns to go through to group to share your skill level. If you are unsure about your skill level as a friend or someone who knows you very well to help rate yourself.

Follow the instructions they shared on page 4. Try to think broadly about your life, your community and your interactions with members of the opposite sex, parents and people with power. Circle on the star the number that corresponds to each answer given. Connect the dots. Someone who is completely empowered (all 5s) will make a perfect, full sized octagon. Someone who is not empowered at all (all 1s) will make a tiny octagon.

http://cdn.worldslargestlesson.globalgoals.org/2016/06/4-Mission-Gender-Equality.pdf

Keep your self-assessment tools will yourself till the end of Lesson 5!

Session 3: APPLY

- Introduce participants to the leadership skills template and have a group discussion of what each skills means, and what actions might show that skill using Malala's example.

Malala Yousafzai is a Pakistani education advocate who, at the age of 17, became the youngest person to win the Nobel Peace Prize after surviving an assassination attempt by the Taliban. Born on July 12, 1997, Yousafzai became an advocate for girls' education when she herself was still a child, which resulted in the Taliban (a terrorist organisation in Pakistan) issuing a death threat against her. On October 9, 2012, a gunman shot Malala when she was traveling home from school. She survived and has continued to speak out on the importance of education. In 2013, she gave a speech to the United Nations and published her first book, I Am Malala, which is also turned into a movie. In 2014, she won the Nobel Peace Prize.

Go through her story and her videos on her website through the timeline on the link below and watch the videos.

https://www.malala.org/malalas-story

Debrief: What are some leadership skills that Malala demonstrated? List at least 10 skills and assess which ones apply to you the most. Which one skill would you like to develop further?

- Proceed with a situation test/ role play format where groups of participants are given a situation to act upon. This will be followed by a debrief on what leadership skills each participant showed in the situation test. (This debrief section of this activity can also be done in the Analyze section)

Session 4: ANALYSE

Watch the following two videos.

Nanhi Kali video about girl child education:

https://www.youtube.com/watch?v=RHOwBIGQUw0

Watch the video "5 Barriers to Girls' Education: Malawi":
https://www.youtube.com/watch?v=iDljot3yvvI

What are the barriers for girl education in your country's context? Are they similar or different?

Session 5: EVALUATE

Privilege walk: The purpose of this activity is for students to recognise the role of power and privilege in life, become more aware of the society and community they live in and reflect ways to overcome hurdles.

Stand in a horizontal line in an open room or outdoors. Read the list of statements one by one. If the statement rings take one step forward and if the statement seems false for you, take one step back. If the statement does not apply to you, remain standing at the same place.

I am a boy.

I go to school.

My father went to school/college.

My mother went to school/college.

I am treated equal as my brothers.

I am supported by my family to follow my dreams.

I can choose my career and what I want to become in life.

I get the same amount food as the opposite gender in my family.

I get the same amount of pocket money as my male siblings in my family.

I can choose whom I want to marry when I grow up.

I can choose to work/have a career when I grow up.

I feel safe when I walk on the street.

I have been discriminated against/bullied because of the color of my skin or the way I look.

My parents can afford to pay for my college/university.

I have access to hygienic conditions for natural and hygienic needs (eg: bathing, toilets, sanitary napkin disposal).

I have access to separate girl's toilets in my school.

Debrief: Ask anyone in the group to share why they think they are standing where they are standing in their position and whether it is reflective of their state of privilege in their society. How do they think they can change their state of privilege? What role does education play in privilege? What were some questions for which they had to take a step back? Ask them to share stories on why? Doing the activity with them while reading out the statements and sharing your story will foster more trust among the group.

Note: It is important that this activity is conducted at a point in training when there is already enough trust amongst the students in sharing, otherwise it can create resentment and a feeling of being undervalued.

Session 6: CREATE

Design for Change: Introduce participants to Design for Change using videos and the Design for Change vision for student leaders. Participants (in groups of 3-5) are asked to identify a problem or intervention area in their communities and design a solution for the same. Students will then design an implementation plan for the solution and identify a timeline to act on their projects after the last session.

http://www.designforchangeindia.com

LESSON 2: STEM for Girls

Summary and Rationale:

There is a longstanding belief that boys are better than girls in Math. This belief is corroborated by OECD's research study titled 'the ABC of Gender Equality in Education' which tries to determine how aptitude, behavior, confidence affects girls to underperform in math. For most, it all stems in childhood where girls are given dolls to play with while boys are given blocks and puzzle to build. It also stems in the fact that there are such few female role models in the sciences through history as compared to men.

The STEM for Girls element of the curriculum aims to build higher order math, science, problem solving and analytical skills through modules focused on applying math and science to solve real world problems and honing analytical skills through tangible hard skills like learning how to code. Having these skills will also strengthen the future job prospects for women in sectors largely male dominated by making them more employable. These modules touch upon not just the SDG 5 but also other SDGs through a series of design thinking challenges and progress upward on the Bloom's Taxonomy.

Time Frame: 6 sessions of 1-1.5 hours each

Subjects: Science, Math, Information Technology, Computer Science, Physics, Chemistry

Standards: Gender Equity, Quality Education, Reduced Inequalities

Competencies: Collaboration, Communication, Scientific Literacy, Creativity, Curiosity, Communication, Social and Cultural Awareness, Communication, Global Awareness, Leadership, Critical Thinking, Higher Order Skills, Leadership

Instructional Goal: To develop a technical, critical thinking and problem solving bent of mind, conceptualise a career and understand the prerequisites for a career in STEM.

Essential Questions: Do you like Math? Do you believe that boys are better than girls at Math? What about at other technical subjects like Engineering, Science & Technology?

Sequence of Activities:

Session 1: REMEMBER

Activity: Using either the internet, an encyclopedia or your subject text books, research information of a female role model you choose (in any field) and present it in any creative form as to why she is your favorite female role model in STEM. You can use any form to present including powerpoint, scrapbook, collage, project, poem, podcast, story etc.

Resources: Sample Material for session:

Until relatively recently it wasn't easy for women to go to university, let alone have a career in science or mathematics. Despite this, there have been women throughout history who have made great discoveries and many more making great discoveries today. Below is an example of 4 such women who contributed towards some groundbreaking work in their own field which helped progress (Wo)mankind.

Science:

Marie Curie (1867 – 1934) was a Polish and naturalized-French physicist and chemist who conducted pioneering research on radioactivity. She was the first woman to win a Nobel Prize, the first person and only woman to win twice, the only person to win a Nobel Prize in two different sciences. Her achievements included the development of the theory of radioactivity (a term that she coined), techniques for isolating radioactive isotopes, and the discovery of two elements, polonium and radium. She founded the Curie Institutes in Paris and in Warsaw, which remain major centres of medical research today. During World War I, she developed mobile radiography units to provide X-ray services to field hospitals. (Source: Wikipedia)

Math:

Florence Nightingale (1820-1910) Florence Nightingale is often referred to as 'the lady with the lamp'. She is famous for being a nurse who was full of compassion and the founder of modern nursing. What is less well known is that Florence was a pioneering statistician who used her work, "the Florence Nightingale coxcomb chart", to dramatically cut death rates.When Florence went to be a nurse in the Crimean war she used statistics to show that lots of the soldiers were dying due to the conditions of the hospitals, rather than from fighting. Florence's use of statistics helped to show governments why people were dying. As a result, she helped reduce mortality rates in both the army and at home. In particular Florence developed lots of innovative graphs and charts which made statistics easy to understand for politicians. Before this time, it was not common to represent statistics in this way. Florence Nightingale's work is so important that for nearly 20 years her image was on the back of the British £10 note. (Source: Math careers.org).[8]

Engineering:

Kalpana Chawla (1962 – 2003) was an Indian born-American astronaut and the first woman of Indian origin in space. She first flew on Space Shuttle Columbia in 1997 as a mission specialist and primary robotic arm operator. In 2003, Chawla was one of the seven crew members who died in the Space Shuttle *Columbia* disaster when the craft disintegrated during its re-entry into the Earth's atmosphere. Chawla is a recipient of the Congressional Space Medal of Honor. Chawla was born on 17 March 1962, but her official date of birth was altered to 1 July 1961 to allow her to become eligible for the matriculation exam. As a child, Kalpana liked to draw pictures of airplanes. Despite humble beginnings, being born in a small town of India, she got her Bachelor of Engineering degree in Aeronautical Engineering from Punjab Engineering College, Chandigarh, India and then she moved to the United States in 1982 where she obtained a Master of Science degree in Aerospace Engineering from the University of Texas at Arlington in 1984. Chawla went on to earn a second Masters in 1986 and a PhD in aerospace engineering in 1988 from the University of Colorado Boulder. And was selected by NASA to carry out their Space Missions soon after. (Source: Wikipedia)

---

[8] http://www.mathscareers.org.uk/article/five-famous-female-mathematicians/

Technology:

Ada Lovelace(1815 – 1852) was an English mathematician and writer, chiefly known for her work on Charles Babbage's proposed mechanical general-purpose computer, the Analytical Engine. She was the first to recognise that the machine had applications beyond pure calculation and published the first algorithm intended to be carried out by such a machine. As a result, she is often regarded as the first to recognise the full potential of a "computing machine" and the first computer programmer.

Between 1842 and 1843, Ada translated an article by Italian military engineer Luigi Menabrea on the engine, which she supplemented with an elaborate set of notes, simply called Notes. These notes contain what many consider to be the first computer program—that is, an algorithm designed to be carried out by a machine. Lovelace's notes are important in the early history of computers. She also developed a vision of the capability of computers to go beyond mere calculating or number-crunching, while many others, including Babbage himself, focused only on those capabilities.Her mindset of "poetical science" led her to ask questions about the Analytical Engine (as shown in her notes) examining how individuals and society relate to technology as a collaborative tool.

Session 2: UNDERSTAND

Activity and Resources: In today's day and age computers and cellphones are ubiquitous. But how many of us really know how they work or why they do what they do? In this session we will need a computer or a cell phone, access to internet and one hour of your time!

Watch the video below, the hour of code:

https://www.youtube.com/watch?v=FC5FbmsH4fw

Now spend one hour on this page and see how many line of code you can write in an hour.

https://hourofcode.com/us/learn

If coding is something that interests you, we encourage you to make an account at any of these sites below and learn a programing language for free in a fun gamified way!

- www.codeschool.com PHP, .Net, #C, Ruby, Java Script, R

- www.codecademy.com JavaScript, html, CSS, Make a website

Session 3: APPLY

Math | From where I stand: Math is a use to solve problems and numbers can be used to tell stories. Statistics is one section of Mathematics that can be used to tell convincing stories rooted in data. It forms the basis for research, evidence-based interventions and large scale policy change.

Refer to the following Lesson Plan and follow the activities.

http://cdn.worldslargestlesson.globalgoals.org/2016/07/Final-Gender-Equality-Lesson-Plan-1.pdf

Share your results here: click on "Participate" and follow a simple step by step process to enter and share your data and findings.

https://worldslargestlesson.globalgoals.org/FromWhereIStand/index.html

Session 4: ANALYSE

Have you ever wondered how and why things around you work? In this lesson we will look at everyday articles and try and understand the math, science, mechanics and technology behind it.

Activity:
Tool box: You will need a tool box for this activity. Find an electronic device or a machine around you. Dismantle it completely and try and fix it together to way it was before back to working condition. (Make sure you have the permission of whoever owns the device to do so with it, otherwise you will be in big trouble!) You can use this as a resource to understand the working of the device you chose: https://www.howstuffworks.com/. Draw, explain and present its functioning and why/how it works!

Session 5: EVALUATE

Read CHAKRA: The comic book.

Read the comic book: You can take printouts, and each be a character and read it out to the rest of the class as role play. Your can also just read it as a class or read it silently.

https://www.yumpu.com/en/document/view/54407965/chakra-the-invincible-gender-equality-comic

Discuss and Debrief:

Are boys and girls truly different? How are they different- Physically, Biologically, Mentally, Emotionally? Are boys as strong as girls? Are boys and girls similar? Are boys and girls equal?

Session 6: CREATE

Math, science, engineering and technology is used in our lives every day to solve a range of problems. Science, Math, Engineering and Technology forms the basis of some of the simplest devices like a water filter to some of the most complex machines like a space shuttle. The use of water filters prevents numerous death from water borne diseases and space exploration tells us something new about our own place in the universe and helps in finding other planets like earth with life on it.

Activity: If you could solve any world problem using Math, Science or Technology, what would it be? With your newly learnt skills in math, science, engineering and technology or existing knowledge create a working prototype of a solution to an everyday challenge! You can use a simple 4 step Design thinking framework you can find the answer for this. Feel. Imagine. Do. Share. Find steps to facilitate the discussion and framework here: http://dfcworld.com/file2015/toolkit_global.pdf

You can also find examples of solutions other students created on their website. Once completed, you can share your solution and project on the Design for Change website to spread the world and help others use your solution.

http://dfcworld.com/SITE

LESSON 3: Financial Literacy

Summary and Rationale:

One of the arenas for making education relevant and value-adding for young girls is financial literacy. While it can be defined in multiple ways, this curriculum attempts to include aspects that are most relevant to girls from low-income households in developing countries. Aflatoun identifies the role of financial literacy for adolescent girls in the context that girls, in ages 11-14, begin to understand to understand themselves as placed in a wider community and country which is wider than their direct experience (OECD, 2011). Further, financial education has the scope to mitigate girls' marginalization in form of domestic violence, illiteracy, early marriage and pregnancy (OECD, 2011).

Thus, the modules involve a combination of awareness, knowledge, skills, attitude and behavior necessary to make sound financial decisions and ultimately achieve financial well-being (OECD, 2011). Additionally, the design of the modules allows for integration of social component with financial literacy. The 6 sessions are scaffolded across Bloom's levels and combine different learning forms to deliver specific learning outcomes in each session, as well as overall learning outcomes. It begins with building personal understanding and exploration, savings and spending, planning and budgeting towards analyzing occupational structures and labor markets, evaluating financial returns of education and culminates into opportunities for designing a financial enterprise in their immediate contexts. Through case studies across the world on women self-help groups and micro financing institutions, field visits to banks, engagement with community stakeholders, the modules aim at capacity building of adolescent girls that ultimately leads achievement of SDG 5.

Subjects: Social Science, Economics, Math

Standards: Quality Education (SDG 4), Gender Equality (SDG 5) and Decent Work and Economic Growth (SDG 8)

Competencies: Collaboration, Communication, Scientific Literacy, Creativity, Curiosity, Communication, Social and Cultural Awareness, Communication, Global Awareness, Leadership, Critical Thinking, Higher Order Skills, Leadership

412

Instructional Goal: The objective of this content is to provide access and exposure to basic economic concepts, financial services, build decision making capacity leading to financial inclusion of girls at an early age.

Essential questions: What is economics and resource allocation? How do people and communities budget? What are the basics of designing a business plan? Why do men and women get paid differently for the same work?

Sequence of Activities and Resources:

Session 1: REMEMBER

What is economics and resource allocation? Identify areas in life where resource allocation happens. How do individuals manage money as a form of resource allocation? Using banking for money management.

Introduction to economic theory and resource allocation using videos and print material. A visit to the bank, interaction with different persons working in the bank and users visiting the bank. Whole group discussion on how individuals can gain access to banks.

The activity will be followed by a questionnaire for participants to articulate working of banks, resource allocation, where how they plan to engage with banks in the future.

Resources: http://ecedweb.unomaha.edu/lessons/lessons.cfm

https://www.youtube.com/watch?v=VttAbSYYIsw

https://www.youtube.com/watch?v=8Pu-mH0nFtU

Session 2 : UNDERSTAND

Savings and Spending - Participants will be able to understand why people save, what are the money management and saving practices in their community. Further, they will connect it to the previous session on the role of banks in money management.

Introduction to what is a budget. Bring a monthly household budget, see what different budgets look like – what are the differences and similarities.

413

This will be followed by a discussion on money management practices, based on experiences with parents and especially women – what are best practices.

They will write a memo on advising someone on how to save and budget.

Session 3 : APPLY

Participants will apply the concepts of resource allocation and budgeting to businesses.

Case study of Self-Help Groups of women in Bangladesh and the role of Grameen Bank. Identify how women cooperatives used resources to build sustainable businesses. In groups, participants work to design a banking system for their group and identify how to use the money saved in a business plan.

Resources: http://www.cds.ac.in/krpcds/w38.pdf

http://www.muhammadyunus.org/index.php/design-lab/about-social-business-design-lab?id=1474

Session 4: ANALYZE

Participants will now move on to studying what different people do to earn money in their community and how they get paid for it. They will identify similarities and differences in pay structures.

Students will then be introduced to the concept of gender inequality in pay structures. In groups, students will identify why it exists – they will interview people employers in their community to understand why differential pay structures exist.

Session 5: EVALUATE

Participants will return to the concept of resource allocation in a situation-based activity. Herein, they will evaluate where to invest their saved money where one of the options is education. Through videos, they will be introduced to the concept of opportunity cost.

Participants will evaluate the opportunity costs for investing in education.

414

Each participant will give a speech on where they would allocate their resources, what is the opportunity cost for their chosen option, and support their decision with adequate decision.

The other participants will be allowed to ask questions to each participant based on the decision.

The activity can be done in whole group of smaller groups depending on the size and time availability.

Session 6: CREATE

The purpose of this session is to allow participants to reflect on their learning from the past five sessions and make a mind map of their learnings. (30 minutes)

Further, in groups of 3-5, participants will work together to create an entrepreneurial model/ business plan — specifying how will resources be managed, who will be the participants, who will benefit from the model/ who are the customers. They will create a 5 year projection of expenses and revenues and their implementation plan.

LESSON 4: Fighting Violence Finding Voice

Summary and Rationale:

According to SDG 5: "On the basis of data from 2005 to 2016 for 87 countries, 19 percent of women between 15 and 49 years of age said they had experienced physical and/or sexual violence by an intimate partner in the 12 months prior to the survey. In the most extreme cases, such violence can lead to death." A United Nations report, covering 65 countries through government data and police reporting found 250,000 cases of rape annually. However, this is still not the full picture since most rapes go unreported for various reasons ranging from the societal shame associated with rape to not wanting the person who caused it to be prosecuted in case of marital rape or by a partner. One in 9 girls as compared to 1 in 53 boys under 18 are sexually abused or assaulted by an adult.

In such a scenario, a content area that strengthens an adolescent girl's resolute, makes them understand the difference between a good touch and a

415

bad tough, teaches them the power of saying 'No' and consent, together with building strength and endurance becomes of prince importance. The content area Fighting Violence and Finding a Voice aims to do just that with activities ranging from doing squats in class as energizers to self-defense techniques and role play to come out of unwanted scenarios and situations.

Time Frame: 6 Sessions of 1-1.5 hours each

Subjects: Physical Education, Social Skills, Life Skills, Self defense

Instructional Goal: What competencies, knowledge, skills, dispositions, do you hope students will gain in this lesson?

Standards: Gender Equity, reduced inequalities, Good Health and Wellbeing.

Competencies: Collaboration, Communication, Scientific Literacy, Creativity, Curiosity, Communication, Social and Cultural Awareness, Communication, Global Awareness, Leadership, Critical Thinking, Higher Order Skills, Leadership

Essential questions: Are girls as strong as boys? Why are girls attacked and eve teased on the street and what should one do in such a situation?

Student Learning Objectives: To stay safe, become mentally and physically strong and find self-confidence to fight any negative situation.

Sequence of Activities and Resources:

Session 1: REMEMBER

What is Consent?

Watch the following video:

https://www.youtube.com/watch?time_continue=65&v=h3nhM9UlJjc

Debrief and discuss: What was the video about? Whom do you think are people who can have consent/permission to touch you and in what context?

Make a list of people who should never be allowed to touch you and talk about the possible situations when this can happen.

Activity: Stand in a circle and one by one say out your choice of word to express a negative response for someone's action or request that makes you uncomfortable. Here are some examples! You can use the same or come up with your own. Be loud and confident!

Some polite ways to say no: No, thank you. I'm ok, thanks. I prefer not. I don't think so. I rather not. You rather not. Unfortunately, not. Not possible!

Affirmative ways to say no: Absolutely not! (Shout Out) NO! It's not a good idea for me. I wish you don't! Walk away or else I will shout. I do not talk to strangers! Leave me alone! Go away.

Remember! these rules all your life, even after you get married. The consent to your body is your decision.

Session 2: UNDERSTAND

Watch the video below to understand the difference between unsafe touch and safe touch:

https://www.youtube.com/watch?v=zNTUMNKSNwk

Discuss and debrief: What is the swimming costume rule? When is it ok for someone to touch you? When is it not ok for someone to touch you? Draw and explain, what are the places where people should never touch you.

Activity: Here is a practice of what you can say when someone asks to touch you in places that make you uncomfortable or touches you without your permission. Flex those Vocal Chords! When you should let the voice come from the stomach and shout as loud as possible. In a group warm up with shouting "HELP!"

1… 2… 3… "HELP!"

Sometimes the word FIRE is more useful in grabbing people's attention in public. Now, shout out the word "FIRE!" together or shout out the word for fire in the local language. 1...2...3… FIRE!! Repeat three times as loud as you can.

Activity: Stand in a circle and one by one say out your choice of word to express a negative response for an action or request that makes you uncomfortable. Here are some examples! You can use the same or come up with your own. Shout out the phrase on the list as loud as possible.

Before the attack: Stop right now or I will shout! *Shout out loud. Just scream.*

During the attack: HELP! STOP! EMERGENCY! FIRE! *High pitch scream!*

Session 3: APPLY

Discuss: Take one minute to think- what would you do if someone were to attack you on the street? Share your responses with everyone around.

Watch: The fact is, when a situation where we sense danger our brain kicks into fight or flight response mode, where the part of the brain the initiates the automatic part of the fight or flight response, the amygdala, can't distinguish between a real threat and a perceived threat. Sometimes the perceived threat is so intense it triggers a "freeze" response and you cannot think fast enough to know what to do and freeze in shock.

Hence, it is always good to be prepared! Watch this video and in pairs of two, take turns to practice the moves shown in the video:

https://www.youtube.com/watch?v=LfWqnPeUfpI

https://www.youtube.com/watch?v=W8BVx2S6IMo

Session 4: ANALYSE

Situational Reaction Test: In the last class we learnt that the part of the brain the initiates the automatic part of the fight or flight response, the amygdala, can't distinguish between a real threat and a perceived threat. Sometimes the perceived threat is so intense it triggers a "freeze" response. But in most situations people do not know how they will respond. Human beings naturally either stay and Fight or run away as fast as possible referred to as Flight?

Here are a couple of scenarios. What would you do in the following situation?

- You are walking on the street and there is someone following you.

418

- You are walking alone, and a group of boys ever tease you, call you names and provoke a response.
- You are walking with a group of friends and a group of boys ever tease you, call you names and provoke a response.

What do you think is the right response- fight or flight? What is the smarter option?

In groups of 4 present different scenarios of your responses in the form of a play/skit.

Session 5: EVALUATE

Which one of these - Whistle, Pepper Spray, Taser and Knowing Martial Arts- do you think is the best response when being attacked. Discuss the pros and cons for each.

Session 6: CREATE

Create a solution to respond to a problem that woman face.

Some examples of a problem can be acid attacks on women, forced labor, domestic violence, sexual violence, eve teasing, discrimination against girl education, lack of female public toilets etc. Some examples of solutions can be making a woman safety device, an innovative chilly powder bond to carry in your bag, a concept cellphone app in case of trouble etc.

Resources for students: List print or online resources that can support students in carrying out the activities.

Resources for teachers: List print or online resources that can help teachers prepare the lesson.

Here are some more resources for teachers:

https://mcc.gse.harvard.edu/files/gse-cc/files/mcc_the_talk_resources.pdf

LESSON 5: Menstrual Health and Hygiene

Lesson Plan Title: Menstrual Health and Hygiene

Summary and Rationale:

According to UN reports, "Girls in developing countries miss up to 5 days of school per month when they menstruate. In a study from Nepal, 41% of girls reported missing school during their menstruation." 2.4 billion people lack proper sanitation including inadequate facilities for hygiene and safety for menstruating women and girls. There are also long-standing myths and misconceptions around periods which often portray women to be inferior to men.

Thus, a need for the building awareness on Menstrual Health and Hygiene becomes important. Menstrual Health and Hygiene concerns not only SDG 5 of gender equity but by addressing it one can positively influence Goal 5 to ensure healthy lives, Goal 4 to ensure inclusive and equitable education, Goal 6 of ensure water and sanitation, Goal 8 of promoting inclusive and sustainable economic growth, Goal 11 of sustainable neighborhood and community, Goal 13 of climate action and Goal 12 of ensuring sustainable production and consumption patterns. All these aspects are weaved into the curriculum through engaging content, case studies, multimedia, projects and discussions.

Time Frame: 6 Sessions of 1-1.5 hours each

Subjects: Biology, Anatomy, Ethnography, Theory of knowledge

Standards: Good Health and Well Being, Clean Water and Sanitation, Responsible Consumption and Production, Climate Action, Sustainable Cities and Communities.

Competencies: Collaboration, Communication, Scientific Literacy, Creativity, Curiosity, Communication, Social and Cultural Awareness, Communication, Global Awareness, Leadership, Critical Thinking, Higher Order Skills, Leadership

Understanding: Understanding the biological process of a menstruation, ethnography and global cultural beliefs, healthy skepticism towards stories and myths and exercise critical thinking towards the world around us.

Essential questions: Where do babies come from? What are Periods and why do girls have periods? How can we best take care of our bodies? Is everything they say about periods true? What challenges do women face due to social sigma? What is the most efficient way to deal with periods?

Student Learning Objectives: Participants will be able to better understand the biology and anatomy of their bodies and lead healthy and hygienic lives.

Sequence of Activities and Resources:

Session 1: REMEMBER/RECALL

The Science Period!
Watch the menstrupedia video "Hello Periods" or read the comic book. Answer the questions prompts.
https://www.youtube.com/watch?v=2Z70rBPkrfQ&t=1s
https://www.menstrupedia.com/

Design Challenge
In teams, build a prototype model using any materials and explain the biology/process behind menstruation in class.

Session 2: UNDERSTAND

Deep Dive: Periods Myth and Culture
Read, Watch and Discuss:
- Documentary Film " The Curse " on Menstrual Hygiene Taboo
https://www.youtube.com/watch?v=1iRlngOAsxo
- Article on the Myth of Periods:
https://www.globalcitizen.org/en/content/8-crazy-cultural-myths-about-periods/
Discuss the following:
- Share some beliefs about periods that exisit in your community and globally.
- Classify these beliefs as Myths or Facts.
- Ask an expert!

What's your First Period Story?
Watch: Komané has her first period or Esuko and this is celebrated with a party dance in which the women from all around take part of this Himba population in north of Namibia.
https://www.youtube.com/watch?v=NlpGWau95Dg
Discuss:

- For those of you who have had your period in class, share your stories in class.
- What are some celebratory practices around the world & in your community for periods?
- Are there any negative practices around first time Periods like social ostracization etc? Where and why?

Session 3: APPLY

Story Telling
Activity: Interview the women in your community and learn their First period story. Dig deeper and ask your grandmother, mother, aunties, community neighbors and older siblings to share their experience on:
- how times have changed through the years
- what kind of hygiene management practices they used
- how do they feel about talking about this issue
- how were they treated while on their period?
Think and Share:
Share their story in any form, a poster, a story book, a comic, a podcast, and interview, a dialogue, a role play.

Session 4: ANALYSE

Men and Periods
Watch the movie Menstrual Man
http://www.menstrualman.com/
Disucss:
- Do men know that woman go through periods? Do the boys in your class know?
- What's the role of men in supporting
women in periods?
- Why is it taboo to talk about Menstruation in some communities?
- What does it take to make a good innovation?

Session 5: EVALUATE

The evolution of Pads
Research and Evaluate: Split in teams of no more than 4 and takes up research on one form of Menstrual Hygiene management
- Tampons
422

- Sanitary Pads
- Menstrual Cups
- Cloth Pads

Metrics to consider:

- Which one out of all is the best?
- List the pros and cons for each?
- Which is most affordable? in the short/long run.
- Discuss the Environmental impacts of each?

Vote to choose which one is most popular and debate as to which one is ideal for you.

Session 6: CREATE

G4G: Girl for Girl

In a group of no more than 4, Design an advocacy project for addressing the taboo around menstrual hygiene?

Your project Efficacy will be based on

- The number of people it reaches.
- The innovative methods you use to talk about an Issue related to Menstruation
- How easy it is to replicate and scale?

List the sequence of events for this lesson. Include an **opener (motivator)**, core events of the lesson and a conclusion. Indicate how students should be grouped and the question or provocation that will guide their work in each event.

Final day:

What did you learn in the past 5 lessons?

Once again, fill the empowerment start self-assessment:

http://cdn.worldslargestlesson.globalgoals.org/2016/06/4-Mission-Gender-Equality.pdf

Compare it will when you started this course several weeks and see how much you have grown on each scale.

Resources for students:

https://www.youtube.com/watch?v=2Z70rBPkrfQ&t=1s
https://www.menstrupedia.com/
https://www.globalcitizen.org/en/content/8-crazy-cultural-myths-about-periods/
https://www.youtube.com/watch?v=NlpGWau95Dg

Resources for teachers:

To build out further:
List print or online resources that can help teachers prepare the lesson.

We all come with our own set of predispositions. As teachers we need to self-reflect to access our stance on issues since self-awareness is the first step to acceptance and change.

Before starting this module; take this quiz and see where you stand on Feminist scale and how use that to reflect on your bias towards the topics we discuss.

Teachers predispositions.

Emotional Maturity/wellbeing.

Teachers moderating the sessions are required to create a safe space. What the students share in this space would remain in the classroom and the teacher should use that information with discretion and only in the best interest of the student.

Formative instead of summative assessment - not during class.

References

Armstrong. P., Article from Center for Teaching, Vanderbilt University, Retrieved on 29th September 2017 from: https://cft.vanderbilt.edu/guides-sub-pages/blooms-taxonomy/

Finkelhor. D., Anne Shattuck. A., Turner H. A. & Hamby S. L., (2014), *The Lifetime Prevalence of Child Sexual Abuse and Sexual Assault Assessed in Late Adolescence*, 55 Journal of Adolescent Health 329, 329-333

Kober, Mary J., "Educational Opportunities for Adolescent Girls' Empowerment in Developing Countries" (2016). Master's eses. Paper 168.

OECD (2015), The ABC of Gender Equality in Education: Aptitude, Behaviour, Confidence, PISA, OECD Publishing. http://dx.doi.org/10.1787/9789264229945-en

Reimers, F. M., & Chung, C. K. (2016). *Teaching and Learning for the 21st Century* (Vol. 5). Cambridge, MA: Harvard Education Press.

UNESCO. (1996). *Learning: The Treasure Within*. UNESCO.

UNICEF. (2012). *Progress for Children: A Report Card on Adolescents*. New York: UNICEF.

United Nations Economic and Social Council. (2017). *Progress Towards Sustainable Development Goals: Report of the Secretary General*. United Nations Economic and Social Council. United Nations.

United Nations Office on Drugs and Crime, (2001 - 2002), *The Eighth United Nations Survey on Crime Trends and the Operations of Criminal Justice Systems*, Retrieved from: http://www.unodc.org/unodc/en/data-and-analysis/Eighth-United-Nations-Survey-on-Crime-Trends-and-the-Operations-of-Criminal-Justice-Systems.html

Global Citizenship Curriculum Prototype: Gender Equality

Pallavi Jhingran and Supraja Narayanaswamy

Overview of the Curriculum

The following curriculum has been developed for a gender-based education program for middle school children in mid-to-high income private schools all over the world. The program will run alongside the mainstream school curriculum over the course of one semester and will be executed through workshops every alternate week. These workshops will be facilitated by school teachers who undergo training sessions on the curriculum by our curriculum team. The aim of the program is to create an engaging and stimulating experience for students, by exposing them to a wealth of knowledge and perspectives surrounding gender and equipping them with 'global competencies' to frame their own ideas and take action. Global competencies refer to essential knowledge, skills and dispositions that students, world-over, require, to thrive in a highly globalized world (Reimers, F. et al, 2016).

We believe that 11-14 years would be the right age to empower school-goers on the idea of gender inequality. Adolescence is a primal life stage for identity formation, usually characterized by the conflict between own-self and social-self. This increases the vulnerability of school-going adolescents to conform to societal and culturally sanctioned roles. Thus, adolescents stand at risk to internalize societal gender roles and norms, without being critical of the implicit stereotypes and biases attached to them. Additionally, adolescence is marked by an array of physical and cognitive changes, placing emphasis on expression of gender-based personality characteristics.

This curriculum has been developed keeping in mind United Nations' Sustainable Development Goals (SDG) for 2030, and more specifically, SDG 5, which aims to achieve gender equality and empower women and girls everywhere. This SDG lists out a string of nine targets to be achieved under

427

the goal. We aim to introduce each target briefly to children of grades 6 to 8 in an age-appropriate manner and allow them to critically think about them. This will be done in the form of activities, discussions and reflection. Through discussing factors that exacerbate gender inequality, such as socioeconomic status, the curriculum also touches upon aspects related to equity and inclusion, as specified in SDG 10- Reduce inequality within and among countries.

We chose to base the curriculum on a pre-existing framework provided in the document, 'Educating for Global Competence: Preparing Our Youth to Engage the World' (Mansilla & Jackson, 2011). The document elucidates the foundation of a global curriculum through the following competencies:

1. Investigation of the world beyond their immediate surroundings

2. Respect and recognition for others' perspectives as well as awareness of their own perspectives

3. Communication of ideas with a diverse set of audiences

4. Take actions to improve conditions as active global citizens

Given below is a brief overview of the curriculum that spans 8 two-hour sessions across the semester.

Week 1: Gender Equality: Does it matter?

Questions: How is gender constructed in society? What is gender inequality and how can we tackle discrimination against girls?

Week 2: Unmuting a woman's voice

Questions: How can we ensure equal representation and participation by women at all levels of decision making in political, economic and social life?

Week 3: Battling Gender Abuse

Questions: What types of violence do women and girls face, and how can we combat them?

Week 4: United against Gender Discrimination

Questions: What are some harmful and discriminatory practices against women? What is the history of these practices, and how can we eliminate them?

Week 5: Let's Talk About Work and Gender

Questions: How can we recognize and attach value to unpaid and domestic work of women all over the world?

Week 6: My Body, My Rights

Questions: What is sexual and reproductive health? How can we ensure universal access for the same?

Week 7: Today, We Can

Questions: How can the use of information and communications technology aid women empowerment?

Week 8: Your Gender Agency

Gender Symposium: Presentation of actionable ideas surrounding gender

Sample Lesson Plan

Lesson Plan Title: Gender Equality: Does It Matter?

Designer(s) Names: Pallavi Jhingran and Supraja Narayanaswamy

Grade Level: Grades 6 to 8 (Ages 11-14 years)

Time Frame: 2 hours per workshop

Rationale: This is the first workshop of the gender-based education program. This workshop aims to build a foundational understanding of gender as a social construct, and covers labels, biases and prejudices associated with gender in society.

Big Idea: The scope of the workshop is not limited to knowledge transmission, but also to provide students with opportunities to engage with, critically think about, collaborate, and take action on prevalent societal gender-based inequalities in the local and global context. By combining their previous knowledge and experiences with new knowledge and global competencies honed through the workshops. students are scaffolded to develop a gender-sensitive way of thinking and doing.

Subjects: Separate module on gender-based education

Standards: This workshop helps make students aware of the first target of SDG 5: Gender Equality, i.e. to end all forms of discrimination against all women and girls everywhere.

Instructional Goals:

Goal	Knowledge	Skills	Dispositions
Investigation of the world beyond their immediate surroundings	Identifying the interplay of gender and society in local and global contexts	Critical thinking skills, Information access and analysis, Curiosity and inquiry	Open-mindedness
Respect and recognition for others' perspectives as well as awareness of their own perspectives	Analyzing diverse perspectives surrounding gender and gender equality	Collaboration skills, Cross-cultural skills	Self-awareness, Reflection, Empathy
Communication of ideas with a diverse set of audiences	Supporting/critiquing renewed understanding of gender to peers, teachers, schools and communities	Interpersonal skills	Adaptability to situations and contexts

Take actions to improve conditions as active global citizens	Creating applicable solutions to real-world gender-related issues	Problem solving skills, Leadership and decision-making skills, Creativity and imagination	Civic and ethical responsibility, Ownership and agency

Student Learning Objectives:

Students will be able to:

1.   Define gender as a social construct

2.   Identify prevalent societal roles and labels associated with gender

3.   Analyze norms, biases and privileges associate with gender

4.   Develop solutions to gender-related problems in local and global contexts

Assessment:

Student assessment for the workshop is divided into formative and summative:

1.   Formative Assessment

Teachers will maintain portfolios for every student to check for concept-based understanding among them. The portfolios will carry outputs created by students, in groups and individually, through the course of the program. Teachers will also follow a set of rubrics for in-class observation and measurement of 21st century skills and global competencies in students (Appendix A). Students will maintain a learning journal, which will be introduced in Workshop 1, to share reflection on thoughts, ideas and feelings as the workshops progress and also as a tool for self-assessment.

2.   Summative Assessment

Summative assessment will involve a review of the final portfolio and a project, which students will work on in groups. The workshop culminates in a Gender Symposium, held at the school, where students will present their final project. In their final project, students will tackle one target of SDG 5 covered during the previous weeks, identify a problem specific to their school or community, and provide an action plan to overcome the inequality in their target population.

Activity 1 - Look around!   **Time: 20 mins**

Purpose: This activity is designed for students to understand gender as a construct and identify the contrasts in labels associated with each gender in society.

Materials required: Picture cut-outs of famous personalities (16), Post-its, sketch pens/markers, pencils

Guidelines for teachers:

-        On the four walls of the classroom, paste pictures of famous personalities (50% men and 50% women) from your country as well as around the world. These should include personalities that students are familiar with from industries such as media, sports and politics.

-        Ask students to walk to as many posters as possible and assign adjectives (using post-its) corresponding to that picture and personality. Guide students to pick adjectives that they think best fit the personality displayed.

-        Next, make students walk around the classroom and read the adjectives that other classmates have used to describe the photos. Based on what they've read, and as part of a larger group, discuss the following questions:

Q. Is there anything significant or unusual that you observe?

-    Facilitate the class discussion towards analyzing difference in adjectives based on gender and derive that some adjectives lean towards one gender. Once the class recognizes these differences, discuss the following question among the entire class:

Q. Why do you think some adjectives are used for females more than males, and vice versa?

Q. Is there a difference between the adjectives used for males and females within your culture and outside? If so, why do you think so?

-    Ask partners to share with each other the following. Walk around class and listen as students engage in discussion:

Q. Have you had any experience where any gender-specific adjective was used to describe you?

Q. How did it make you feel?

-    Engage with the group to discuss gender labels and implicit biases existing in society. Derive the conclusion that gender is a social construct, and that girls and boys are perceived differently in society.

Activity 2 – Look Within!   **Time: 40 mins**

Purpose: This activity is designed for students to have a nuanced understanding of gender inequality, question biases and privileges associated with gender, and conclude that poverty exacerbates gender inequalities.

Materials required: Sheets with fictitious case studies of individuals from different countries and backgrounds (as many chits as there are students); Video link - https://www.youtube.com/watch?v=4viXOGvvu0Y&t=3s

Guidelines for teachers:

2.1 Privilege Walk   **Time: 25 mins**

- Ask students to stand horizontally in a single line. Hand over the case study sheets to them (in a random order).

[Example:

(i)   You are Vikram. Vikram lives in new Delhi with his family and studies in an international school. His parents both have MBA degrees and work at a prominent MNC. His younger sister studies in the same school. Currently he is studying for his SATs to apply to a college abroad. Vikram's parents are willing to pay for his tuition abroad but are unsure of sending his sister abroad.

(ii)   You are Mayu. She is a fifteen-year old school-going girl who resides in a small village in Vietnam, with a population of close to 10,000 persons. Both her parents are illiterate. She goes to a public school where she studies in Class 8. Mayu takes special interest in Science and Math and hopes to become an engineer one day. However, Mayu has been recently told by her father that she has to drop out of school and help with the family farm. Further, her parents have been talking about her marriage. They feel that if they don't marry her off to someone in a year, it would be too late.]

- Read out a series of statements; if they correspond to the information of the individual as assigned to their sheet, then students should take a step forward/backward. If the statement is irrelevant to them, they remain in that position (Appendix B).

[Example:

(i)   Take a step forward if you are not the first-generation learner;

(ii)   Take a step backward if you are from a low-income household]

- At the end of the exercise, ask students to look at where they're standing and reflect on what the distance between them signifies. In pairs, students talk about their character's existence or lack of privileges.

435

-       Have a whole group debrief with the following questions:

Q. Does your assigned gender increase or decrease your privilege status?

Q. What are girls and boys in our community "expected" or "not expected" to do? Do traditions and beliefs play a role in these expectations?

- BREAK (10 minutes) –

2.2 Video
15 mins

-       Show students a video on gender and socioeconomic inequality: https://www.youtube.com/watch?v=4viXOGvvu0Y&t=3s

-       Based on the video, derive the concept of 'inequality' in terms of gender, socioeconomic status, race, etc. through responses to the following questions in groups of 3-4:

Q. What are the factors that exacerbate gender inequalities?

Q. Why are girls more disadvantaged than boys, especially in developing countries?

Q. How can countries move towards a more "gender transformative" approach to development?

Activity 3 – Look Beyond!   **Time: 35 mins**

Purpose: This activity is designed to give students, both girls and boys, the agency to participate in solving problems relating to gender in their schools and communities.

Materials: Chart papers (as many as there are students), sketch pens, color pencils, pencils, crayons, rulers, erasers, sharpeners, reflection journal (one per student)

Guidelines for teachers:

3.1 Class Norms   **10 mins**

-        Together, teacher and students come up with a set of rules or norms they will follow in their classroom to make it more gender-inclusive. E.g. (a) There will be equal representation of boys and girls in the class leadership team. (b) Boys will not bully girls.

-        This list is then printed and hung up on the walls of the class to be followed throughout the course of the semester by every student.

3.2 Poster Activity   **25 mins**

-        Read aloud one case study from the privilege walk, i.e. Mayu's story. Pass around sheets with Mayu's story to groups with 3-4 students in each group.

-        Ask students to imagine they're studying in Mayu's school and create a poster depicting what actions they would undertake to develop awareness within the school and among neighboring communities on the importance of treating girls the same way as they treat boys. They should keep in mind the social and cultural context while developing solutions.

-        Get a few student volunteers to present their ideas to the entire class. Inculcate a culture of inquiry by encouraging other students to ask questions to the groups presenting.

-        All posters with be shared with the entire school through a 'gallery walk' as part of the Gender Symposium.

Activity 4 – Reflection & Sharing   **Time: 10 mins**

This is the last activity of the first workshop. Ask students to reflect on their experiences from the day and share their new understanding and experiences to the class. Introduce a reflection journal for students to maintain through the semester to jot down their thoughts, ideas and feelings as the workshops progress.

Activity 5 – Look Deep! (Take home)   **Time: 5 mins**

Purpose: The purpose of this activity, which is a take-home research activity, is to identify gender representations in social, political and economic spheres across the globe.

Materials: Chart papers (as many as there are students), sketch pens, color pencils, pencils, crayons, rulers, erasers, sharpeners.

Guidelines for teachers:

-      In pairs, ask students to research on their computers at home or school, select a country of their choice, and collect information on the following:

1.   Name and gender of Presidents/Prime Ministers in the past 2 decades

2.   Name and gender of eminent award winners (e.g. Bharat Ratna) in the past 5 years

3.   Name and gender of the highest earning members of the country in the past 5 years

4.   Name and gender of highest paid media personalities (actors, actresses) in the past 5 years

-      Next week, encourage students to participate in a discussion to compare the gender inequalities prevalent in different spheres across a variety of countries. This activity is elaborated in the next lesson plan.

References

Mansilla, V. B., & Jackson, A. (2011). *Educating for Global Competence: Preparing Our Youth to Engage the World.* Council of Chief State School Officers' EdSteps Initiative & Asia Society Partnership for Global Learning.

Reimers, F., Chopra, V., Chung, C. K., Higdon, J., & O'Donnell, E. B. (2016). *Empowering global citizens: A world course.* North Charleston, SC: CreateSpace Independent Publishing Platform.

Appendix A: Formative Assessment Rubrics

A. Critical Thinking Skills Rubrics (per student)

Read and follow the given description while marking the rubrics. You can observe this skill at multiple points and mark the level of achievement at the end of every workshop. Tick the option (Level 1, 2, or 3) in the spaces provide.

Stages of Critical Thinking	Level 1 (Not Yet Achieved)	Level 2 (Developing)	Level 3 (Achieving)
Identifying the problem and clarifying	Unable to identify or summarize the problem.	Summarizes the problem but some aspects are incorrect/disorganized, key information is missing or poorly understood.	Formulates core aspects of the problem with clarity, and relates it to the context.
Analyzing and drawing conclusions	Conclusion is simplistic or is attributed to an external authority.	Conclusion describes ideas with superficial relationships.	Conclusion shows well-developed thoughts that are related to each other and demonstrates relationships between them.
Applying knowledge			

and skills	Unable to apply knowledge to scenarios introduced.	Basic application knowledge, but unable to effectively use skills to solve problem.	Is able to relate knowledge to given context and utilize skills developed in the process.

B.   Creative Thinking Skills Rubrics (per student)

Read and follow the given description while marking the rubrics. You can observe this skill at multiple points and mark the level of achievement at the end of every workshop. Tick the option (Level 1, 2, or 3) in the spaces provide.

Levels of Creative Thinking	Level 1 (Not Yet Achieved)	Level 2 (Developing)	Level 3 (Achieving)
Combining ideas			
	Ideas show no originality or imagination- copied from existing sources.	Ideas show some imagination but are derived from the thinking of others (or ideas show originality but display a very low level of imagination).	Ideas show high level of imagination and originality.

C. Collaborative and Interpersonal Skills Rubrics (per student)

Read and follow the given description while marking the rubrics. You can observe this skill at multiple points and mark the level of achievement at the end of every workshop. Tick the option (Level 1, 2, or 3) in the spaces provide.

Aspects of Collaborative and Interpersonal Skills	Level 1 (Not Yet Achieved)	Level 2 (Developing)	Level 3 (Achieving)
1. Participation			
	Only 1 to 2 members actively participate.	Team defines tasks for each member but everyone does not contribute meaningfully.	Team clearly defines tasks for each member, they understand their role and contribute meaningfully.
2. Decision-making			
	Individuals make their own decisions, which do not reflect the thinking of the team.	All members' thinking is not considered while making decisions; 1 or 2 persons take decisions for the entire team.	Clear process for making decisions are established and articulated, process reflects thinking of every team member.

3. Accommodating diversity	The team atmosphere is competitive and individualistic rather than cooperative and supportive.	General atmosphere of respect for team members, but some members are not heard as much as others.	Every team member is treated with respect and their work is acknowledged. Members feel free to seek assistance from others.
4. Effectively communicating ideas	Unable to clearly articulate ideas/opinions within a group or in class.	Articulation, but lack of clarity and synthesis in ideas/opinions.	Clarity in communicating content and in synthesis and presentation of ideas/opinions.

Appendix B: Instruction Statements for Activity 2.1

Take a step forward:

- If you are not the first-generation learner
- If you are male
- If you live in an urban area
- If your family falls in the medium to high income group
- If you go to a private school

Take a step backward:

- If you are female
- If you are illiterate
- If you are from a low-income household
- If you have faced societal pressure such as child marriage and forced school drop-out
- If you are unemployed/doing domestic work that is unaccounted for
- If you have faced sexual abuse

Author Bios

Fernando M. Reimers

Fernando M. Reimers is the Ford Foundation Professor of the Practice of International Education and Director of the Global Education Innovation Initiative and of the International Education Policy Masters Program at Harvard University.

Professor Reimers is an expert in the field of Global Education. His research and teaching focus on understanding how to educate children and youth so they can thrive in the 21st century. He studies how education policy and leadership foster educational innovation and quality improvement. As part of the work of the Global Education Innovation Initiative he leads, he and his colleagues conducted a comparative study of the goals of education as reflected in the curriculum in Chile, China, India, Mexico, Singapore and the United States, published as *Teaching and Learning for the 21st Century* by Harvard Education Press, a book which has also been published in Chinese, Portuguese and Spanish. A forthcoming book, *Preparing Teachers to Educate Whole Students*, published by Harvard Education Press, studies programs around the world which support teachers in developing the professional competencies to teach holistically for the 21st Century.

Three recent books present innovative global citizenship curricula aligned with the UN Sustainable Development Goals. *Empowering Global Citizens* a complete K-12 curriculum of global citizenship education, examines why global citizenship education, aligned with helping students advance human rights and contribute to the achievement of the Sustainable Development Goals is an imperative of our times. *Empowering Students to Improve the World in Sixty Lessons. Version 1.0*, presents a strategic framework and protocols to help teachers and school leaders develop strategies and curriculum for global citizenship education. The most recent book Learning to Collaborate for the Global Common Good, discusses the global challenges to democracy and articulates who curriculum and pedagogy can help students develop the competencies to sustain democracy and advance human rights.

His recent book *One Student at a Time. Leading the Global Education Movement*, is an analysis of the leadership challenges faced by those advancing global

447

efforts to equip students with essential competencies to our times.

Professor Reimers has worked to advance the contributions of colleges and universities to develop leadership that advances cosmopolitanism, democracy and economic and social innovation. He has led the development of several innovative programs at Harvard University, including the masters degree program in International Education Policy and various executive education programs, including a program to support education leaders working for UNICEF and a collaboration with the Universidad de Juiz de For a in Minas Gerais, Brazil, to develop a masters degree program in education leadership. He is a founding co-chair of the Advanced Leadership Initiative, a program which brings to the university outstanding individuals who have retired from a primary career and who are interested in devoting themselves to addressing significant social challenges. As chair of the Strategic Planning Committee of the Massachusetts Board of Higher Education he works with all public institutions of higher education in the State developing institutional strategies to enhance the relevance of their programs. He has advised a range of institutions of higher education on strategies to advance the global awareness of undergraduates and serves on the board of Laspau, a Harvard affiliated organization whose mission is to strengthen institutions of higher education in Latin America.

He has advanced the development of programs to provide students and recent college graduates opportunities to engage in service and to develop civic, global and leadership competencies through his service on the boards of numerous education organizations and foundations inclluding Teach for All, World Teach, the Global Scholars Program at Bloomberg Philanthropies, Envoys, and of Facing History and Ourselves.

In 2017 he received the Global Citizen Award from the Committee on Teaching about the United Nations for his work advancing global citizenship education. In 2015 he was appointed the C.J. Koh Visiting Professor of Education at the National Institute of Education in Singapore in recognition of his work in global education. He received an honorary doctorate from Emerson College for his work advancing human rights education. He is a fellow of the International Academy of Education and a member of the Council of Foreign Relations.

Noah A. Barr

Noah holds a BSc. (Hons) and MSc. from Royal Holloway University of London, and an LL.B (Hons) and J.D. from the University of Law in London. He is currently working towards his Master of Liberal Arts in International Relations at Harvard Extension School. As a qualified New York attorney, Noah has acquired more than 15 years of experience in international development both in the public and the private sectors. In his current role, Noah serves as Senior Sustainability Consultant for a leading investment fund based in the UAE, advising on forced labor, workers' rights, the right to water, the right to education and gender equality in the MENA region. Throughout his career, he has advised corporations, educational institutions and non-governmental organizations on human rights and sustainability issues, including on the U.N. Sustainable Development Goals. Noah has a deep commitment to education. He contributed to the implementation of large-scale education schemes for impoverished or isolated populations in India, Pakistan and MENA in partnership with UNICEF, Save the Children and the British Council. More recently, he has worked with the Council of Europe on a broad educational program for youths on human rights, gender equality and inter-religious peace. Since 2015, Noah lectures on human rights and the 'No Hate' speech movement at various universities and colleges in the U.K and teaches international development at several universities in Ukraine.

Jessica Bergmann

Jessica is from Chicago, Illinois. She completed her undergraduate studies in Secondary Education and English with an endorsement in English as a Second Language from Loyola University Chicago in 2012. She began her career as a high school English teacher with experience in curriculum development, assessment design, behavior interventions, and college access. Jessica transitioned from the classroom to working for the non-profit organization, Chicago Scholars, where she developed a community engagement and recruitment strategy that engaged over 175 high schools and organizations in Chicago. Throughout her career, Jessica has continuously volunteered with the non-profit organization Pangea Educational Development, whose model serves to empower schools and unify communities in Uganda through sustainable and quality education. She has

449

served as a volunteer coordinator, the Director of Marketing, and most recently completed her term as a board member. Jessica is currently an Ed.M. candidate in International Education Policy at Harvard's Graduate School of Education. Her interests lie in the recruitment, retention, and professional development of educators worldwide, as well as trauma-sensitive school models.

Katy Bullard

Katy Bullard is a Ed.M. candidate in International Education Policy at the Harvard Graduate School of Education and a Child Protection Certificate candidate from the Harvard FXB Center for Health and Human Rights. She received her BA in Peace and Justice Studies from Tufts University and is passionate about exploring how education can promote peace and sustainability. She has taught or conducted research in Kenya, South Africa, and Bangladesh. She has also worked on an education for social cohesion project at the UNESCO International Bureau of Education and developed a social-emotional learning policy proposal for the Maryland State Department of Education. She is passionate about the power of engaging curriculum and pedagogies to promote well-being and peace.

Isabelle Byusa

Isabelle Byusa is an international youth development professional who specializes in entrepreneurship education, economic development, and 21st century skills development. She is committed to developing the next generation of entrepreneurial leaders in Africa. She currently serves as Director of Youth Development Programs at Wheaton College (MA), and has supported Fernando Reimers as a Teaching Fellow in his course offerings at HGSE. Prior to joining HGSE, Isabelle was leading IDEA for Africa as country director in Rwanda, where she focused on developing youth entrepreneurial leadership programs. Isabelle's experience also includes working with Babson College's Social Innovation Lab to create education materials geared to improving teaching activities in classrooms related to entrepreneurship. Isabelle holds a Ed.M in International Education Policy '17 from HGSE and a B.S in Business Administration from Babson College '13.

Allison Casey

Alli currently attends the Harvard Graduate School of Education and is working to earn a master's in international education policy. Alli is a native of Southern California and developed a passion for children's rights advocacy as she earned a B.A. in English at UCLA. After graduating, Alli travelled to Cambodia to work with a local NGO, producing reports on violence against women and the role of technology in increasing awareness on the issue. In her most recent position, Alli served as a Global Citizen Fellow at UNICEF USA, where she worked to empower high school students across the U.S. to educate, advocate, and fundraise for children around the world.

June Chung

June Chung (Hyun-June Chung) is an international marketing and educational consultant. June graduated from Stanford University in 2014 with a degree in Political Science, focusing in comparative politics and international relations. During his four years of undergraduate studies, he also worked as a research assistant at the Hoover Institution. Fluent in English, Japanese, Korean, and basic Mandarin Chinese, June has worked with various educational corporations and Ed-tech startups over the last few years, including several projects with the Ministry of Education of Japan (MEXT). Mainly, he has been the international manager for codeTakt, a LMS and Ed-tech solutions provider to K12 schools, and marketing manager for HelloTalk, the largest language exchange community in the world with over 6 million members. Apart from business, June is an event coordinator for the One Asia Foundation, that provides scholarships and funds to over 300 universities around the world to promote the formation of a wider Asian Community. He is also the representative for a United Nations-affiliated NGO, promoting SDGs by hosting fine arts and performance productions. June is currently a candidate for a master's in Education in International Education Policy at the Harvard Graduate School of Education.

Pilar Cuesta

Pilar is a business major, passionate and driven by the power of education. She has served underprivileged students as a full-time business administration teacher in a technical vocational school and understood firsthand the effects of education as a social mobility tool. She has also had experience in the private sector working for the largest airline in Latin America as a senior business analyst, evaluating and deciding the long-term strategy of the company. Her experience both in the public and private sector have driven her to study a master's in public administration at the Kennedy School of Government at Harvard University. An experience that will enable her to develop skills to impact the educational sector, designing and implementing programs to improve the educational sector from the public sector.

Beatriz Giraldo

Beatriz is a strategy and education consultant with relevant experience in sustainability, non-profit organizations, teacher training and formal and non-formal educational processes of children. She is a project manager specialized in assessing and designing frameworks and action plans for for-profit and non-profit organizations in strategy, corporate governance, shared value, and organizational structures and processes. Beatriz spent the last two and a half years designing and implementing teacher training material for the National Ministry of Education on Colombia, based on four aspects: Pedagogical Content Knowledge, Cooperative Learning, correct use of texts and Charlotte Danielson's Framework for Teaching. Also, a great part of her experience as an educator comes from leading educational travel programs for K-12 students, using outdoor education and travel educational methodologies to create learning experiences for young global citizens. Her studies in the International Education Policy program in the Harvard Graduate School of Education, will further her preparation to become an agent of change in addressing access and quality education inequalities in developing countries, particularly in contexts of conflict.

Ben Gulla

Ben began his career as an Americorps Teaching Fellow serving in New York City public schools. During his two years of service, Ben helped NYC DOE teachers implement curricula, manage classrooms and design lessons. In New York, Ben also worked for Citizen Schools, a nationally recognized non-profit organization which extends learning time for underserved communities across the US. In 2014, Ben took on a full-time English teaching at a private school in Cape Town, South Africa where he helped to lead the middle-school and high-school English department. Currently, Ben is a Master of

Arts candidate at the Harvard Graduate School of Education with a focus in International Education Policy.

Rachel Hunkler

Rachel is currently a M.Ed. student in the International Education Policy program at the Harvard Graduate School of Education (HGSE). She is originally from Nashville, Tennessee, and received her bachelor's degree in K-12 Spanish Education. She comes to HGSE with four years of experience teaching in middle and high school classrooms in Spain and the U.S.A. As a Fulbright English Teaching Assistant (ETA) in Madrid, Spain, for two years, she taught English literature and composition at a bilingual school and helped lead the Madrid school system's Model UN program, training teachers and running conferences. Upon returning to the U.S., Rachel taught English and Spanish for two years at a high school in Nashville, Tennessee, and directed their summer study abroad program in Salamanca, Spain. Besides her two years teaching in Spain, Rachel has also spent time in classrooms in Ecuador and Costa Rica. She is passionate about using global citizenship education, bilingual education, and literacy to foster 21st century skills and build mutual understanding. In addition to her studies, Rachel works part time as a curriculum consultant for the United Nations Association of Greater Boston, developing Model UN curriculum for students in the Boston area.

Idia F. Irele

Idia Irele is a Nigerian-American dual national who specializes in civic education, intercultural cooperation, and youth leadership. Prior to pursuing her degree at Harvard, she lived in the Principality of Andorra where she taught English and leadership to upper-secondary school students as a Fulbright Fellow. Her professional experience is rooted heavily in the nonprofit sector, having worked as a social justice educator and community organizer in Boston, and as an English language teacher at the high school and university level in Bilbao and Madrid, Spain. She also sits on the executive board of UPLIFT Africa, an education nonprofit that brings academic resources to impoverished students in Liberia. In 2017 Idia was identified as a global Emerging Leader and invited to speak on the state of African education at the annual Atlantic Dialogues Conference held by the OCP Policy Center in Rabat, Morocco. Idia brings to her work a passion for equity and human rights, development, youth empowerment, and intercultural exchange. In addition to working with youth, Idia enjoys traveling, writing fiction, and learning new languages. Drawing from her experiences living and working in Nigeria, Boston, Spain, Andorra, and Mexico, she hopes to dedicate her career to serving the world's most vulnerable populations through the use of cross-cultural collaboration. This cross-national engagement, she believes, is the key to sustainable peace.

Aakriti Kalra

Aakriti Kalra belongs to Hisar, India. She is currently an Ed.M. candidate of International Education Policy at Harvard University, Massachusetts. She is committed to improving public education in India by focusing on teacher quality through training, and skills-based curriculum. She holds a strong belief in student-centric learning in classrooms and the role of research in informing policy practice. At Harvard, she is specializing in Data Analysis and Program Implementation. One of her current projects is with the Ministry of Education of Peru, to develop a pre-service teacher training program curriculum for public school teachers in Peru. Additionally, she is also developing a pilot project to implement a skills development program for youth girls from rural areas. She was working with School Management Committees in New Delhi, India between 2015-2017 to increase community investment and develop stronger instructional practices with the government school she was working at. As a Teach for India fellow, she was teaching in a government school in Delhi for 2 years, as well as working with the staff team on teacher training and development. At Teach for India, she also developed a Science Curriculum in line with National Curriculum Framework. She holds a Bachelor's in Journalism and Development Communication from Lady Shri Ram College, Delhi University. She hopes to continue working in India on policy analysis and implementation after completing her graduate education.

Ameya Kamath

Ameya is a young education consultant, passionate about the power of global education. He received his BSc in Economics at UCL and graduated on the Dean's List in his cohort. His undergraduate research focused on analyzing education policies such as conditional cash transfers in Latin America using an econometric approach. Subsequently, he served as an Economics and

Business teacher at an Oxford Summer School for young students of over 22 different nationalities. His passion for teaching and research continued at Teach for India where he taught in resource-constrained settings whilst simultaneously interning with the impact evaluations team. Currently, Ameya is an Ed.M. candidate in the International Education Policy Program at the Harvard Graduate School of Education. In addition to his studies, he works part time for a global education firm in developing curriculum for experiential education programs. He aims to continue to advocate for the power of global citizenship education in his life beyond Harvard.

Ashira Khera

Ashira holds a bachelor's degree in Software Engineering and has work experience of over 8 years as a software engineer at Intel. She is an independent and entrepreneurial thinker who has led several teams of developers in the US and Costa Rica to create and deliver innovative solutions to complex problems. She is currently a graduate student in International Relations at the Harvard Extension School and is committed to the use of technology in improving people's lives. Her recent interests have allowed her to travel around the globe to work on several development projects including an integrated village development project carried out in a cluster of small villages in North East India. Here, she worked with farmers and several NGOs to understand the role of training workshops in deepening farmer's understanding of building a market chain. During this time, she also worked with local NGOs and several primary school teachers to understand the impact of technology on school children and the local economy. More recently, she has worked with the Ministry of Education in The Gambia providing them with policy recommendations on how to best improve the training of their teachers in order to improve student learning outcomes. Ashira is committed to finding innovative ways to bring positive impact on people's lives through the use of technology and the advancement of public-private partnerships.

Jennifer Kuang

Jennifer is currently pursuing an Ed.M in International Education Policy at the Harvard Graduate School of Education. She is originally from Richmond, California and received her BA in psychology and East Asian Studies from

Stanford University. Since then, she has worked in Washington, DC on US-China education exchange, implementing programs that foster cross-cultural dialogue between American and Chinese academia, journalists, and policymakers. She was also at Save the Children as a grants manager for a global portfolio of education and child protection projects. Outside of work, Jen has served in a number of community programs focused on expanding education access for marginalized communities in the US, including first-generation low-income college students and students of color, particularly Asian/Asian-American & Pacific Islander (AAPI) youth. She is passionate about the power of community programs, and how community development, grassroots organizations, and non-formal education can address the gaps in access and equity for marginalized populations.

Josué Lavandeira

Josué studied Computer Systems Engineering and Industrial Systems Engineering and worked in those areas in the manufacturing industry before going into education. For 8 years he's been working for the Autonomous University of Coahuila in Mexico, where he got his bachelor's degree. He is very passionate about improving education access and quality in the Latin America and the Caribbean region. He's a very avid learner who's taken over 23 certified courses in edX and Coursera, he's finishing a Data Science Specialization, he holds a master's degree in Administration and Leadership and is currently a M. Ed. candidate in the International Education Policy Program of the Harvard Graduate School of Education. He will go back to his country of Mexico upon termination of his master's program and continue to work in improving public education systems in Mexico and the LAC region.

Hui "Helen" Liu

Helen is a 2018 Ed.M. Candidate in International Education Policy at Harvard Graduation School of Education. While at Harvard, she advised UNICEF Romania on early childhood education, ideated an NGO to improve the quality of early education in India communities, researched on the comparative education between China and India, and organized student activities to promote global perspectives on education systems. Prior to Harvard, Helen was a McKinsey communications specialist in China, where she translated complex business ideas into accessible knowledge and
456

supported foreign and Chinese senior executives in strategic communications. Her project experience included leadership capacity building, organization structure optimization and operations transformation, etc. Prior to McKinsey, Helen worked for University of Maryland and assisted the implementation of leadership development programs for leaders in K-12 and higher education systems. She is passionate about using her strength in project management and communications to serve learners who have adverse early experiences to achieve their full potential through education and become competent global citizens in the 21st century.

Ana Marcela Lozano

Ana Marcela is currently a master's Candidate in International Education Policy at the Harvard Graduate School of Education. Ana's background is in the field of architecture where she worked mostly on the design of learning spaces. Ana's passion for education, however, began early in her life as a student in Texas. Originally from Reynosa, Tamaulipas, a Mexican town bordering Texas, Ana had the opportunity to receive her education in the United States. With this unique dual perspective, Ana came to appreciate the value of a quality education throughout her successful career as a student. Ultimately, her background and experiences led her to shift her professional focus into the field of education where she seeks to use her creativity, design-thinking, and problem-solving skills to empower students to become the architects of their own lives and futures.

Dahlia Maarouf

Dahlia is a Leadership Development specialist at Al Fakhoora program at Education Above All Foundation. Her area of expertise is civic leadership for youth living in conflict/ post conflict states. She has recently designed a unique civic leadership programme to help ensure that youth in Palestine and Syrian refugees in the Middle East have the skills necessary to become positive civic leaders and global citizens in the 21st century.

Dahlia has over ten years' experience in international development designing and managing a wide range of programmes an delivering training workshops to implementing partner within the Middle East. She founded a British registered charity that works specifically to reintegrate and rehabilitate children living in precarious situations in Morocco. Her passion is working towards providing sustainable opportunities for youth living in conflict/post conflict regions through providing them with access to quality higher education programs. She holds a BSc in Economics, a BA in Arabic and Middle Eastern studies and a Ed.M. in International Education Policy from Harvard University.

Florencia Mingo

As a psychologist and a high school English teacher, Florencia has made her ultimate mission to ensure all children develop to their maximum potential. The last four years she has led Impulso Docente, a teacher training initiative that transforms the way new teachers jump-start their career: shifting from a theoretical and one-way learning approach to a hands-on and collaborative experience among in service teachers. Her Foundation has promising results so far: 90% of their budget is covered by sales, 1,800 teachers as part of an ongoing learning community, 5,000 students positively impacted and 86% of recommendation of their workshops and methodologies. Florencia currently undergoes International Education Policy postgraduate studies at Harvard University and hopes to find innovative ways to achieve highly effective professional development for teachers around the world, making sure children succeed and flourish.

Victoria Gale Modesto

Victoria Gale's experience is grounded in classroom learning and teacher training. As Manager of Teacher Leadership Development at Teach For America, she has coached early career bilingual literacy teachers through pre-service and in-service training. Working with Enseña por México, Victoria built out an in-service training model and progress evaluation system for their primary literacy teachers. Additionally, she has spent some time in Guatemala studying non-governmental schools and provided in-service literacy trainings for teachers and administrators. At Harvard, Victoria is a master's Candidate in the Graduate School of Education studying International Education Policy with the aim of leveraging teacher training programs to promote bilingual/multilingual literacy, particularly in indigenous communities in Latin America.

Shannon O'Brien

Shannon has a Bachelor of Arts in Spanish and has been tutoring and teaching languages (Spanish and ESL) since she was in university. Upon graduation, she spent a year volunteering for AmeriCorps in the education sector and has volunteered teaching English in Brazil and translating documents for an educational NGO in Colombia since then. She has spent time living in Mexico, Italy, Korea, Brazil, Colombia and Japan and has furthered her studies by taking courses through Stanford and Harvard's online programs, as well as learning Portuguese while in Brazil. Her ultimate goal is to find new ways to bring equitable, high-quality education to children in every party of the world.

Nell O'Donnell

Nell O'Donnell is a doctoral candidate at the Harvard Graduate a School of Education. Her research focuses on parenting knowledge and beliefs in relation to early learning. Her dissertation research seeks to understand what American adolescents know about parenting and child development. Her previous work has been on global citizenship education, curriculum development, and early childhood education. Nell holds an EdM in International Education Policy from the Harvard Graduate School of Education and a BA in International Studies and French from Washington University in St. Louis.

Tina Owen-Moore

As the lead teacher and founder of The Alliance School in Milwaukee, Wisconsin, Tina Owen-Moore has worked hard to ensure that all schools are safe and accepting places for all students. Founded in 2005, The Alliance School was the first school in the United States started with the mission of addressing bullying and teaching others to do the same. Tina has received numerous awards and recognitions for her work, including receiving a Shepherd Express Milwaukee, 2015 LGBT Progress Award, the 2008 Young Alumna Award from the Marquette University School of Education, and being recognized by the Wisconsin Charter School's Association with an Innovation Award for her co-creation of the Teacher Led Network. Her school was also named the 2011 Wisconsin Charter School of the Year, Platinum Award and in 2015 was named one of the 41 Most Innovative

Schools in America by Noodle.com. Through her studies in the Harvard Ed.L.D. Program, she hopes to learn how systems change can be a lever for ensuring that all schools are safe, accepting, and academically challenging environments to meet the needs of all students.

Mitsuko "Mimi" Peters

Mimi is an ALB candidate at Harvard Extension School focusing on Government and minoring in psychology. Her expected graduation is March 2018. Mimi is a dedicated and compassionate individual with over 18 years of volunteerism in public and private schools and within her community both internationally and domestically. She is devoted to causes that aim to improve education and social conditions for disadvantaged children. Her volunteer experiences include: Reading tutor with the United Way Reading Buddy Program in Houston, Texas (2017 to present), volunteer at Mama Muxima orphanage in Luanda, Angola (2014-2016), patient companion at Texas Children's Hospital (2012-2014), reading mentor with Wright to Read in Alexandria, Virginia (2009-2012), PTA Treasurer at American School of Doha in Doha, State of Qatar (2007-2008), and parent volunteer at various elementary schools in London, U.K., Texas, Connecticut (1999-2014). In January, Mimi will train to be a court appointed special advocate with the Child Advocates organization in Houston. After graduation from the Harvard Extension School, Mimi plans to work in non-profit organizations that directly impact policy development and research to better serve underprivileged children. Mimi is married with two sons. She enjoys running, skiing, golfing, tennis, playing cards, and traveling.

Aarati Rao

Aarati Rao believes in making this world a better place and the causes she associates herself with are what define her. With over four years of experience in the nonprofit and education space in different capacities and geographic locations worldwide and Education Policy Implementation in a developing nation, Aarati recently co-founded E-base Kodagu to promote sustainable learning spaces. She is an active member of the Global Shapers Community, was a part of the International Antarctica Expedition 2016 and volunteers her time with varied causes like the Rio Paralympics 2016. Her passion lies at the intersection of Social Enterprise, Education Equity, and Environmental Sustainability.

Lauralee Y. Roddy

Lauralee is a marketing professional with a passion for innovation in education, industry educational support programs, and understanding the impact of family strength on societal strength and education. Lauralee has worked for more than 10 years at a Fortune 10 company in the Oil and Gas industry, and in her career has done significant work on internal employee training and knowledge sharing, as well as, customer training and learning programs. In her career, she most enjoys the opportunities she has to teach, train, develop and mentor others. Lauralee has actively taught in her church for the last 15 years including adults and children, and enjoys the learning and development process, regardless of subject matter. Lauralee graduated Summa Cum Laude with a BBA in Marketing from Texas A&M University and is currently working towards a master's in liberal arts from Harvard University's School of Extension Studies in International Relations with certification in Nonprofit Management. In the future, Lauralee wants to further study and do work in instructional design and educational leadership.

Tatiana Shevchenko

Tatiana Shevchenko believes that every young professional should do work they thrive in with people they admire. To advance this idea she started www.adastragroup.org, a youth employment organization in the Republic of Moldova. Tatiana is a teaching and research fellow at Harvard Graduate School of Education and Boston University. Her research focuses on developing learner confidence and designing peer-to-peer career guidance materials. Tatiana holds an EdM in Education Technology and Innovation from the Harvard Graduate School of Education and a BA in International Communication and Political Science from Franklin University Switzerland.

Aarushi Singhania

Aarushi is passionate about issues of women empowerment and leadership development. She has worked on designing a conceptual framework for evaluating the most effective teacher training practices with UNICEF headquarters. She also co-founded her startup 'Pehchan' to educate a community of women and young girls from high need, low income backgrounds - equipping them with financial and digital literacy, entrepreneurship skills and 21st century skills that they need to lead an

461

empowered life. At Teach for India, Aarushi worked with 180+ low SES students. Apart from teaching, she also co-designed several teacher capacity building workshops and trainings in India, Bangladesh and China. Prior to education sector, Aarushi was working for a leading hedge fund, D.E. Shaw Group.

Aarushi holds a BBA (Finance) as a rank holder from Christ University, India and Ed.M. International Education Policy from Harvard University, USA.

Sonya Temko

Sonya Temko is a research assistant at Harvard Graduate School of Education's EASEL lab, run by Dr. Stephanie Jones. Sonya has worked as a Social-Emotional Learning (SEL) specialist and consultant for international organizations supporting education in emergencies, such as the International Rescue Committee and Open Learning Exchange. Sonya has taught various age groups in the United States, Morocco and France, including as a Fulbright Grantee. She has a Master's in International Education Policy from Harvard Graduate School of Education and a Bachelor's in English Literature and French and Francophone Studies from Mills College.

Sarah Thang

Sarah is a teacher and nonprofit professional passionate about ensuring that all students have equal access to a high-quality education that will equip them with the necessary 21st century skills. Her current interests include the research of early childhood, language, and teacher training practices, as well as educational policies around the world. She began her career in education teaching grades 6-9 at a public charter in inner-city Houston, where she designed and grew a Mandarin program, taught Reading Intervention, coordinated the English Language Learners program, and mentored new teachers. She subsequently worked as a Development Officer in higher education, raising funds for a variety of causes, as well as helping to design new initiatives to increase alumni and donor engagement. Outside of work, Sarah has volunteered with organizations that serve refugees and international students, as well as taught music to low-income students. Originally from Singapore, Sarah earned her bachelor's degree, *magna cum laude*, in Music Composition/Theory, English, and East Asian Studies from Vanderbilt University, as well as a Certificate in Nonprofit Leadership from

Rice University. She is currently an Ed.M. candidate in International Education Policy at the Harvard Graduate School of Education.

Michelle A. Ward

Michelle began her career in education as a teacher in Dallas, Texas. She taught early elementary for five years and was a Teach For America corps member. During that time, Michelle taught first grade in two public charter schools, one of which she helped found, and second grade in a bilingual public school, gaining experience in curriculum and assessment design and academic and behavior interventions. While working as a classroom teacher, she taught all subject areas and was the team lead for reading and writing content for several years. Additionally, she wrote curriculum for first grade writing instruction, which was used in classrooms across the Uplift Education charter school network. Michelle also developed and implemented teacher training sessions in reading and writing instruction at the school and district level. Prior to entering the field of education, she graduated from the University of Missouri in 2012 with degrees in Journalism and Political Science. Michelle is currently a master's in education candidate in the International Education Policy program at the Harvard Graduate School of Education, where she is interested in teacher training and support, specifically related to student and teacher mental health, socio-emotional learning, trauma-sensitive learning environments, as well as media literacy for students.

Gillian Foster Wilkinson

Gillian Foster Wilkinson is an international development professional specializing in knowledge management, project management, and technical assistance. Originally from Oklahoma, Gillian graduated from Colorado Christian University in 2014 with degrees in Business Administration, Political Science, and Global Studies. Gillian is committed to human flourishing through educational and economic opportunity, and currently works for HOPE International, a 16-country nonprofit microenterprise development network. In her current role, Gillian provides technical assistance to microfinance institutions for client training, leads trainings-of-trainers, and coordinates resource sharing and collaboration among peer organizations. With certifications in adult learning and design thinking, Gillian is passionate about the intersection of economic development, entrepreneurship, and non-formal youth and adult education. Gillian is a 2018 candidate for master's in Education in International Education Policy at the Harvard Graduate School of Education.

Veena K. Wulfekuhle

Veena is a Board Member of two of her Alumni chapters and holds a BA in English, a BBA in Accounting, a master's in taxation and has attended her first year of law school. This is the third class she has taken through Harvard Extension. She has personally launched the professional speaker series for two of her networks and was featured as a nationwide leader in one of the alumni magazines. Prior to her not for profit work, she worked for ten years in the private and international corporate tax consulting sector. She has sat on the school Board for her children's schools and has volunteered with Junior Achievement and has assisted in teaching elementary classes. Her hobbies include traveling, photography and cooking. She has been to over 20 countries She has two children and has been married for 22 years. Her utmost passion are the orcas in The Salish Sea whom she visits every couple of years.

Jesella Zambrano

Jesella Zambrano is a California native who completed her bachelor's degree at Cornell University where she majored in History and Spanish, and minored in International Relations, Law & Society, and Latin American Studies. As an undergraduate, Jesella spent a summer working with nonprofits in southern Brazil, where she developed programming for at-risk youth and furthered her interests in empowering marginalized communities. Following her graduation from Cornell, Jesella worked as a Fellow for The City of Temecula's Economic Development Department before moving to Brazil to as a Fulbright English Teaching Assistant (ETA) at the Federal University of São Carlos. As an ETA, Jesella assisted in curriculum development, created a basic-English course, and organized and hosted a series of cultural workshops for university students with the aim of promoting mutual understanding across communities. Upon returning to the United States, Jesella began working for a low-income school district, primarily populated by immigrant communities. Her work primarily focused on assisting with progress monitoring and intervention services, but also included developing a leadership program for elementary school students. She is currently a master's

Candidate in the International Education Policy program at Harvard University with the goal of learning how to most effectively empower communities, while being culturally sensitive to their contexts.

Shengnan "Cicy" Zhang

Cicy is an international trainer in youth leadership and cross-cultural communication from Beijing, China. Leveraging her work experiences in international development organizations including AIESEC, Volunteer In Asia, and Atlas Corps in 25 countries, Cicy founded an Chinese educational NGO, YouthPower, where she designs and leads social entrepreneurship and leadership training programs for over 5,000 high school and college students covering over 300 schools in China. Before joining Harvard Graduate School of Education, Cicy worked with the Stanford Design School as a trainer of Design Thinking for Social Innovation, and was a high school English teacher in Bogota, Colombia, working with a national program of the Ministry of National Education of Colombia. In addition to works in education, Cicy is also a trilingual interpreter and has translated in many international conferences such as the APEC Summit and State Visits of government officials from the U.S and was a Rhode Scholar Finalist of 2016. Cicy is a now a candidate of Master of Education in Specialized Studies at the Harvard Graduate School of Education.